PATTERNS OF POLITICAL BEHAVIOUR

Patterns of Political Behaviour

ALEC BARBROOK

Martin Robertson

First published 1975 by Martin Robertson & Co. Ltd.
17 Quick Street   London   N1 8HL

ISBN 0 85520 050 2 (paperback)
ISBN 0 85520 051 0 (case)

Printed in England at The Pitman Press, Bath

PREFACE

Most of us who teach specialized courses in a university setting feel, sooner or later, that the ideal textbook for our course does not exist. Rather arrogantly, we then try to fill the gap. This book has grown out of a course in Advanced Political Analysis which has formed part of both a first degree and an MA degree in Politics and Government at the University of Kent at Canterbury over the last few years. It promises to be no more than a survey of a proportion of that vast literature which has grown out of the attempt to analyze political behaviour in a manner which purports to emphasize description rather than prescription. Whether or not such attempts at descriptive analysis are fully practicable is a question which is discussed in the body of the text but there is little doubt that much literature of significance has been produced by the movement known as the 'behaviouralist' one, that students of political science should be aware of its range and that they should be acquainted with the major themes that run through it.

This commentary is in no way a substitute for a study of the work cited hereafter but, since the sum total of this literature is substantial, it may be thought useful to commence any examination of the writing with an introduction to the field.

Although the book sprang from the structure of a particular course taught to undergraduate and graduate students, it does try to reflect a general way of approaching this considerable, and often daunting, body of literature. Historically, there have been two principal strands in the development of analytical theory. One has been to develop a methodology for the examination of whole political systems and the way in which the parts relate to the whole. The alternative and ancillary approach has been to take a certain aspect of political behaviour and to develop a corpus of theory about that aspect in relative isolation from the remainder of the political system, often using case-work or localized studies to illustrate the theoretical models being advanced.

For the first of these two approaches, the thread of the argument may be obvious but the choice of areas of partial theory (tending to the micro rather than the macro) may seem arbitrary. In fact, the three chosen—voting and elections, democracy, bureaucracy—have provided the richest veins for the behavioural theorist looking at parts of the political system.

By following in turn these two approaches, I have been able to review a considerable portion of the writings of those who have favoured the behavioural interpretations of the way in which the political system works. There are omissions, especially of work which has exploited mathematical interpretations of politics, yet to extend the coverage into these fields would have injured the thematic unity of the book and—in the case of mathematical modelling—would have taxed my own abilities more than my own assessment of their limits.

During the several years during which the concept of this book has taken shape, I have been fortunate in the classes of students who have attended my seminars and I am grateful for their shrewd comments on the major themes which comprise the book. I am especially grateful to colleagues who have read and criticized parts of the manuscript, particularly Dr. Christine Bolt, Dr. William Jenkins and Mr. Richard Scase. I have also been helped considerably by the secretarial assistants at Rutherford College of the University who typed the finished manuscript and some preliminary drafts.

Many of the key terms in Political Analysis receive a different spelling in the United States from that accepted in Great Britain. I have adopted the practice of retaining American spelling in quotations where appropriate and using the conventional British ones in the text.

Alec Barbrook
Canterbury, October, 1974

CONTENTS

CHAPTER 1
INTRODUCTION

It is now over a decade since Robert Dahl published his 'epitaph for a monument to a successful protest'. That was a time when the behavioural approach, or the behavioural revolution as some termed it, had virtually taken over American political science and was just beginning to be a force in Europe. Dahl's summary of the forces bringing about this new wave or emphasis remains both relevant and perceptive but what one notices now is a faint air of complacency in the assumption that the 'revolt' was already being assimilated and that 'it will slowly decay as a distinctive mood and outlook'.[1] It is true that there are fewer virulent 'behaviouralists' about than there were in the early 1960s and that the phrase 'behaviouralism' is no longer regarded as being in the vanguard of fashion. Yet the behavioural approach is still sufficiently distinctive for the growth of what we might term a counter-culture dedicated to the downgrading of the behavioural approach to the study of politics.[2] In the long run, Dahl may well be right and the present and sometimes carping criticisms may abate with a disappearance of the dichotomous schools of political analysis that now dominate the scene. Whatever the long-term value of the behaviouralist approach some evaluation of the mass of theory that it has spun off is now essential if only to place it in context in the long history of speculation about political arrangements.

One of the more evident advantages of behaviouralism has been its concentration on the political system as such. 'Empiricism' and 'scientific method' as strands of behaviouralism have been fed into a central concept which may bear some relation to older concepts such as 'the state' but is sufficiently fresh in the writings of the mid-twentieth century to provide a focus for at least part of the behaviouralist thesis. It is our belief that the most lasting effect of the behaviouralist approach will be this attempt to see politics as a system.

1

2 Patterns of Political Behaviour

Like any 'school', systems analysis has had its lunatic fringe and the very phrase itself is often a confusing one. Nevertheless, if one thinks of the macro-level of behaviouralism as comprising an attempt to analyze parts of the political system or to study the interrelationship of the specific parts by a model of the whole, then a systems approach is far less absurd than it may seem at first sight. Much of the behavioural thesis involved fieldwork geared to the micro-theory end of the spectrum and this had two aims, one to solve the specific minor problem that was of passing interest, and secondly, to feed material into larger models of the political process. These models have tended to be of two kinds, either fully fledged macro-theories which tend to pull together all the separate sections of the political system and show how they interrelate, or partial theories (i.e. more than micro- but less than macro-) which attempts an analysis of one aspect of the system.

In drawing together these investigations one has tried to use the political system as a core of the analysis and to choose the more interesting areas of partial theory to supplement the examination of general theory. The ensuing treatment is therefore rather different from that of the political sociologist who may cover a similar area of concern but with a different emphasis. Political sociology has become a highly eclectic field and the comment that its extent is defined by its practitioners more than are most academic specialities is undoubtedly true. Political analysis is somewhat more restricted in scope. It is difficult to conceive of an overall view of politics without some recourse to the normative considerations that have been the staple of political thought for many hundreds of years, and it is often alleged that the study of politics in particular—but perhaps social science in general—is meaningless unless pre-eminence is given to the place of ideas in the governance of social behaviour.[3] One can consider this an overstatement while recognizing that analytical approaches depending on behavioural theory are not necessarily complete as paradigms of political life.

It was noted above that behavioural theory has frequently been identified with empiricism and the 'scientific' approach to politics. Although the development of the latter concept will be examined in the body of the text, it is worth pointing out at the outset that it is less of a novelty as a term than is usually realized. Even Disraeli used it: 'It is a peculiar class, that; £1,200 per annum, paid quarterly, is their idea of political science and human nature. To receive £1,200 per annum is government; to try to receive £1,200 per annum is opposition; to wish to receive £1,200 per annum is ambition.'[4] Much the same point could be made about empiricism, but it was not until the twentieth century that a concerted attempt was made to provide general and specialized theories of politics that were dependent on case studies and were relatively low on normative precepts. The advance of methodology in the natural sciences was obviously attractive to social scientists hoping to emulate their pure science colleagues. The improvement of data-gathering, the obvious advance of abstract theory in the social science of economics and the dissatisfaction felt with the legalistic and philosophical strangleholds on the study of politics all contributed to the search for a new methodology to help in the understanding of the phenomena of politics. It is also evident that intellectual trends, especially in the United States, contributed to the 'mood' that many see as the main distinguishing feature of behaviouralism.

Many writers have charted the dominant position of pragmatism in American intellectual developments of the first quarter of the twentieth century.[5] The long-term optimism that stemmed from the Progressive movement, suggesting that all social problems were soluble in time and given good faith, the intellectual influence of William James and certain of his contemporaries, combined with a deep-seated emphasis in American life which gave importance to the individual's capacity to overcome all but the greatest obstacles. John Dewey's faith in scientific method came to be reflected in wider applications than philosophical thought. By the 1920s, with the decline of progressive values in public affairs, academic life seemed to be the last holdover for pragmatism; reinforced by newer concepts beginning to stem from positivism, the way was clear for a theoretical advance based on scientific method to take some hold of the study of politics. The intellectual climate became even fairer for this general approach for the next thirty years or more. The fashion has now changed and normative considerations are again at a premium in political theory. Despite this trend, we have been left with a considerable range of behavioural theory, some of which has been completely accepted into the methodology of political science and some of which is regarded by many as dubious in its application. By taking the idea of the political system and the interrelation of its parts as a key to the technique of political analysis, it is possible to order this vast mass of material and examine the relative utility of particular sets of analytical theory. This is especially true when one considers that there have been two broad areas of approach, as described earlier, and that it is therefore possible to separate out broad strands for survey purposes.

Many general questions about the study of politics can be illuminated by an examination of behavioural theory, its assets and its shortcomings. If the behaviouralists were short on some of the 'gut' issues of politics, such as the effects of class and privilege inside certain political systems, they made up for it by focussing on problems like power distribution thus reawakening interest in basic questions of the discipline. Even those who most dislike the behavioural approach tend to use a more analytic approach than their predecessors of a generation or two ago. The most bitter legacy from the disputes carried on in the name of political science and anti-science is still that of the value content of political theory—can we presume to develop Weber's 'wertfrei' prescription in our theorizing about politics? There may have been something of a 'straw man' created here, for few writers of the stripe regarded as 'behaviouralist' wished to throw out the baby value with the bathwater imprecision. Held values are the stuff of any overall discussion of political preferences and the political analyst generally tends only to separate them out from general structural *and* functional patterns. Any full view of a political process must reinstate them at some stage, yet it may be that the development of analytical theory has brought us nearer to an understanding of what the study of politics is about. Definitions like Easton's 'authoritative allocation of values' and the recent concentration on the decisions made as being the central focii of government activity lead to a limited clarity at least, and this is something that we did not possess in the past.

It was remarked above that intellectual trends in general had a great deal to do with the development of behaviouralism in the United States; a different tradition in Europe has certainly slowed down any crude transference across the Atlantic of a great deal of this theory. Any extreme claims for the analytical school were probably themselves a reflection of the 'end of ideology'[6] phase in the United States which is now seen as highly premature at the least. Similarly, the disgust of the young with what seemed an arid and anaemic brand of theorizing was at least partially due to the Vietnam war, and the less radical generation which now seems to be emerging may be more inclined to a synthesis of styles in political theory. Meanwhile we need to try to digest some decades of theory in this mould, if necessary abandoning any that no longer seem relevant to our purpose. This exercise may help us to understand the political system and its actors; Weber's other well-known tag, *'verstehen'* (understanding), is still one of the most important words in the political scientist's vocabulary. Despite hundreds of years of heated discussion about the nature of politics, we still have an imperfect understanding of the complexities of the subject as it is, leave alone as it should be.

A survey of behavioural theory can never be more than a selection of 'other men's flowers' but the very mass of material flowing from the United States in particular over the last few decades does require distillation. If it provides some sense of the wood where there were only many different kinds of tree before, then it will have served its purpose.

CHAPTER 2

THE SEARCH FOR VALUE-FREE POLITICAL THEORY

It is comparatively rare that one can pinpoint the beginning of an intellectual movement to a particular year but there is a good reason to trace the behavioural movement in political science back to the year 1908. As we tried to show in the introductory chapter, it did not even then spring fully armed from the heads of a few but was a natural outcrop of trends existing in the American culture. It could even be argued that there is a strain of behaviouralism going back to the earlier days of political theory; how often has one heard the comment that Niccolò Machiavelli was the first behavioural scientist? Yet the virtues of 1908 depend on two solid contributions to this relatively new movement in the study of the political process, two books which were not to be challenged in their lonely isolation until the 1920s. Graham Wallas and Arthur Fisher Bentley are the two writers who share the eminence of this pioneer spirit and it is good if chauvinistic to note that the former was British, unlike the majority of his successors who came from the United States.

David Easton placed Wallas's major book in context when he wrote: 'Only within very recent times, however, with the publication of Graham Wallas's *Human Nature in Politics,* if a rough date is to be set, has a body of thinking arisen in the United States which uses psychological categories, not to lay the foundations for later specula-tion or research but as an intrinsic part of that very research.'[1] Wallas opened up many of the areas that would interest political scientists in the twentieth century. Quantitative method, the use of psychology, the border between rational and non-rational inference are three aspects of the study of politics which are the very stuff of that cooler, analytical side of political science emphasized by the

6

behavioural movement. The basic contention of his book *Human Nature in Politics* is that the study of politics is nothing without the study of man, for man's personality and behaviour patterns dominate the development of political actions.

It is ironic to note Wallas's plea for the greater use of sociological method in the study of politics when one considers the influence of many of the major sociological thinkers over the last generation of political scientists but the plea does indicate this Englishman's capacity for unconscious forecasting of future developments in the discipline.[2] It would be unreasonable to expect Wallas to spell out all the implications of his inferences; the equipment to transfer his general aspirations into operational terms was not there in the first decade of the century and some of the examples that he gives are not far from the ludicrous at times. His suggestion that the optimum size of a debating hall for a legislature can be decided by quantitative method would seem to be of this order although, on the other hand, his citation of the 'normal curve' as a pattern of the distribution of variables does look forward to the type of statistical analysis favoured by many recent political scientists.[3]

Wallas is a refreshingly concise writer, lacking the verbosity and pomposity of many who try to prove that the study of politics is a 'science' by excesses of jargon and flamboyant phrasing. He is even able with the simile, as when he likens the 'laws of political economy', dominant in British econo-political thought from 1815 to 1870, to a 'gigantic stuffed policeman, on guard over rent and profits'.[4] There is a gentle, polemical strand in the book, however, and this is contained in the insistence that, because rationality on the part of members of a political system cannot be assumed, there must be substituted for this lack a definite act of will, a mental effort which can reinforce the patterns of democratic choice that face the electorate. When Wallas came to write the preface to the third edition, he was especially depressed that mankind seemed farther than ever away from a self-conscious attempt to develop rational modes of thought and, since the date was 1920, he had even fewer illusions about the inherent rationality of man than he had pre-1914.[5]

For all of this, Wallas expresses a certain long-term optimism, at least in his pre-war writing. He was a one-time Fabian socialist, a 'liberal democrat' and even something of a utilitarian. His other book of note, *The Great Society,* has for its title a phrase which became famous in another context when it was adopted by Lyndon Johnson for his mid-1960s reform programme for the United States. In it, Wallas took up some of the themes of the earlier book, though still without any worked-out analytical system. One has suggested that he owes something to the utilitarian strands of nineteenth-century English philosophy because of his insistence that 'happiness', in the widest sense of the term, is synonymous with the good life, but he did not follow their narrow pleasure–pain dichotomy and was highly critical of the effects of utilitarian doctrine, 'the intellectual bias' of the nineteenth century, which encouraged the worst evils of the factory system.[6] In its place, Wallas saw happiness as the general factor to be maximized but largely through incremental means by devices ranging from proportional representation to the expansion of public education. Therefore, his prescription, if it be such, is in the end a fairly standard liberal one, perhaps not unlike those American programmes of governmental action for community improvement typified by the Lyndon Johnson effort which took over Wallas's phrase (although Wallas feared that the 'Great' in 'Great Society' spelled impersonality rather than opportunity).

It is likely that Wallas will be remembered not for his individual prescriptions that lead to the good life but for his twin interests in methodology, the need to quantify political problems and the dependence of analysis on recognizing human behaviour as it is, rather than creating ideal citizens who will act in the manner of angels rather than of men. If man is an imperfect being, it is necessary to recognize his imperfections and to try to canalize those which lead to the general happiness of the whole community; the ordering of society may similarly restrict the more unpleasant tendencies of the human animal. If the remedy is 'social engineering', Wallas was something of a social engineer but one who believed in the practical solution of specific problems as they arose and not, despite a nod occasionally in the direction of philosophic values, in the creation of normative patterns to which society should conform.

Unlike Wallas, the other 'pioneer' who concerns us here is more definite in his belief in a general analytical tool for analysis in political science. There is a tendency among the practitioners of political science to be tempted by what one can term the 'Holy Grail' myth. This is the feeling that politics can be explained by a relatively simple concept which is awaiting discovery; when it is discovered, a convincing 'general theory' of politics will become possible. As yet, no single-term explanatory theory has achieved any sort of general acceptance but it remains unlikely that this fact will deter those who feel that *the* major discovery in political science is just around the corner. It is true that politics has been highly resistant to explanatory theory of a concise nature and that most general theory has been wordy stuff, saying a great deal to describe but little. For all of the hopes that still exist, it seems unlikely that explanatory theory which covers the political system as a whole will be anything but complex; a degree of parsimony is all that we can hope for. Perhaps it all seemed easier seventy years ago, for Arthur Fisher Bentley based much of his major work in political science (for he wrote across a number of disciplines) on a main concept, that of 'the group'. Although it is sometimes disputed that this idea is the core of his major book, it is certainly the one for which he is remembered and the one which has cemented his place in the development of analytical theory.

Interest in Bentley's work has mainly been generated since the Second World War. His *The Process of Government* had little influence for thirty years after its appearance in 1908 but by the 1950s it had begun to assume the status of a classic and had spawned a virtual 'school' of theorists. This interest has meant that Bentley's life and work has now been well examined, even to the point of assessing unpublished work still only available in manuscript. Since he lived for eighty-seven years—1870 to 1957—Bentley survived from a time when political analysis was in its relative infancy to one where he was hailed as the founder of many of the strands of modern political science. His full-time academic career ended in the 1890s and it is often suggested that the long spell that he spent as a newspaperman after this sharpened his ability to detect the real nature of the political process. However, this shortened academic career must have made acceptance of his interpretation of the political process a slower one than if he had remained a teacher at a well-known university; it must be admitted that he would possibly have been less ready to stake as much as he did on single-dimension explanations of the political process had he been part of a large academic unit.

Bentley is usually regarded as the father of group theory, the belief that the group is the single most powerful explanatory factor in the political process. This is encapsulated in the best-known line from his best-known book: 'When the groups are adequately stated, everything is stated. When I say everything I mean everything. The complete description will mean the complete science, in the study of social phenomena, as in any other field. There will be no more room for animistic "causes" here than there.'[7] Writers like A. J. Beitzinger have occasionally argued that the most important aspect of Bentley's interpretation of politics is not its dependence on the group but the sense that he gives of politics as a 'process', and it is true that this dynamic viewpoint is a vital one in his work.[8] However, it is the notion of group behaviour as being the essential motivating political force that has persisted and influenced political scientists since Bentley's work first came to be noted by the profession. Bentley insisted that the essence of political and social life was 'activity' (a later generation of social scientists might have preferred his alternative, 'action'). To make sense of the activity, one needed some frame of reference, something which was tangible and which was measurable in terms of things done. The 'group' was such a reference-point, if a fluid and shifting one. It could not be otherwise than fluid for Bentley rejected the Marxist concept of hard-and-fast classes, preferring to see the 'mass of men' slipping in and out of specific groups depending on their situation. In a more recent pattern of terminology, these groups can be regarded as 'cross-cutting'; one man could be a member of many groups, according to his place of residence, nationality, religion, his reaction to major issues of the day and so on.

Bentley believed that the 'process' of government was activated by the conflict between group and group. This was real whereas many of the 'ideas' and 'feelings' that cannot be directly rooted in human action were not real in the same way. The group was isolated from the rest of humanity in order that its propensity to exert pressure could be noted (though Bentley seems to have disliked the narrow confines of pressure or interest group theory as such). One of his followers, Charles B. Hagan, has described the group in these terms: 'A group is a segment of human activity focussed upon by the analyst or the investigator for the purposes of his political inquiry.'[9] Bentley's description of political action in this way may appear to be a statement of the obvious today, but in 1908 it provided a radical departure from the formalism which pervaded most discussions of governmental activity.

Where one tends to part company with Bentley's paradigm of political activity is when he tries to equate group activity with the whole of political life. Even so, one would not agree with all the criticisms that have been levelled against his tendency to arrogate supremacy to the group. For example, Bentley denies the existence of what is often termed 'the national interest' as against specific group interests. Not only are there 'no political phenomena except group phenomena', but 'The society itself is nothing other than the complex of the groups that compose it.'[10] This allegation has caused many writers to attack Bentley for what they believe to be a form of arrogance. One of the best-known ripostes was Robert MacIver's: ' . . . As we have sought to show, the whole logic of democracy is based on the conception that there is still a national unity and a common welfare. The fact that the interest in the common welfare cannot be organised after the fashion of specific interest should not conceal from us either its existence or the need to sustain it.'[11]

Many of the received views about democracy have stressed the need to put some abstraction such as 'the people' or 'the public interest' above what are often viewed as selfish and sectional interests. Yet this is usually defined in the last resort as what a majority of the voting public will accept or even what a large minority will back, where there are more than two solutions to a problem which has a 'national' dimension. Much of the writing on democratic theory—such as Dahl's 'intense minority' dilemma (see Chapter Six)—has highlighted the question of who should win in a democracy where this division on alternative outcomes is apparent. Most political issues in a modern state do not have a clear 'national interest' solution, but rather a range of alternatives which will often benefit some but impose costs on other members of the society. The best illustration of this can be seen in a developed country which has problems of planning new forms of transportation or of preserving run-down segments of the economy to stave off local unemployment. Except in a few cases—the 'special interest' of a handful of 'fifth columnists' at a time of enemy invasion could be one example—it is difficult to conceive of a national interest that has not been reached by debate or conflict between specific interests inside the polity.

A much more debatable precept, but one which has aroused rather less controversy, is the following: 'Leadership is not an affair of the individual leader. It is fundamentally an affair of the group.'[12] It is true that a leader is generally impotent without the led ('The power of the boss lies in his machine'[13]), yet it could be argued that without leadership, parties, armies and other powerful groups in the state can dissolve into a rabble with less effective force than a well-knit, well-led group. When discussing pressures on the Executive, Bentley suggests that the President at the time of writing, Theodore Roosevelt, was a significant figure in so far as the various groups could function 'through him'.[14] The picture of Roosevelt as a neutral channel for warring factions is surely belied by all contemporary accounts of the man. The assassin's bullet which killed McKinley and brought Roosevelt to power made 'little difference' in Bentley's view; person-alities pale before the power of the group. One does not need to play the game of 'great figures of history' to presume that, at least on occasion, it is significant that X has wielded power rather than Y in terms of a political event. Action theories make more sense when they are built around actors, whether groups or significant individuals being backed by, and influencing, groups.

Bentley's quest for the Grail is eventually defeated by his own presumption. To state that the group is a powerful force in the political process is indisputable. To state that it is the only one is not proven and is highly suspect as a working model of the way in which political interaction takes place. In Leo Weinstein's words, there is 'a sense of unfulfilled promise' in Bentley's book, unfulfilled because he comes so close to an understanding of the mechanics of politics and then spoils it by a degree of overstatement.[15] Perhaps the real advance in Bentley's early writing as compared with that of his contemporaries is the sense that it gives of the dynamic aspects of 'government' (hitherto a somewhat static term) rather than the 'tool' that he fashioned out of the group concept. It is Paul Kress's view that only the 'secondary strains in Arthur Bentley's social thought have been accepted' and, as we saw earlier, this view seems to be gaining ground.[16] One would still argue that the major influence that Bentley has had on the development of analytical thinking was the concept of the group as a 'heuristic' device, something which enables us to understand the phenomena that we observe. Two versions of 'group theory' are apparent in the literature, one which emphasizes the group as appearing in any part of the political system, the other stressing the importance of the group as part of the 'pressure' or 'interest' sector of the system. Although Bentley's emphasis is on the wider interpretation, he recognized the especial significance of the group in what, *pace* Gabriel Almond, is termed 'interest articulation'.

In a book published in 1969 (posthumously), he took the progressive platform of the day and made a case for its furtherance by 'non-partisan organization operating behind the formal parties', with organizations such as the Municipal Voters League and the National Non-Partisan League given among the examples.[17]

The writers who took Bentley's 1908 book as what one of them called 'the principal bench mark for my thinking' tend to fluctuate between these two viewpoints.[18] David Truman, whose phrase we have just quoted, opted for the 'interest group' approach as the most useful development of group analysis, though not without recognizing that a wider application was possible.[19] Truman refines the Bentley approach in accordance with the more sophisticated attitudes of mid-century. Excesses are tamed and a more moderate view of the political system appears, with familiar landmarks restored. The basic line is modest as compared to the mentor: 'Yet without some working conception of the political role of interest groups, their functions, and the ways in which their powers are exercised, we shall not be able adequately to understand the nature of the political process.'[20] Leadership, as a 'functional relationship', and even public opinion are rescued from the constraints under which Bentley had put them.[21] In fact, few could dispute that Truman's description of the role of interest groups was lucid and reasonably accurate, although the emphasis of the book may tend to arrogate more power to these groups than recent research would suggest that they wield.

Two contemporaries of David Truman tend to take a wider interpretation of group theory and spread its influence to encompass, and almost dominate, the political system. Earl Latham's assessment is a sweeping one: 'Beginning with Alfred [sic] Bentley in 1908 American writers on politics have increasingly accepted the view that the group is the basic political form.'[22] Latham believes that, in 'private' as well as 'public' government, the group is the major dynamic unit and this is summarized at the opening of his book: 'The chief social values cherished by individuals in modern society are realised through groups.'[23] Latham combines the group interpretation of politics with the sense that the real stuff of the discipline is the study of the exercise of power: 'The ubiquity of power in human relations and its manifestations in group forms other than the state are the reason for believing that the subject matter of politics is power, contrary to the view that its subject matter is the state, which is only one of the engines through which power is exercised.'[24] As we shall see, the 'power' strain in this analysis comes in through another body of writers and will concern us later in this chapter. Latham uses the group framework as a way of tracing through a specific case study in which a variety of groups inside the system compete and contend to influence the outcomes of the system. Similarly, Bertram Gross, in another early-1950s genuflection to the Bentley thesis, portrays the legislative process as one which is essentially a 'struggle' of competing groups, not only 'pressure' groups but groups inside the legislature and elsewhere.

Fashions in political analysis tend to reflect in diluted form the major trends in thinking of the day, and it is perhaps no accident that Gross, writing in the early 1950s, tends to reflect something of the high tide of the American consumer economy with its emphasis on a competitive ethos. The subtitle of his book is *A study in social combat,* and the thesis implies that free competition in the legislative field is as natural as it is in American economic life. This is perhaps reasonable if one is trying to be relatively value-free, though Gross recognizes that values tend to come poking in and that the best that one can do is to recognize this: 'True objectivity consists not of trying to withhold judgement but of recognizing one's biasses. Straightforward analysis requires an effort to state these biasses as candidly as possible.'[25] The final apology for the group thesis therefore was that it gave a relatively objective viewpoint from which to analyze the political system, allowing one to segregate the normative considerations from the descriptive and to assess each as data which provides the final configuration.

Group theory shares with pluralism the status of a near-ideology in the views of many critics. The one is heavily dependent on the other since pluralism is based on the concept of group competition for the achievement of political goals. Yet even if we accept it as a framework for analysis, it still seems incomplete. Although it identifies the actors or the players of the game, it does not supply us with the 'rules' or the scenario in enough detail to see how the various outcomes of the political process are reached. To use another metaphor, group theory is rather like a recipe which provides a list of ingredients but fails to add the quantities and the method of cooking them to produce the final dish. Group theory seems to invite this metaphorical type of criticism, for it gives one a picture of large objects—icebergs, perhaps? —clashing blindly against each other and with a 'happy ending' in the way in which the political system contends with the conflict. It is a peripheral pattern of analysis, useful in its identification of the protagonists and important in extending the range of actors involved away from the purely governmental ones to the many 'private' organizations which have political influence. Yet it fails to identify the internal dynamic of the system and it has lost influence as an overall explanation because of this fact.

For all the criticisms that one has made of the development of group theory, its domination of a great deal of mid-century American political thought has to be recognized; without it, the whole concept of pluralism, for example, would mean little. The Bentley influence has persisted and he remains the one writer from the earliest part of this century who has directly influenced his compatriots looking for analytical methods in political science. The only other important figure to appear before the evolution of the 'Chicago School' is Walter Lippmann, though it is only in his initial writing that one detects a real analytical approach.

Lippmann has been a man of many parts on the American literary scene for more than sixty years, straddling journalism and philosophy, and as adviser and critic to the major public figures of our times. His early influences included Freud, Wallas and William James; all three are drawn upon in a book published in 1913, especially Wallas, and parts of the book seem to come directly from the work of the older man who taught Lippmann at Harvard in 1910 and became a friend and mentor to the young American: 'In other words, we must put man at the center of politics, even though we are densely ignorant both of man and of politics.'[26] At this stage of his development, Lippmann was firmly set in the pragmatic mould, tending in fact to a socialistic view of the world. This was heavily modified, even by the end of the First World War and, for most of his life since then, Lippmann has remained a free-enterprise liberal with a suspicion of 'big government' balanced by a recognition that some governmental intervention is inevitable to preserve liberal values in the twentieth century.

Up to the publication of his book *Public Opinion* in 1922 Lippmann retained an interest in the more analytical side of political thought, and that book did exercize some influence on the development of theories of voting and democratic behaviour (see later chapters). Lippmann then moved across the philosophical spectrum to a point which was finally summarized in his obsession with the 'public philosophy', a reversion to the thesis that the good society is dependent on the observance of natural law. One cannot do better than give Reinhold Niebuhr's criticism of this:

> Traditional concepts of natural law presuppose a classical ontology, which equates history with nature and does not allow for the endless contingencies of history and the variety of its configuration. If we do full justice to these contingencies, our norms are bound to be no more precise than the general feelings that there are standards of justice which transcend any conceivable positive law.[27]

Lippmann travelled, in thirty years or so, from the twentieth century to the eighteenth in his quest for a basis for his belief in a type of liberal democracy. In a series of books, he passed from early pragmatism, through a penetrating assessment of the real place of public opinion in modern society to his final ambiguous retreat into a less-than-satisfactory attempt to isolate a democratic ideology based on generalization. As a spoiled political analyst, he flirted with concepts like political culture in his first book, with a concise description of its nature that one looks for in vain in his philosophic writing of later years:

> Culture is the name for what people are interested in, their thoughts, their models, the books they read and the speeches they hear, their table-talk, gossip, controversies, historical sense and scientific training, the values they appreciate, the quality of life they admire. All communities have a culture. It is the climate of their civilization. Without a favorable culture political schemes are a mere imposition. They will not work without a people to work them.[28]

There speaks the pupil of Wallas and we hear something of a foretaste of later approaches to behavioural theory. When the United States gained a 'philosopher–journalist' and a conscience for its statesmen, it also lost a potential political scientist who might have added much to our real knowledge of the working of the political system.

The 'Chicago School' and their associates

At least two of the social sciences owe a great debt to the University of Chicago, which has been a great forcing-house of theory in the twentieth century. Although it may be that the Chicagoan economists have left a more formidable mark on their discipline than the political scientists on theirs, any assessment of comparative influence would probably conclude that it was a close-run thing. Undoubtedly, the 'dean' of this school was Charles Edward Merriam, who was a dominant force at the University during the first four decades of this century and even after his retirement, down to his death in 1953. Merriam remains a controversial figure, praised by many as a great figure in the development of American political science, denigrated by others as a poor, imprecise writer who promised much in analytical terms but delivered little. As a teacher and counsellor, he is remembered by a whole generation of academics who were encouraged to press ahead with research projects, fired by his enthusiasm and assistance. Harold Lasswell, the late V. O. Key and Gabriel Almond head a long list of those who worked with him in their youth. It may be that it will be for inspiration of this type, and perhaps also for his work in helping to set up the Social Science Research Council in 1924, that Merriam will be best remembered. Despite his deep involvement and participation in Chicago city politics, a severe practical school if there ever was one, and his advocacy of political behaviour research in the 1920s, his written work is generally disappointing, much of it lacking the exactitude and clarity that he sought for the descipline as a whole.

Merriam's seminal book is *New Aspects of Politics*, published in 1925. It is basically a checklist of topics for future investigation, including: ' . . . the relation of politics to psychology, the use of the quantitative method in political inquiry, the relation of politics to the study of environment and of biology, the organization of political prudence. . . .'[29] At this time, Merriam was insistent on basing the study of politics on the study of human behaviour though he bemoaned the fact that a 'scientific' development of the subject was not possible until data-collection, precise standards of measurement and a degree of objectivity were automatic equipment of the political scientist.[30] By this time, the question of 'value-free' analysis was becoming a critical one in any discussions of the science of politics, and Merriam's view, for example, that the political system might possess a configuration repeated the world over is a critical advance towards comparison which emphasized objectivity and sought similarities as well as differences in regimes wherever and whenever they were found: 'While it is sometimes asserted that history does not repeat itself, the political process appears to be much the same in different periods, making allowance for certain variables that must be calculated.'[31] In Merriam's view, it was essential that a more precise approach to both governing and the study of politics was developed, if only because of what he saw as the spread of democracy. He seemed to be an optimist about the degree and the benefits of such a movement: 'The democratic movement, the larger leisure of mankind, the broader education of humanity, the new forms of intercommunication, the larger resources available for scientific inquiry—these are factors which are likely to force a readjustment of the bases of the political order. . . .'[32]

Merriam did not see himself as an isolated pioneer, for he felt that a pragmatic strain had already established itself in the humanities and social sciences with the work of men like Charles A. Beard and E. R. A. Seligman. In 1931, when the second edition of his book was published, he could point to a whole corpus of recent writing which pursued the lines that he had recommended a few years earlier.[33] For example, in 1928 Stuart Rice's *Quantitative Methods in Politics* had appeared. This was an important landmark in the development of research into mass voting and other political situations where quantification was possible, and we will need to refer to it again later in this context. Rice was quite definite on the need to distil out one's value system when examining a political situation: 'As a social philosopher, one may be keenly interested in furthering child welfare, good government, and other "reforms". As a social scientist, one is indifferent to furthering them.'[34] Rice was not unrealistic about the extent to which objectivity in the social sciences was possible. He understood the difference between the natural and social sciences as well as anybody and did not underrate the difficulties faced by the student of the latter in getting to grips with his subject-matter. The fact that the social scientist can become easily involved with the material that he studies, whereas the natural scientist rarely does, was recognized by Rice and, because of this, he felt that experimentation, for example, was not possible in his field to the extent that it was for natural scientists.[35] This has been a constant theme for argument since early in the century, though it is now evident that the distinction is one of degree rather than kind. One could instance the case of a zoologist—surely a 'natural' scientist—becoming involved in the question of preserving from extinction a species that he was studying. The whole question is still far from settled.

Another of the contemporary works cited by Merriam in 1931 is of especial interest because it marks another rare incursion into the field of political analysis by an Englishman, though one who worked at this time at Cornell University. George (now Sir George) Catlin supported the view that an exact science could be made of the arrangements by which political power is exercized, and indeed went rather further than, say, Rice in seeing the possibilities: 'There is no inherent reason why the study of political data should not reveal natural regularities of process; the field admits of treatment by scientific hypothesis, with the causal connection of "if . . . then"; and its conclusions are not incapable of being tested by controlled experiment.'[36] This is a little sanguine since, even today, 'controlled experiment' in the way that the natural sciences know the term still presents enormous difficulties to the political scientist. Understandably, people dislike being 'guinea-pigs' in anything but the simplest form of game-playing or simulation exercises; it is not easy to reproduce the real relationship of the political arena in an artificial context.

In his autobiography published in 1972, Catlin reminisced about this early period of his professional life when he was involved in the apparent take-off in American political science, marked by a new and increasing interest in methodology. It is a long passage, but as the creed of the new optimism in the discipline it could hardly be bettered:

> We distinguished the empiricism of political science from the speculation of political philosophy; we stressed the fundamental and methodological identity (of some administrative importance) between political science and political sociology; we emphasized anew, aided by Stuart Rice and Jacques Rueff, the challenged importance of a quantitative approach . . . then dismissed with contempt.
>   We defined again what we meant by 'power'. . . . We took note of the contributions of psychology. We found in the Concept of Power the central hypothesis of our science, and around this construed our conceptual system—as economics had done around the pursuit of wealth—our abstractions and our models.[37]

This 'concept' is one which has long fascinated political scientists. For Merriam and for some of his associates, 'power' was the Holy Grail, as 'the group' had been for Bentley. In 1934 he published a book devoted to its examination. The concept was a tempting but a tantalizing one, used by students and practitioners of the political process with rarely any clear definition of its meaning. Later writers, such as Robert Dahl, were able to give a clearer idea of its nature, but Merriam failed to do this, and we are left with a hazy idea which is difficult to 'operationalize'.[38] Merriam recognizes that the word calls for definition but cannot bring himself to be exact: 'Political power possesses a peculiar and *indefinable* integrating quality, important for the individual personality and for the social group of which he is a part' (our emphasis).[39] Little of Merriam's later writing approaches the verve and style of *New Aspects*. Virtually nothing of the promise of that book is sustained in written form, whatever may have been the verbal impetus that he is supposed to have supplied to those who worked with him. His last major book, *Systematic Politics,* published in 1945, is anything but systematic, as many have pointed out. Once again it promises much: 'I propose to analyze political behavior in the light of the factors that surround institutional forms, ideologies, political patterns, or clusters of patterns in particular political societies.'[40] Measurement, and even concise definition, are noticeably absent and, although a shrewd phrase appears here and there, the overall impression is of a rambling collection of thoughts about politics.

Merriam's star pupil and main disciple was Harold Lasswell, who has long been one of the most venerated elder statesmen of American political science. He took up many of the themes that Merriam had 'floated' in the 1920s and made a little more of them than his mentor had done. Like Merriam, he was interested in the application of psychological method to the study of political acts and was also something of a follower of the 'politics is power' concept that Merriam had popularized. An even more prolific writer than Merriam (including fields that lie outside our immediate jurisdiction), it is worth isolating certain themes which illustrate the main trends of his thought.

Lasswell moved even further away from the undiluted 'group' approach to politics than had Merriam. He has been interested in the classification of personality types as revealed in the careers of political activists, and shows a decided Freudian bent in the way in which he has traced back certain of their public attitudes to childhood with its intra-familial tensions and sexual repressions. In an early book he summed up the contention that exists in political life between the 'rational' and the 'irrational' forces that coexist in the individual psychology:

> Politics, moreover, is the sphere of conflict, and brings out all the
> vanity and venom, the narcissism and aggression, of the contending
> parties . . . politics is the process by which the irrational bases of
> society are brought out into the open. . . . Politics seems to be
> irrational because it is the only phase of collective life in which
> society tries to be rational.[41]

We might feel less confident than Lasswell did forty years ago in
defining the line between these two supposed dichotomous areas of
human behaviour, but his insistence on our understanding the well-
springs of individual psychology as it affects political behaviour is as
relevant now as it was then. Lasswell came back to this theme later in
his career but, for many years, he was more preoccupied with the
distribution of that political commodity which he and his mentor liked
to describe as 'power'.

As suggested above, 'power', though attractive as a key concept
(mainly because there are few people who deny its presence in political
operation), is inherently clumsy if we are looking for something which
will give an exact idea of the nature of specific or general political
relationships. One way in which Harold Lasswell tried to make it more
precise was to take over the concept of 'the élite' from those European
political theorists who had first developed it and apply it in what, for
the Chicagoans, was a surprisingly succinct manner. In Lasswell's
view, as set out in what is probably his best-known book, the distinction between the small group with the ability to direct public affairs
and the large one with no direct influence on the outcomes of politics
is the most crucial one in the polity and defines society in a way that
other forms of analysis cannot do:

> The study of politics is the study of influence and the influential.
> The science of politics states conditions, the philosophy of politics
> justifies preferences. . . . The influential are those who get the most
> of what there is to get. Available values may be classified as
> *deference, income, safety.* Those who get the most are elite; the rest
> are *mass.*[42]

Lasswell absorbs stratification by social class into his model of society
and allows it as one means of distinguishing between the élite and the
non-élite, together with the adoption of special skills by the élite and
the power, if we dare use the word in a non-Lasswellian sense, of the
individual personality which is likely to predominate among élite
groups. Thus Lasswell has here absorbed both group and more

individualistic views of the nature of society into a general picture of its shape.

The mal-distribution of the ability to change direction of a polity is inevitable in the Lasswellian view, but he does not appear to have argued from this point to a lack of faith in democracy. The democratic society can survive, but only if the 'enemy'—'human destructiveness' —is kept in check.[43] In a later book he tries to distinguish between power good and power bad, power which is used for worthy as against unworthy purposes. He also comes close to that idea of 'power' which contemporary theorists, while downgrading its paramount position, have clarified: 'At this point we narrow our conception of power, using the term to designate relations in which severe deprivations are expected to follow the breach of a pattern of conduct. This eliminated an enormous range of relationships in which a breach is assumed to be of trivial importance.'[44] Lasswell eventually felt confident of being able to relate power to the whole of the political system in a scheme which progressed like a mathematical proof from definition to definition. He reiterated the distinction present in his earlier work between the theory that he was propounding and theory which contained a strongly normative strain, what he termed 'political doctrine': 'It [the book] contains no elaborations of political doctrine, of what the state and society ought to be. Historically . . . such doctrines have served chiefly to justify the political philosopher's own preferences.'[45] By 1950 Lasswell had clarified his view of power to the point where it still remained the base value of the political system but had a number of others circling around it (respect, rectitude, affection). It could now be defined—or rather described—in terms which complemented the attempts of post-Second World War political science to adopt the standards of measurement once advocated by Merriam: 'G has power over H with respect to the values K if G participates in the making of decisions affecting the K-policies of H.'[46] Of course, it is still difficult to quantify a proposition such as this but it is relatively precise, relative that is to the generalizations of a generation earlier.

Yet by this time the need for a 'deference value' which would define the nature of politics was beginning to loom less large in Lasswell's work. He was now toying with ideas which would be taken up with enthusiasm by younger colleagues and which became the basis of much behavioural theory of the 1950s and 1960s. Two such ideas are the act of decision-making as the central one in the political process, and the 'developmental standpoint' which provided a setting for the process. Power, as we have suggested earlier, is an amorphous concept by itself but when allied to the act of decision-making it takes on a new meaning. It looks forward to the systems theories which took 'input' and 'output' as their main strands, for the decision is the essential link between the two phases of such a systemic view. Similarly, the belief that political systems are in a constant state of change or 'development' provides a necessary dynamic strain to the static nature of much political theorizing. It contrasts with the Parsonian stress on 'equilibrium' which we will examine in the next chapter and links up with the latest patterns of behavioural analysis which are discussed in Chapter Four.

These two themes are not only apparent in the 1950 book with Kaplan but also in much of Lasswell's later, episodical writing that Heinz Eulau has managed to draw together. There is yet a third theme which appears but this is less useful—the redefinition of the social sciences as 'policy sciences' because they are of use in policy-making; surely this once again confuses the value–fact division and smacks too much of social engineering!

The abundance of themes in Harold Lasswell's writing has made him one of the most influential of American political scientists; his later evolution towards a more dynamic view of the political process provides an essential bridge into the patterns of analysis favoured in the last twenty years among the so-called 'behavioural' school. Yet there are defects in Lasswell's method of presenting ideas which make him an infuriating writer at best. Heinz Eulau sums it up well: 'On the negative side, it seems to me, Lasswell's undisciplined ways of presentation have tended to make his total work seem disjointed.'[47] Although ideas are there in abundance, few are ever worked out with the rigour that is required if they are to be useful in the analysis of concrete political issues and situations. There is, even in Lasswell's work, that tendency to slide off into generalities or vague abstractions that marred Merriam's work even more. He does mark an advance on the work of the 1920s that is little more than aspiration but, reading much of even his later work today, one can be exasperated by hares that are started but rarely caught.

Conclusion

Apart from T. V. Smith, the political philosopher and colleague of Merriam and Lasswell, whose pragmatic brand of philosophy contributed little to methodology as such, we have tried to examine the principal American and British contributors to the 'American science of politics'. This half-derisive label was the title of a well-known critique of what is, in effect, the early development of behavioural political science and the attempt to distinguish between normative and analytical approaches to the study of politics. Bernard Crick's attack was aimed principally at Bentley, Merriam and Lasswell. His implication is that their work is confused, empty of content and—in the case of Lasswell—near to being totalitarian in its ethos.[48] While one would agree with some of his milder strictures and even with his reluctance to admit a close identification of social science methodology with that of the natural sciences, the criticisms are too sweeping to be acceptable. There is a tendency to throw out baby, bathwater and bath all in one go. Why is it that writers such as Key, Odegard and Herring, who were associated with the above and who derived some of their academic motivation from their work, are acceptable and the begetters not acceptable? Quality of academic writing is the real test here but the case studies associated with the younger men might not have appeared without the formal statements of theory that stemmed from their predecessors.

Crick would probably be the first to agree that there is a slightly dated air about his book now, since there have been many developments in political analysis since the mid-1950s when, presumably, the bulk of his research was completed; the 'windmills' tilted against have moved. If the attempts to create a relatively value-free political science depended solely on the work of those whom we have sampled in this chapter, one might agree that political analysis was an interesting by-way in the study of politics and little more. However, the work of Bentley, Merriam and the others was little but a foundation, perhaps not even the complete foundation, and a sturdier edifice than even they could have hoped to see has been erected in the last generation.

In short, one can recognize the value of the pioneering efforts of the self-styled 'political scientists' of the first half of the twentieth century at the same time that one recognizes their limitations. Without the new orientation that they brought to the study of politics, much of the more valuable work produced in the last twenty years would not have been possible. Speaking about the Fabians, Alfred Zimmern is supposed to have remarked that 'Mr and Mrs Webb are interested in town councils; Graham Wallas is interested in town councillors.'[49] For a rounded view of the political process, both the institution itself *and* those who operate it are worthy of study and if these 'border scouts', to use Crick's definition of Lasswell's role, did little more than chart a passage for future exploration, then it was surely a useful exercise in the development of a greater understanding of the nature of politics.

CHAPTER 3

SOCIOLOGY AND POLITICAL THOUGHT

Political analysis is essentially an eclectic discipline or sub-discipline, and it has tended to borrow its methodology without shame from whatever source seemed appropriate. In particular, there was a considerable period during which it drew almost exclusively from sociology and social anthropology for new ideas which would order the data collected into understandable patterns. The tendency for the study of politics to overlap its sister social sciences, despite their comparative youth, has led to some confusion in the minds of those with only a nodding acquaintance of them. For example, that branch of sociology known as political sociology has a subject-matter which is very similar to that which we are describing under the heading of political analysis. With the increasing tendency for social scientists to become interdisciplinary in their work, the overlapping of disciplines is of far less importance than it once may have been, and the fact that political scientists tend to talk of political analysis where sociologists talk of political sociology is mostly a question of semantic convenience, though it does indicate a slight shift of emphasis depending on one's starting-point. Other differences in emphasis are noticeable since sociologists have tended to become sceptical of the validity of systems theory at a time when political scientists still find themselves tempted by this approach, but hard-and-fast divisions have not existed and the line between the sociologist's and the behavioural political scientist's interests becomes increasingly blurred.

Sociologists, developing their 'science of society', were inevitably students of the way in which political arrangements impinged on the relationships between the various actors, individually and in groups. Many of the major pioneers of sociological thought—Michels, Mosca,

Pareto and others—have been absorbed into the development of various aspects of the 'partial' theories in political analysis, touched on in the latter part of this book. One of the 'founding fathers' of sociology, Max Weber, is noteworthy for his influence over developments in specific subject areas, particularly administrative theory, and also for certain general concepts which still permeate analytical thinking in the study of politics. For this reason, it is difficult to discuss the ways in which we study political behaviour without general reference to his work.

Max Weber

Since the span of Weber's life (1864–1920) almost exactly paralleled the rise and fall of the Second German Empire, it is not surprising that some of his writing reacted to events which occurred during that short-lived imperial dream. Yet he was also a great eclectic and in his interpretation of the political arrangements of societies ancient and modern he ranged over a considerable gamut of human experience. It is difficult to find, in Weber, a coherent framework into which all his major tools of analysis will fit. Although he has been captured by Parsonian sociology as the ancestor of the 'action' frame of reference, Weber's approach is more general and less stilted than 'action' as it has been translated by structural functionalism. Weber starts from the concept of the actor 'understanding' his own acts or, in one of the German tags that are associated with him, this is the *verstehen* approach to the way in which society works; Gerth and Mills have summarized this: 'Man can "understand" or attempt to "understand" his own intentions through introspection, and he may interpret the motives of other men's conduct in terms of their professed or ascribed intentions.'[1] Therefore, this is a world in which rationality can exist and in which men sometimes say what they mean and do what they say they are going to do, though not always! From a general principle such as this Weber could try to isolate political action as a phenomenon worthy of study. Runciman has argued that we must accept *verstehen* in what he calls 'the harmless sense', that we should '. . . understand the meaning of someone's words or thoughts before being able to explain them, it then becomes possible to reconcile his doctrine of '*verstehen*' with an acceptance of the relevance to the social sciences of presumptive psychological laws'.[2] But the concept implies more than that; as we argue elsewhere, it supports those who believe that a degree of rational action is to be expected in political life.

Certain of Weber's ideas about political action are to be found summarized in a lecture given late in his life. '*Independent* leadership in action' is his starting-point, but he prefers to limit this to the exercize of such leadership in a 'state' rather than in *any* group which acts in a corporate manner. This leads to one of his most famous definitions, one which illuminates both the nature of political activity and the physical bounds inside which it is normally conducted: 'We have to say that a state is a human community that (successfully) claims the *monopoly of the legitimate use of physical force* within a given territory.'[3] To some extent, we can see the influence of Weber's immediate background here, for he never attempted to belittle the position of the nation-state in political life, either descriptively or in normative fashion. Power (*macht*) and the state dependent on it (*machtstaat*) feature heavily in his writing on the nature of politics. He sees power relatively simply as the right to use physical force legally within this geographical limit, and he quotes the then contemporary saying of Trotsky (at Brest-Litovsk) that 'every state is founded on force'. Inside the state, political actions are dependent on the exercise of power, dividing up the right to use it between those groups and individuals who are politically most effective; internationally, politics also deals largely with this power relationship between nation-states. There is little in this description of the stuff of politics that any statesman of the period would have found offensive, and one's main criticism of it today would be that it implies that politics is of concern almost exclusively to the formally constituted officers of the state, once again a less than surprising emphasis when viewed against the received views of the time. In particular, the German state with which Weber was inevitably concerned *was* a veritable 'power-state', hierarchical and bureaucratic, conducive to Weber's adoption of the belief that 'the concept of power is highly comprehensive from the viewpoint of sociology'.[4] There has always been a certain amount of dispute over the degree to which Weber believed in the parliamentary strain in recent German history, such as it was, as compared to the 'Caesaristic' one which, in the views of some, resulted in the eventual domination of the *Führer-prinzip* under the Nazis. Yet it has been argued convincingly that Weber favoured strong leadership backed up by parliamentary majorities which give the leaders a mandate as long as success ensues in political terms: 'The whole broad mass of deputies function *only* as a following for the "leader" or the few leaders who form the Cabinet, and obey them blindly *as long* as they are successful. . . . This "Caesaristic" ingredient is (*in mass states*) indestructible.'[5]

It would seem therefore that power is, for Weber, not an aggressive force but the inevitable concomitant of politics, the 'stuff' that allows society to operate in those areas where collective decision-making and enforcement is necessary. He never states it quite as succinctly as this, and there is a tendency to describe political activity within a very wide parameter without much concern about the ends or goals that are proper—even in a descriptive, non-normative way—and when he writes about the distribution of power there is little sense that power must be used for specified ends such as the provision or redistribution of valued things in the community. Possibly, Weber would have assumed that the redistributive nature of the political system was to be taken for granted, but he left it for later writers to define political activity more accurately. At least, *his* concept of power is simpler and more understandable than the attempts of the Chicago School writers who postdated him. His definition of power is at least as parsimonious as those put forward by American political scientists thirty or forty years later: 'Power is the probability that one actor within a social relationship will be in a position to carry out his own will despite resistance, regardless of the basis on which this popularity rests.'[6] One can sense the beginnings here of the 'probabilistic' theories of later political scientists and an aspect of the relationship between the natural and social sciences that appears in much of Weber's writing. The difference between them is one of degree rather than kind, and it is not true that the natural sciences can possess an exactitude which far outstrips the social sciences. Yet Weber recognized that the number of variables in the causal chain that made up social phenomena was usually more considerable than in the natural sciences and that this meant that inferences had to be 'probabilistic', that is, one could make a more-than-educated guess at the causes of a phenomena but one could not be absolutely certain that weighting and choice of causes was correct (in the power context, one cannot always be absolutely sure that B does something because A has power over him and A desires the end).

It is true that, as Carl Friedrich has pointed out, there is some ambiguity in Weber's concept of power though it is one that he might have eliminated had he lived longer. There is less ambiguity—though some controversy over its implications—about the analysis of authority that complements it. This analysis is contained in a set of 'ideal types', a pattern of analysis of which Weber was very fond. From a picture of the state and of the power which it represents, it was perhaps inevitable that Weber would look at the relationship between the rulers and the ruled that keeps the state intact, at least between revolutionary upsurges which challenge authority. First, though, one must be clear about Weber's meaning when he uses the term 'ideal type'. It can be distinguished from the Platonic ideal, the 'bed in Heaven' to which all earthly beds only approximate; nor is it a completely idealistic concept, but rather a distillation of reality for study purposes. It is a little more than a classificatory system for the 'types' can be combined and, in fact, one should not expect to find an ideal type in the real world but a reality which contains (in the vast majority of cases) traces of more than one type even if one dominates. In Weber's own words: '. . . sociological analysis both abstracts from reality and at the same time helps us to understand it, in that it shows with what degree of approximation a concrete historical phenomenon can be subsumed under one or more of these concepts.'[8]

The essence of the Weberian analysis of 'authority' is that he concerns himself exclusively with legitimacy and, by inference if nothing else, relegates authority with a low degree of legitimacy to an unimportant category. Legitimacy implies that the ruled recognize the right of the rulers to command and will obey these commands while the relationship endures. This is quite distinct from what some would term the ruler's right to rule, for this has a normative connotation; it involves an ethical dimension that has little place in such a descriptive model. If the mass of the ruled obey the commands of the rulers then legitimate authority exists in the state at that time. In effect, it is granted by the subjects or the people at large to the ruler or the government of the day and can be withdrawn by a variety of methods, ranging from electoral defeat to revolution. Anything that can be termed 'illegitimate' authority (almost a negation in terms in the

Weberian construct) would be unstable and quickly resolved into a degree of legitimacy. This relationship, amounting to domination of a large group by a much smaller one, has been finely distilled from Weber's references to it by Reinhard Bendix in one of the best-known glosses on the master's works. Isolating the components of the 'reciprocal relationship' into rulers, ruled, command structure and compliance, Bendix emphasizes the beliefs and expectations of both sides in a behavioural pattern of anticipated reactions:

> In addition to the fact that they issue commands, the rulers claim that they have legitimate authority to do so, and hence they expect their commands to be obeyed. In the same way, the obedience of the ruled is guided to some extent by the idea that the rulers and their commands constitute a legitimate order of authority.[9]

The sub-division of the relationship into three ideal types provides what is probably the best-known set of categories derived from Weber's writing and one of the most useful classifications that sociology has provided for the political scientist. Weber terms them 'inner justifications', three types of domination that tend to be accepted: 'traditional', 'charismatic' and 'legal'.[10] The first of these is the easiest to understand for it flows from the tendency of communities to accept that which has always been accepted; that which has been handed down through chiefs, elders or pure custom tends to continue while that social system endures intact. The rulers in a traditional society tend to inherit their power or be chosen by a customary procedure, 'patriarch and the patrimonial prince of yore', and be served by a household or by a set of feudal retainers. Until the rise of the modern nation-state, and even during its early phases, the traditional pattern of authority was obviously the predominant one. Feudal society was perhaps its most refined variant and it is now rare in a comparatively pure form, though many societies retain an element of tradition, Britain being an obvious example.

Although members of the general public are unlikely to recognize much of Weber's work in popularized forms, his second type of legitimate authority has percolated their consciousness. 'Charisma', once a term to describe that 'gift of grace' possessed by religious leaders, is now thrown about indiscriminately to explain the hold that particular politicians, or any personable public figures, have on the masses. It is not many years since the best-known of American newspapers ran a Sunday feature on the major political figures of the day as a sort of game, arguing which were charismatic and which were not—for example, Castro (early) was and Castro (late) was not. Charisma clings to the individual leader—it is difficult to think of a charismatic group—and it is the prophet, the great war leader or the spellbinding political demagogue, who typifies the charismatic leader in practice. Weber described this process as a 'calling' and suggested that the charisma was retained as long as men at large believed in the leader and his right to lead them. Such leadership, as he says, 'has emerged in all places and in all historical epochs'.[11] His definition is, of course, more tightly organized than the popularized version and it would apply to comparatively few of the examples that are cited in the press or in casual comment. Once again, authority that is completely dependent on charisma is rare and it is often an adjunct to political power produced by more routine means.

The 'legal' or 'rational–legal' type of legitimate authority is the variant that many of us like to think is prevalent in the modern world. 'The rule of law' is a claim made by many polities, ranging from 'liberal' to 'people's democracies' and beyond. Constitution-making, surely an epitome of the 'legal' approach to authority, is the necessary concomitant to every new nation, even if in practice such nations are often steeped in tradition or subject to charismatic take-over. If laws are laid down and observed, if conduct follows the prescriptions of the constitutional and statutory powers, then a high degree of 'legal' authority is present in the state. Parsons has summed it up:

> Under this pattern of authority political leadership is itself legally bound in the framework of something like a constitution, but equally by virtue of this legal framework it is in certain respects independent of ethical and religious control in either the traditionalistic or charismatic senses.[12]

It is the 'legal' type which is especially identified with the growth of the bureaucracy, that infrastructure of administrative officials who implement the system and who are responsible, in theory at least, to the elected representatives who head the constitutional framework. There is a degree of bureaucracy in any organized state and therefore administrators are often responsible to traditional or 'charismatic' rulers, but the bureaucracy really comes into its own in the state with an ordered constitution and a considerable dependence on legal procedures. Weber's major role in the early development of administrative theory is elaborated in a later chapter; one needs do little more here than to note it as a key element in his contribution to political analysis.

In assessing the importance of Weber's typology of legitimate government, a major factor must be the influence it has had on later analytical constructs. Most of the major post-war American political scientists who have tried to frame models of the political system have at least genuflected in the direction of the ideal-type statement of legitimate authority even though some (for instance Almond and Eisenstadt) have found it more useful than others (for instance Easton and Deutsch), the latter tending to be critical of the lack of depth, or indeed of any extensive dimension, in the construct.[13] As an overall framework, with a terminology that is now taken for granted in the language of political science, it remains one of the bases of our understanding of a significant relationship in politics, that of the mass of the governed towards the governors. The ideal-type pattern of analysis, in this instance at least, did provide a useful tool to chisel away at the nature of political power, rather in the way that H. H. Brunn has summarized its usefulness: 'What apparently makes the ideal types particularly useful, in Weber's view, to the presentation of scientific results is their ability to retain and reproduce the *significant* parts of reality, the parts, that is, which are of special interest to the historical sciences.'[14] The confusion has often been between the nature of reality and the abstractions that are used to order reality into a comprehensible pattern. It is understandable in this instance because of Weber's insistence that the types rarely appear in isolation from one another. Most of Weber's interpreters would accept this as a necessary *and* useful aspect of the framework. Bendix, writing on this occasion with Guenther Roth, has pointed out the way in which the 'Kennedy clan', epitomizing personal power, exercize it via charisma, patrimonial traditional authority plus a considerable organizational infrastructure; even George Washington is not allowed the 'gift of grace' unalloyed: 'Genuine as Washington's charisma probably was, it was acted out in a framework of received political and legal institutions.'[15] No one would claim that the threefold typology is a complete analysis of the nature of political power. It tends to be static, snapshot-like in its depiction of society, lacking the mobility of a fully developmental construct; yet, in such an aspect of the theory as the 'routinization of charisma', Weber does explain change within a relatively limited framework.[16] What is important is the facility provided by the theory to see how authority is held in a society and how actors tend to view themselves in a society where certain ideal-type characteristics operate. In fact, there is much in common between this approach and the concept of 'culture' which is a factor of much of the writing on political development. Weber, by implicitly suggest-ing a continuum of societal types, based on a range of characteristics, is heading in a direction which is opposite to uni-causal theory (hence his suspicions of certain parts of the Marxist dogma); instead, it is pointing clearly to the more eclectic systems theories of recent years.

Although Weber eschewed one overall grand theory to explain society, the selected ideas mentioned above have wielded enormous influence on behavioural theory in political science; one should emphasize 'selected' because much of Weber's writing has distant connections only with the political life of the state. Before leaving his work, some emphasis must be laid on an all-pervading aspect of it, the aspiration for it to be *'wertfrei'* or 'value-free'. Considerable dispute has raged over the credibility of Weber's contention that the presentation of facts and the evaluation of desired ends should be kept distinct 'because fact-finding and evaluation happen to be two different things'.[17] This simple distinction is often ignored, and the bone of *'wertfrei'* is worried over by many who either wish to refute the division entirely or to modify it, or even to justify an even greater importation of value-judgment into social science than 'descriptive' social science already possesses.[18] Perhaps the modifiers provide the most interesting glosses even when it is not fully sympathetic with their point of view. Runciman, for example, seems to argue that the distinction is usually self-evident and only of vital importance where facts are interpreted by actors specifically in terms of their held values, yet one would think that this has been a basic problem in social science. As Runciman emphasizes, one must be clear what is a fact and what is a value.[19] It is very easy to mistake a Boojum for a Snark with the sort of disastrous fate which befell Lewis Carroll's Baker. It should be possible for the observer to recognize that the social sciences perceive a certain range of phenomena as facts and another range as values and that, as far as possible, they should be kept apart when analysis is being carried out. It is doubtful whether Weber would have wanted to go beyond this comparatively limited aim though, at this late stage, it is impossible to be certain about this. Of course, facts are interpreted according to the value systems of participants and observers, but the social scientist, when in an observing capacity, should possess the training to detect the vital overlap of the two discrete items. This tends to bring us round full circle again to that sense of understanding the behaviour and intentions of the actors in a systemic context. To possess this is to be able to order the phenomena one is studying in a meaningful context, one which will be intelligible to the outside world.

For someone who did not provide a clear-cut model of the social system as a whole, it may seem surprising that Weber has had such a profound influence on the behavioural aspects of the social sciences. Part of the answer to both of these factors may lie in the historical context in which Weber wrote: '. . . given the intellectual situation of his time, it is exceedingly unlikely that Weber would have presented a work of symmetrically rounded perfection at all.'[20] Parsons' comment reflects Weber's reaction to the formalistic and metaphysical strains present in the German academic world of the late nineteenth century. It was the beginning of a reaction which made much of the development of sociology a possibility (though Weber was one of a handful of scholars in several countries who can be said to have 'fathered' this development). It also led into the newer approaches to political science which were eventually dubbed 'behavioural'—at a time when later Weber-inspired sociologists were exercizing an independent influence on the methodology of the discipline. Therefore, Weber's influence can be said to have been cumulative and probably unequalled in this relatively narrow line of the influence of the one discipline on the other. Whether by luck, judgment, historical inevitability, or a combination of these, Weber's choice of political phenomena to study chimes in with those that concern political scientists of a more recent period. His terminology and certain of his constructs have now become a significant part of the analytical approach to the study of politics and may in fact be more fundamental in their influence than more recent phases in sociological thought.

The input from social anthropology

On the face of it, the study of primitive society might appear to offer little to those seeking knowledge of modern political systems, but in fact some substantial sectors of recent methodology owe their origins to the writing of certain social anthropologists, even those studying the primitive survivals among twentieth-century inhabitants of this planet. In fact, the more interesting developments in methodology seem to have come from those anthropologists who are identified with relatively undeveloped societies rather than those who have now transferred their attentions to contemporary civilizations which are considered to be relatively 'developed'.

The major strands of methodology which originate mainly from the social anthropologist are the concepts of culture and the various tenets of functionalism; others used by this range of social scientists, such as the concept of 'the group', have a more general origin inside social science as a whole. It is not difficult to see why anthropologists felt the need to acquire a framework of study and reference for the societies that came under their examination. Basic questions in the discipline demanded this. Were societies, especially those remote in time or because of the poorer transport conditions prevalent in the early twentieth century, to be regarded as *sui generis,* or were there patterns of institution and/or behaviour which one could expect to find in all societies once one had delved beneath the surface of custom, ritual and ceremony? Even if each social system was completely idiosyncratic, some frame of reference was needed to condense the many characteristics visible into a pattern capable of comparative usage; hence the use of the idea of each society possessing a culture which could be described. Responses of groups and individuals could be seen to bear a relationship to the cultural base of the society, a base which, in its turn, changes over time. Because it is such an all-embracing term, 'culture' is sometimes cumbersome to handle and, although essential to any comparison of societal systems, it can be little more than a catch-all if some degree of precision is not built into the way in which it is used. Bronislaw Malinowski based his interpretation of the concept on the fact of man as a creature with biological needs; he writes:

Whether we consider a very simple or primitive culture or an extremely complex and developed one, we are confronted by a vast apparatus, partly material, partly human and partly spiritual, by which man is able to cope with the concrete, specific problems that face him. These problems arise out of the fact that man has a body subject to various organic needs, and that he lives in an environment which is his best friend, in that it provides the raw materials of man's handiwork, and also his dangerous enemy, in that it harbors many hostile forces.[21]

On top of this, and to satisfy these basic needs, man creates an apparatus which has a life of its own and tends to elaborate the cultural pattern in its turn. Malinowski sees this leading to the creation of institutions which become organized around the basic needs and values of a specific community at a particular time and which will then tend to persist until pressures bring about substantive changes or even elimination of the structure. Cultural constructs tend to emphasize those recurring patterns of behaviour which adopt the same outward form in a society over a range of years and which lead one to expect certain reactions to stimuli rather than others. The essence of cultural study is that one must keep close to the context; in other words a custom, belief or practice means little unless one relates it to the society under study. In its turn, culture has a reinforcing quality which enables societies to survive certain short-term stresses. Malinowski's near-contemporary, A. R. Radcliffe-Brown, emphasizes this point:

The function of culture as a whole is to unite individual human beings into more or less stable social structures, i.e., stable systems of groups determining and regulating the relation of those individuals to one another, and providing such internal adaptation between the component individuals or groups, as to make possible an ordered social life.[22]

Political scientists have taken over the concept of culture with some enthusiasm, as we shall see in the next chapter. In so doing, there has been the usual process of modification that has occurred with all—or almost all—of the borrowing that has taken place from the sister social sciences during the time that the study of politics has tried to make itself into a more exact discipline. On the whole, political analysis tends to use the theory as less of an all-embracing framework than did the anthropologists earlier in the century, and especially Malinowski and Radcliffe-Brown, who had taken it up enthusiastically.

It is obviously narrower in the sense that political culture should refer principally to political objects rather than the wider social symbols of basic drives that the anthropologist studies. Also the emphasis on traits like stability has become less marked with the increasing desire for dynamic theories of the political system, ones which will explain change rather than laying emphasis on the persistence of certain characteristics over time, important as that may be. It is, of course, an even stronger criticism levelled at the theories of functionalism which are joined to a degree to the cultural approach. Yet one would not disagree strongly with Malinowski's dictum that: '[Culture] is a large-scale moulding matrix; a gigantic conditioning apparatus. In each generation it produces its type of individual. In each generation it is in turn reshaped by its carriers.'[23]

The functional theories developed by the anthropologists mentioned above do contain certain faults which have been carried over into sociology proper and even occasionally—but far less often—into political analysis. Evans-Pritchard has claimed that the functional approach in anthropology is in error when it ignores the history of the institutions which make up a particular culture and, if this is so, it would be a grievous fault. It is arguable that, although there is a tendency to downgrade the value of history as an explanatory variable (perhaps because the functional anthropologists tended to concentrate on primitive societies without written records), these writers do not ignore it entirely.[24] The essence of the functional approach is the use of equilibrium to explain the way in which the social structure operates, the state of equilibrium only persisting by continual renewal rather 'like the chemical-physiological homeostasis of a living organism'.[25] Radcliffe-Brown admits that a particularly strong disturbance may result in a new equilibrium 'which differs from the one previously existing.'[26] As we shall see, the study of historical development has made a distinct come-back in the overall study of political systems and, where functional analysis downgrades it as an essential ingredient of understanding the nature of a specific social system, it would seem to be at fault.

Functionalism in social anthropology operates at a more elementary level than the later complex and more elaborated concepts prevalent in sociology for several decades. It stemmed from the belief that in all behaviour patterns there are limits within which variation can take place if the organism is to survive and conditions that must be met if the organism is to flourish. In society, there are certain roles that need to be played out if the societal balance is to be maintained, although the outward manifestation can differ from society to society. Basic needs have cultural responses and these tend to throw up organizations which contribute to the overall institutional structure of the society. A secondary set of needs, what Malinowski terms 'derived needs', slowly develops as society copes with the elementary wants and tries to extend its potential for satisfying wants on a higher plane, in effect maximizing secondary wants—comfort as against simple shelter, elaborate armies rather than armed guards. It is from this increasing complexity that political organization tends to develop; the need to establish a formal pattern of authority with sanctions available in the form of authorized violence leading to the primitive, then less and less primitive, institutions which make up the state. Schapera's suggestion that 'there is a broad correlation between the political system and mode of subsistence' is not, as he takes pains to point out, pure economic determinism but a fairly obvious correlation showing that larger and more involved communities inevitably need more functional specificity in government.[27]

The relatively narrow range of ideas selected from early twentieth-century social anthropology had a far-reaching effect on the elaboration of general theoretical constructs which attempted to explain the overall workings of the political system. In particular, the way in which these ideas related to one another conditioned the development of systematic theory. Radcliffe-Brown claimed that: 'You can study culture only as a characteristic of a social system. Therefore, if you are going to have a science, it must be a science of social systems.'[28] Translating this approach to the study of politics, one can see how the 'system' as an over-arching concept has proved to be as persuasive to political scientists as it was to these anthropologists of a generation earlier. 'Political culture' has become a vital reference-point in comparing political systems, a set of political behavioural patterns as vital to the student of politics as the more general theory of 'culture' was to this group of anthropologists, and adaptations of the 'functional' view of the social system have similarly left their mark. However, it is from sociology itself that the strongest influence of functional theory has applied itself, and, briefly at least, political science was much affected by the work of writers such as Levy, Merton and, especially, Talcott Parsons.

Modern sociology and structural functionalism

Political science has borrowed extensively from sociology, mainly because the latter descipline has made an effort to develop methodology with a lower content of normative thought than has the main stream of philosophic political thought. This is a comparative rather than an absolute difference for sociology has had its normative theorists; who more so than Marx, claimed as a sociologist by many of that profession though surely exceeding its confines? From sociology, the political scientist has selected what has seemed to be useful for the problems facing him; this is why the overlap has tended to include some of the prominent names in the history of the younger discipline and, at the same time, virtually ignores others. Compared to the diffusion of Weber's ideas among political scientists, for example, the writings of Emile Durkheim are of less influence despite his elaboration of certain concepts which have carried over the divide between the two disciplines, especially that of 'anomie' and also some contribution to the development of functional analysis. Durkheim has lacked the expert commentary in English that Weber has enjoyed for so long— at least until recently when the balance has been redressed somewhat.[29] Also, his main concerns seemed of less interest to the political scientist when compared with, say, Weber's preoccupation with authority and the organizational basis of government. A re-examination of Durkheim may well alter this state of affairs, but that is where it stands at the moment and it does not detract from the fact that Durkheim's indirect influence is considerable, due to his position in the early foundation of sociological methodology.

We are concerned here mainly with the ways in which general theory in political analysis has been influenced by sociological writing over the last few decades. This brings us back to the analysis of whole systems afforded by the functional approach. This is now inextricably linked in the minds of those with a general interest in methodology with the name of Talcott Parsons, a theorist whose writings are a byword for obscurity in the eyes of many who have read him casually and even by those who have tried to use his measures of analysis.[30] In fact, Parsons has used functionalism as a part of a larger design and would probably dislike the rigidity with which he has been tied to it. The key to his model is that phrase which forms part of his first major book, 'social action'. Although it has been modified over the years, it remains in outline similar to this early description. There is some circularity in the definition of the 'act' which is central to action theory for it is said to 'imply' an actor, to have an 'end', to take place in a developing 'situation' and to be pre-selected according to the norms of the actor.[31] 'Social action' is, in fact, Parsons's umbrella term for the nature of human behaviour as it occurs between individuals and groups. From it one spirals down, so to speak, to the social system itself, for social action encompasses the elementary biological and social processes by which the actor tries to attain gratifications or avoid the deprivations that form an attraction–repellence force in human activity. It would be just possible to think of social action in a Robinson Crusoe situation, though perhaps only if there was another actor, a Man Friday, hardly enough to form a social system but enough to represent a setting for the action.

Parsons uses the concept of 'culture' to emphasize the orientation of the actors to a social system, for culture implies a set of symbols by which the actors can get their bearings. There is a comparatively succinct definition of the social system in one of Parsons' best-known books and it sums up, as far as this can be done briefly, the relationship between his general concept and the societal application:

> Reduced to the simplest possible terms, then, a social system consists in a plurality of individual actors interacting with each other in a situation which has at least a physical or environmental aspect, actors who are motivated in terms of a tendency to the optimization of gratification and whose relation to their situations, including each other, is defined and mediated in terms of a system of culturally structured and shared symbols.[32]

As well as the social system, the general structure is said to have two other components, the cultural system and the individual personality system. They are held to be independent yet indispensable to each other, therefore interdependence is perhaps the best overall description of their relationship. Following the general point of view of the anthropologists, Parsons tends to use culture as a basic attribute of his action system, with the emphasis on its transmittability, its transfer across the system by the learning process and subsequent sharing within the boundaries of a common culture. The social system itself is merely held to be the mode of interaction of individual actors and, though obviously a basic sector of the whole Parsonian schema (and one of his books has that very title, *The Social System*), it is subsidiary to the concept of action itself. Most political scientists have tended to relate their model-building to some overall view of a system —'political' by choice—rather than a concept which is somehow superior or senior to the system itself, and this is perhaps one reason why the outline that Parsons developed has had a relatively limited impact on them in its unadulterated form, though its indirect effect has been more considerable.

Inside the social system, actors are said to take up 'roles' and this is used as a major unit of analysis. A lengthy definition sums up the Parsonian view of roles:

> The role is that organized sector of an actor's orientation which constitutes and defines his participation in an interactive process. It involves a set of complementary expectations concerning his own actions and those of the others with whom he interacts. . . . Roles are institutionalized when they are fully congruous with the prevailing culture patterns and are organized around expectations of conformity with moral sanctioned patterns of value-orientation shared by the members of the collectivity in which the role functions.[33]

For the political scientist, this has become a useful concept. The political system demands that activation should be instigated by individuals and groups which expect certain satisfactions from it. The culture and the basic institutional pattern both tend to circumscribe and determine the nature of the part that an active member of the system plays in the process of political action, and this sense of role-playing, in which competition and co-operation with other members of the system are both called for, can be viewed inside the general description given in the quotation. Whether this treatment by Parsons is a sufficiently dynamic interpretation of the 'role' as it operates in the political system is a question which is linked to much of the criticism that has been levelled at the writings of Talcott Parsons as used by political scientists.

It is when one turns to the next stage of Parsons' schema that one sees some of the more controversial features which have ranged supporters and critics up against one another. A contrast is set up between a social system which has 'a persistent order' or which undergoes 'an orderly process of development change' on the one hand and one which is close to disintegration on the other.[34] Since this is the stage when a functional dimension is introduced, it is worth remembering the nature of the chief ideological objection (there are others) which is levelled against this style of analysis when used by men like Parsons. Percy Cohen expresses it thus:

> The chief criticism of this kind is that functionalism encourages or reflects a conservative bias. The argument behind this is that functionalism, by emphasising the harmonious relationships between different parts of a social system, tends to treat each system as though it were the best of all possible worlds.[35]

In order to analyze social systems and to explain the reasons for their persistence, Parsons argues that societal differentiation 'must be functional', and he puts forward a 'master scheme of four functions' which will show how societies tend to divide into sub-systems which make analysis easier and clearer.[36] The four have become probably the best-known section of Parsons' constructs, and much of the criticism of Parsons' ideas rests on their interpretation.

The first of them, 'pattern-maintenance', which acts primarily through the cultural system and which sets up the main symbols and codes by which members of the system operate, is often looked upon as an invitation to retain the status quo at all costs, though Parsons argues that it 'is by no means incompatible with a great deal of social change—quite the contrary'.[37] The general social system is the main carrier of the 'integrative' function, although on the one occasion that Parsons looked at voting studies he claimed that they illustrated this aspect of his theory, political support stemming mainly from what he terms 'the structure of solidarity groups in the society', that is the reference and small groups identified by Lazarsfeld, Berelson and their colleagues as the chief sources of influence in voting terms.[38] Presumably, voting makes the individual feel a part of the system and encourages him to feel that his demands on the decision-makers are being listened to and that his support is valued by them, all factors that cut down anomic tendencies and intensify integration.

The third function, 'adaptation', embraces the relation of the actors to the conditions in the external world and is said to be best typified by the economic sub-system and the exchanges that go on between that sub-system and the others in the whole system. 'Goal-attainment', the final function, is that most closely associated with the political sub-system and the main contributions of the political to the social system are contained in the basic political components of the system. Parsons expresses this in the following words:

The main output of the polity to the integrative system is effective leadership, which is a form of power, and the main input into the polity from the integrative system is generalized support. Or, to put it a little differently, the *goal* of the polity is the production or generation of effective leadership and, on the less general level, of binding decisions.[39]

For many political scientists, this way of looking at social systems in general does give an idea of the functional necessities present if a social system is to persist and also some idea of the interrelation between the various sub-systems which carry these functions. It is not easy however to 'operationalize' the Parsons schema in political science terms. As Lipset has commented, the Parsons theories are 'very general', perhaps because of the emphasis given to conditioning and socialization in the Theory of Action.[40] It is true that a device such as the 'pattern variables' tries to provide a picture of certain social attributes that are present in a given system and that these are useful for comparative purposes. For example, one of Parsons' original five sets of pattern variables is the ascription–achievement axis, and it could be useful in comparing political systems to understand that one derived from a social system in which individuals were ranked on the basis of heredity qualifications (which would be 'ascriptive'), while another was much more achievement-oriented and merit was rewarded with places and material reward; governing élites would be likely to reflect this contrast among other groups. Similarly, the remaining four of the original set (others have been suggested)—universalism–particularism, diffuseness–specificity, neutrality–affectivity, self-orientation–collective orientation—refer to characteristics in social and political systems which are useful for reference and broad comparison. One could in fact draw a 'sawtooth' profile of a range of societies according to the position that each takes up (in approximate terms) along each of the five continua. But it remains a generalized pattern of comparison and does not tell us a great deal about the operation of the political sub-system, even in relation to the grand design which Parsons puts forward.[41]

It is true that there are one or two political scientists who take the view that the Parsons framework provides a particularly sharp tool for the analysis of political systems. The two that especially spring to mind are the American William Mitchell and the late Peter Nettl, an Englishman who died in the United States. Mitchell is perhaps the major political science disciple of Parsons, having written a survey of American politics in a framework mainly derived from the master and also a handbook of Parsonian theory in its application to the study of politics.[42] In fact, Mitchell's inquiry into the 'American polity' tends to show up some of the drawbacks of Parson's methodology as applied to the breakdown of a political system. Although Mitchell can fit the various components of the American political system into the broad categories laid down by Parsons, he continually needs to draw on more specialized models to show how the institutions and other components operate, and there is therefore almost as much drawn from the work of men like Dahl and Almond as from Parsons himself. There is of course no reason why such an eclectic approach should not succeed and the only cavil is at the original assumption that so much of a functional analysis of the system could be based on Parsons. Similarly, in his guide to Parsonian theory for political scientists Mitchell tends to apologize profusely for the shortcomings of the model in certain key areas. For example, he admits that Parsons' paradigm of the input side of the political system is 'more ambiguous than others', the latter being systems theorists like Almond and Easton, yet input analysis is one of the most fruitful areas where empirical research and methodology have converged in recent years.[43] Elsewhere he states that, by implication, the political sub-system is ambiguously defined, that the conversion process has not been set forth in detail, and that his theories are more in the nature of 'ground-clearing' than empirical tools.[44] These are comments which would meet with a fair measure of agreement from students of Parsons though they are balanced, as would be expected, by claims for the value of the design in fitting the political system into the grander action system which summates man's activities and its especial utility in explaining political change which originates outside the polity.[45] Mitchell is highly articulate in the defence of his mentor but, in the last resort, he is not able to convince one that the Grand Design offered by Parsons is the best single way to analyze political systems.

Nettl's review of systems theories in a famous, almost notorious, paper covered four alternative system concepts in political science: Parsonian functionalism, analogue or circuit theory (as found in Deutsch or Easton), 'specific performance' theory (Almond, though Easton would surely fit here too), and general systems theory (Bertalanffy, Ashby) though the latter is regarded as marginally important as far as political analysis is concerned. In fact, his second and third alternatives seem to overlap so much that it could be argued that the only real alternative posed in the paper is between the Parsonian approach and the purely 'political' one developed by the range of writers with which the next chapter concerns itself, especially Almond, Easton and Deutsch. Nettl sets up a number of criteria to show how he reached the view that the first of his four systems is the one to be preferred but, although the criteria are relevant, his application of them is suspect to some degree. 'Comparability' is a vital criterion since much systems theory was developed in order to aid comparison between political systems, and one would agree with Nettl that what one might term the 'purely political' approach is suitable for comparing systems through time and with one another. Yet his suggestion that Parsonian theory is suited to the latter type of comparison as well as to comparing sub-systems of the social system with one another (say, political with social) is surely not true, since the degree of comparability offered by Parsonian types between one political system and another, although not negligible, is limited when one compares it to Almond's or Easton's typologies.[46] Admittedly, Nettl claimed that there were three stronger criteria for preferring Parsons to any other systems theorist. These were its range of application, the purely political systems approaches being too narrow in his view; the referent criteria of each, the second and third categories here being 'relatively old wine in new bottles' because they tend to refer to structures rather than functions; and the question of organizing power, where he plumps for the strictly functional model on the grounds that it provides for an assessment of values, whereas one of the most persuasive arguments against it is that it has a degree of value-implication built into the system. Although closely, almost meticulously, argued, one's feeling is that Nettl turned some of the obvious arguments on their heads in order to press the validity of the systems approach which he favoured.[47]

We have been critical here with those who believe that a wholesale adoption of the Parsonian approach is the best course for producing general systems theories for the examination, delineation and comparison of political systems. On the other hand, there is little doubt that Parsons' influence on general theories of the political system has been considerable. His ideas on the interrelation between the sub-systems of the social system, the use of the concepts of role and culture, and the need to understand the working of a system in functional terms have all rubbed off on later theorists who have tried to frame the political system in some sort of analytical setting. He remains a highly controversial figure in sociological circles, but it is difficult to imagine any contemporary examination of the systems approach and its applicability to political analysis without a considerable genuflection in his direction.

Although Parsons is not the only sociologist associated with the 'functional' approach to have influenced analytical political science, he is the major one. Others were often his close colleagues (Smelser and Bales) or those who travelled along lines which were similar (Marion Levy). One figure of the broadly 'functional' school who does stand out, from our point of interest, is Robert Merton; Merton does offer an alternative use of the method, one rather more restricted than Parsons' in its parameters. Merton tends to start from small sectors of the system under study and tries to understand why the items looked at persist and how they should be interpreted. His division of functions into 'manifest' (intended and recognized by members of the system) and 'latent' (neither intended nor recognized) is extremely interesting to the political scientist because of one of his major examples, the political machine. He points out that the machine has usually been regarded in the United States as being 'bad' and 'undesirable' yet that it has continued in being for a considerable time (presumably, he would interpret many of the contemporary characteristics of American political organization as holding over from the great days of the machines). His generalization about the needs and wants that the machine satisfies stems from a general argument:

> Proceeding from the functional view, therefore, that we should *ordinarily* (not invariably) expect persistent social patterns and social structures to perform positive functions *which are at the time not adequately fulfilled by other existing patterns and structures,* the thought occurs that perhaps this publicly maligned organization is, *under present conditions,* satisfying basic latent functions.[48] (Author's emphasis.)

The machine offers personalized and local services which, in Merton's view, the official structure fails to provide; it also services business, legitimate and illegitimate, and provides a degree of social mobility for certain sub-groups who otherwise would find it difficult to use their talents to the full. Merton first propounded this thesis in the 1940s and, already, it has become less applicable to American politics than it was then, although it is unlikely to disappear entirely as a phenomenon. The growth of more effective political organization and the 'manifest' regard for the personal service function in the political system, such as improved welfare services, have led to the decline of the machine in its cruder forms. Yet Merton's analogy explains the long life of the political machine in more direct and accurate terms than any non-sociological model could do. In addition, his final conclusion of the section using the machine as an example of this division of functional types is one which bears examination in a wide area of analytical operation; 'structure affects function and function affects structure'.[49]

Conclusion

Political scientists have pirated sociological method unmercifully in order to improve their analysis of political systems. Any review of this process must come to two general conclusions. One is that the borrowing of certain overall concepts has been enormously useful; it has enlarged the vocabulary and increased the general understanding of the relationship between politics and the rest of the social system in many ways. Without its penetration of the structures which bring men together, it is doubtful whether even the limited advances made in the analysis of political systems over the last two decades would have taken place. However, the second conclusion is one that qualifies the first to some degree. It is that sociological method of itself has been less useful than some of its protagonists have claimed it would be. This is best seen in the balance sheet of the Parsonian school as it has covered the political enterprises of society. The problem here is that politics emerges as a relatively small part of a large design. As mentioned earlier, one spirals down from the overall action system to the social system to the political system along one side of a considerable pyramid of systemic apparati. This is useful when looking at the question of interchange but less so when one is examining the political system itself, for the methodology is rudimentary in the extreme by the time one is down to this junior level in the hierarchy.

Without the impetus of sociological thought, it is doubtful whether the material which forms the basis for the next chapter would have been written, at least not in the profusion in which it appeared in the 1950s and 1960s. Yet its elaboration indicates that sociological method by itself was not adequate to the examination of the fine tuning of the political system. Even this elaborated theory is still very much a rough-and-ready set of methodology and it is still questionable whether a really effective macro-theory has emerged to cover the whole system as against its component parts. Compared to what was available twenty years ago it forms an impressive whole; a review of its range will show that modern political science is beginning to be a valid methodological approach to the age-old problems of how states and similar political organizations operate in practice rather than in philosophical theory.

CHAPTER 4

GENERAL THEORY AND THE POLITICAL SYSTEM

Although many of the ideas originating in the work described in the last chapter form a starting-point for much of the general theory which has been a major influence in political analysis since the later 1950s, it formed a foundation rather than the main structure. As suggested in that chapter, there has been a concentration on the political aspects of the social system in the newer patterns of general theory. In the first place, attention was paid to the political system as such, attempts were made to delineate its nature and to show how it operated, principally as a process which reacted to pressures but depended on the support of its rank and file, eventually making decisions which its authority could enforce, modifying the political environment as it did so. The 'circuit' analogy, rather like the diagram of a piece of electronic equipment, was, and to some extent still is, a popular entry into the analysis of the political system, for it was neat and seemed to tie up loose ends as well as stressing the dynamic nature of the system. Certain of its assumptions remain though the stress has moved to a type of model which is multi-dimensional, including the essential one of time, in the more extended sense than the working-through of a short-term demand. In other words, a degree of neatness is now sacrificed to a more comprehensive, if slightly more amorphous, type of construct. The frame of reference has been enlarged to take greater note of historical development and even to try to embrace the question of problem-solving through held value positions in a way that borders on the normative.

The Political System

A useful starting-point for the examination of the later stages of the elaboration of general theory is to take a book written by David Easton in the early 1950s with this very title—*The Political System*. With Gabriel Almond, Easton has been one of the two most influential writers on general theory of the last twenty years, and his work in its successive phases has helped to mark stages of thought along the way to constructing a full-blown theory of politics which will have a major explanatory force. The subtitle for the 1953 book is *An Inquiry into the State of Political Science* and the book summarizes both the problems and the possibilities inherent in the development of general theory as they could then be seen. Although it is now evident that David Easton would qualify some of the statements made in the book in the light of the events of the last twenty years, it would seem to be generally agreed that much of its import is still relevant and that it remains an excellent primer for its times.[1]

Easton saw the state of American political science in the post-Second World War period as lacking in real conceptual tools with which to understand the nature of politics, despite the advances in fact-gathering and general empirical research which had occurred. He argued that: 'Without a conscious understanding of the role of theory and its possibility . . . political research must remain fragmentary and heterogeneous, unable to fulfill the promise in its designation as a political *science*.'[2] In order to clarify the direction which theoretical inquiry should take, the author argued that one must try to narrow down the subject-matter of political science since definitions had failed to give any clearer idea of the political aspects of the social system as a framework in itself. Easton puts forward what has become probably the best-known single definition of the role of the political system, that which equates political acts with those which relate 'to the authoritative allocation of values for a society'.[3] For a clear understanding of what this phrase means, one must isolate its three main components, 'authoritative allocations', 'values' and 'society'. Taking them in reverse order, for this is the order of ascending complexity, 'society' is involved because rules and other authoritative decisions made in small groups which are of interest only to them may have little effect on the society as a whole (and, though Easton does not labour this point, membership of small groups may be voluntary, membership of the overall society is not). 'Values' in this context may be best understood as 'valued things' rather than moral values although, in certain circumstances, the latter could be relevant; societies often try to impose moral codes on their members. 'Authoritative allocations' suggests that the political system is enforcing distribution of valued things over which there is dispute and when, for example, distribution cannot be left to the economic system. With this minimum of glossing, Easton's explanation of the political process in terms of the making and enforcing of decisions, by implication resting on the Weberian idea of 'legitimacy', gives a clearer picture of its nature than almost any other.

Although the phrase just examined is the one for which this text will be long remembered, much of the subsidiary discussion is equally worthy of preservation. There is a lengthy examination of the use of the equilibrium concept in the creation of a general theory of politics. This is somewhat of a cliff-hanger, for Easton saw certain attractions in the idea of a moving equilibrium which would eliminate some of the problems found in the more static view of equilibria found elsewhere in scientific theory. Finally, though, he is persuaded that, despite its uses on the road to the development of general theory, 'its ultimate value can lie only in the very fact of its inadequacy for a systematic political theory'.[4] The suggestion is that the value of the moving equilibrium lies in its emphasis on political change and this is, in retrospect, the most important advance made by Easton at this time. Although he presses for use to be made of the behavioural data which were beginning to become available through empirical research, he does not claim that political science can be value-free in every respect and he is ready to admit that 'the development of systematic theory will normally be related to the moral views of the theorist'.[5] Although no clear model of the political system is put forward in the book, the ground is prepared carefully and the focus of the problem —that is, the need for a dynamic general theory of the political process—is sharply indicated and it remained then for Easton to show how this might take shape.

An outline of such a general theory was first put forward by Easton in an article published in 1957 and eventually amplified at length in two books, both of which appeared in 1965. In the 1957 article one can see a blend of the old and the new. Use is made of the concept of culture derived from some of the sociological models referred to in the last chapter, culture here being used as a setting 'that shapes [the members'] general goals, specific objectives, and the procedures that the members feel ought to be used'.[6] Socialization, of the political variety, is also used to show how role-playing and a level of expectation are built up, how in fact members of the political system are conditioned to an attachment to the system. The use of the theory of systems itself is a carry-over from sociological thought as well as taking off from *The Political System*—although the latter gives few hints on how the analysis of the political system is to be elaborated. What is new (though it has some origin in economic thought) is the input–output framework now put forward as the most comprehensive way to view the political system. As advanced by David Easton, it is a beautifully clear and lucid concept, which is probably why it has been so readily adopted and why the terminology used quickly passed into everyday use by political scientists.

The Eastonian input–output model is usually illustrated by a diagram which looks something like an Indian war-arrow, a small box with two sets of inputs, a single output, plus a 'feedback' to the input side. The thesis is that political systems make authoritative decisions (outputs) on prompting from the input side, chiefly from the demands that are made on the decision-makers. The second set of inputs—supports—consists of people's actions and attitudes of mind which enable demands to be transformed into decisions. 'Support is fed into the political system in relation to three objects: the community, the regime, and the government'; this is Easton's summary of the tripartite division of the system needing support.[7] 'Regime', often used by other writers as a synonym for the government of the day, means here the principles upon which the political system bases itself, including for example a well-established written constitution. There is very little in the article about the output–feedback sector of the loop, the accent in the explanation being laid down on the input side and on the relation between the political system and the environment. The latter has some affinity to the Parsonian concept of the social system as a whole for, according to Easton: 'In the environment we have such systems as the ecology, economy, culture, personality, social structure and demography.'[8] It is the exchange between these sub-systems and the political system that provides much of the demand 'push' for the political process, although some demands are generated from within the political system itself (this is a division expanded in later work).

The obvious attractions of the Easton model include its immediacy, that is, the fact that one can quickly comprehend it and establish its relevance to the facts of political life as one knows them, and the sense of dynamism that pervades it. One can see how an issue may be generated, probably from some sector of the environment, become intense enough to demand a decision, and then how this output can be fed back to modify the input side, at least to the point where the demand will be modified. Much of the process is suggested rather than spelt out in this early article, although the sense of movement is clearly indicated: ' . . . inputs give a political system its dynamic character. They furnish it both with the raw material or information that the system is called upon to process and with the energy to keep it going.'[9] Despite its attractions, there are a number of criticisms that one might make of the model on the basis of this article. However, since it was expanded considerably by Easton's later work, it is essential to look at that to see how far the model is amplified before trying to assess its place as a major analytical instrument.

Easton moves from an approach to a framework and, finally, to a full-blown systems analysis in the work which we are reviewing here. His framework is one of the definitive behavioural theory documents, emphasizing the analytical value of treating political life as 'a system of behaviour' and establishing the set of interactions which allocate authoritatively the valued things in a society. In a definition which remains his basic one, he states that: 'The political system is the most inclusive system of behavior in a society for the authoritative allocation of values.'[10] Members of the system act politically when they are engaged in activities relevant to this definition. Of course, they operate in other systemic patterns as well but it is possible to isolate the systems, political and otherwise, that form an environment, either within the general society (when they will be intra-societal) or outside the immediate society (when they will be extra-societal).

Since the emphasis now is on the mobile nature of political systems, the idea of a political system as continually tending to a state of equilibrium is finally discarded. However, the system as a system persists over time despite the inevitable stresses that occur; this must not be confused with change which can take place all the time but lays emphasis on the degree of continuity of the form; the point is made best by stating the antithesis: ' . . . it appears that nonpersistence points to a condition that involves more than mere change. It suggests the complete breakdown and evaporation of a political system.'[11] Stress comes across the boundaries from the environment or from within the political system itself. It may be contained or it may, in some instances, push what Easton terms the 'essential variables' (an adaptation from the writer on cybernetics, W. Ross Ashby) to the point where the system itself is basically changed. For example, if stresses on a Western democracy led to serious curtailment of freedom of speech as presently tolerated, an 'essential variable' would have been displaced and the system would appear to be moving from one that was comparatively democratic to one which was nearer to a totalitarian state.[12] It is emphasized at this point that the Parsonian concept of exchanges across boundaries as of necessity being of mutual benefit is not part of the Eastonian model; the latter regards exchange as being neutral in meaning, though not of course in effect.[13] Easton here comes back to the flow model which he sketched out in the 1957 article and suggests that inputs act on the political system so as to create disturbance, the system reacts to the stress and, unless the stress is too great, responds by producing outputs to relieve it. Movement, dynamism is all in this model; as Easton says, 'it [the system] is able to get something done'.[14]

Many of these points are further amplified in Easton's subsequent (and to date, final) book in the series. He reiterates the essential behavioural basis of his model: 'We have been interpreting political life as a system of behavior set in an environment and open to the influences stemming from that environment, as well as from internal sources.'[15]

The dynamics of the system now occupies a central place in the model with doubt placed on political theories which have emphasized allocative aspects as such. This may seem a little confusing to the casual reader of Easton—if such could exist—for he uses the 'authoritative allocation' phrase continually. What he sees as allocative theory of the past is the 'who gets what, when and how' variety as compared to the systems approach, which 'draws us away from a discussion of the way in which the political pie is cut up and how it happens to be cut up in one way rather than another'.[16] In other words, research based on interest in distribution of valued things without interest in the way that the political system gathers in total resources and the way in which it persists under stress is bound to give an incomplete view of political life. It is this book in particular which tackles the problems of systemic stress and the nature of support for the system in a way that the previous ones did not. 'Demand input overload' is an obvious type of stress on the system, the latter being unable to cope with the volume generated at a particular time, but the kind of demand generated can also generate stress, if for example demands come from a specialized quarter with vehemence but lack a general consensus (this discussion contains echoes of Dahl's comments on the 'intensity problem' in *A Preface to Democracy Theory*). But stress can also come from basic divisions in the community which cut into support for the system.

If one is concerned, as Easton is, with the persistence of the political system under conditions of stress, the changing nature of potential support for the system is of major importance. Outputs would have no effect if members of the system united in rejecting them, that is, if support was completely withdrawn. Other necessary conditions for persistence are the stability of the regime and the cohesion of the political community as the ongoing processing of demands is taking place.[17] This might appear to be a plea for stability of the equilibrium type, but in fact the point being made is that the processing of demands is only possible if there is a minimum structure with continuity to carry through the necessary decisions and their implementation. It does seem though that Easton puts considerable store by legitimation and he seems to suggest that, as against any well-established structure, even one which is poor on producing the outputs demanded, a revolutionary movement has an uphill task to produce a similar range of support to replace that which time has helped to build up for the structure under attack.[18]

Easton introduces what he terms a set of structural regulators into this edition of his model. These 'gatekeepers' sit astride the flow from demand to output and, via the feedback loop, back to the input side; the strategic points at which they operate are, naturally, gateways where demands can be stopped, winnowed down, combined or otherwise altered. Most of the major roles in the political system can be seen in terms of gatekeeping. Parties and interest groups, for example, do this task, and at the same time can also gatekeep support for the system. As a concept, gatekeeping is useful in the comparative politics field; it can be said, for example, to be widely diffused in democratic systems and severely restricted in authoritative or dictatorial ones.[19]

Although much of the model seems to depend on the usual Western democratic convention of the vitality of competing interests inside the political system, Easton does expand this to some degree, especially with a chapter which attempts to find something beyond perceived self-interest, what he terms 'the belief in a common interest'. This has always been difficult for analysts schooled in Western democratic methodology to define, but Easton sees its existence as a type of support not unlike the legitimating effect that certain ideologies possess for specific systems. Where belief in the common good does exist, it encourages some moderation of demand by specific groups which, otherwise, would foment division enough to damage political solidarity. Thus it is especially useful for governments in developing countries to try to persuade their citizens that they are operating in the general interest and that failure to satisfy demands in the short run must be balanced by long-run gains which will benefit the whole political community. This is rarely possible if authorities are seen to be identified with a narrow class or caste, but the creation of symbols of the common good, such as are often found in developing countries enshrined in leaders, parties, ceremonies, etc., can sometimes be effective in encouraging this range of 'diffuse support'.[20]

The foregoing is an outline of what had become quite an intricate scheme by the production of the book just mentioned. There were signs by 1970 that David Easton was modifying slightly the intensely behavioural flavour of his model, but the basic structure is still one which he, and many others, see as a valid way forward to improving general analytical theory. The virtues of Easton's writing are many and one hopes that some glimmering of these have survived the rough summaries that one has made of his thinking. The sense of movement, so vital to an understanding of the political process where little stands completely still, pervades the shape that he has discovered in the system while the linking together of such a variety of structures and roles, once translated into his mobile brand of quasi-functionalism, shows us how the system can operate in a way which few other models can encompass. It is perhaps more effective in short-term than long-term analysis, that is, it throws comparatively little light on the sort of developmental change in political systems that takes place over time. It has also some defects which are common to systems analysis as a whole, particularly the lack of information given by these models of the conversion process, inputs into outputs. This is something that needs to be looked at in more detail but, first of all, we must survey the models which emphasize developmental change, plus one or two more idiosyncratic ones.

Gabriel Almond and the 'developmental' approach

Like David Easton, Gabriel Almond has provided an approach to analysis based on theories of the whole system which appear in a number of his books and papers written over the years. Rather more rooted in the comparative politics approach and aware of the problems which appeared to be presenting themselves to political scientists in an era of so many 'new' systems, he has elaborated sets of theory which as he puts it, attempt 'to draw the notions of system and function closer to the main currents of empirical research in political science'.[21] Both Easton and Almond were influenced by the work of some of the writers covered in the preceding two chapters, Parsons and the Chicago theorists for example, but both have moved on to develop theories which stand on their own as distinct bodies of work, models with certain unique features. Gabriel Almond admits to influence from the separation of powers doctrine in the creation of his seven-stage functional model, that part of his work which has had the most far-reaching influence on current thinking in political science. He has probably been subjected to more criticism than any other writer who upholds a systems approach to political analysis, much of it from Great Britain where senior members of the profession like S. E. Finer and W. J. M. Mackenzie have been quick to show Professor Almond where, in their view, he has erred. The fact that his work has attracted such critics tends to suggest that his ideas have been lively enough at least to warrant a highly serious examination. In fact, many of his assumptions and neologisms have now passed into the vocabulary of general political science and have enriched the way in which one can discuss the way in which political affairs are arranged.

The take-off point for Gabriel Almond's scheme is an article which he published in 1956. He starts from two premises, one, now commonly accepted, that there was a need to expand the horizons of methodology in comparative politics, and, secondly, that 'certain sociological and anthropological concepts' could usefully be applied to the study of political systems.[22] There is an assumption that 'action', 'system' and 'role' should be used as bases of a system of analysis and the last concept is singled out as 'the unit of the political system'.[23] Finer implies that 'role' is a newfangled way of saying that a polity (he dislikes 'political system') is made up of a number of institutions in which individuals participate, but once one starts to try to use his terminology it is easy to become vague about what exactly enters into the political aspects of a society and the confusion between individual and multi-individual arrangements seems compounded.[24] 'Role' is a useful shorthand to suggest that a range of interactive processes exists and that the individuals and groups which form the polity automatically assume these, not in any absolutely fixed pattern but in a varying one within certain confines, that is, certain roles are pressed on the total membership to assume as circumstances dictate.

Perhaps the most vital and far-reaching concept put forward in this early paper is the adaptation of the 'culture' idea from anthropology into what Almond terms political culture, that 'particular pattern of orientations to political action' in which political systems are set. One of the useful characteristics of this piece of jargon is that it provides one with a variable that is not tied specifically to a political system as such. Almond points out that it can sprawl across several political systems and it has been suggested more recently that systems which nestle inside each other—such as a federal system—are prime examples of this phenomenon.[25] At this stage, Almond was especially concerned with the contrast between the political culture of the Anglo-American political area and that of certain other parts of the world. The Anglo-American culture is said to be essentially pragmatic, with specialized role-playing, a certain diffusion of power and a series of institutions with a considerable degree of continuity over time. As a contrast, the 'European' model of political culture (that of Western Europe) is less specialized in the roles adopted (parties and pressure groups overlapping) and is more likely to throw up strong sub-cultures than the Anglo-American political culture. These contrasts—and others are suggested as with the 'totalitarian' model—give certain shapes which Almond felt were routes to more exacting comparisons between sets of political systems, and the fact that 'political culture' is now an acceptable way of distilling certain aspects of a political system shows that he had discovered a most useful shorthand to summarize a considerable range of characteristics.

From this point on, Almond's work in the methodology of comparative politics has tended to diversify. Cultural comparison was especially enshrined in the study of five political systems published in 1963 with Sidney Verba. Here the concept is redefined and put into a form where actual empirical comparison can more easily be made: 'When we speak of the political culture of a society, we refer to the political system as internalized in the cognitions, feelings and evaluations of its population.'[26] Here Almond isolates the political element in the general cultural pattern of a social system, complementing the sense of general culture as developed by the social anthropologists touched upon in the last chapter and by their successors in the social anthropology field such as Ruth Benedict and Margaret Mead. This element is inevitably tied to the idea of political socialization, that method of inducting individuals into the adult political world by means of their experience in their pre-adult lives, at school, with their families and elsewhere. In particular, a range of what are virtually ideal types is used to point up cultural difference; these are developed via the input–output technique. The 'parochial' political culture contains those orientated mainly towards their immediate localities if anywhere and not orientated to the main inputs and outputs of the overall system at all. In a 'subject' culture, orientation is towards outputs, not inputs, and only in the most sophisticated culture, the 'participant', is there a general orientation to both the inputs and the outputs of a political system. In practice, the tendency is for a political culture to be placed somewhere on one side of a triangle constructed around the three points, participant, subject, parochial. For example, Britain is looked upon as a mixed subject–participant culture because, on the one hand, it retains 'persisting deferential and subject orientations' yet it also tends to the type of 'balanced political culture' which is close to the 'civic culture' of the book's title. It must be admitted that there are aspects of this latter idea which almost invite criticism. An empirical study of the political culture of five 'democracies' does not always sit comfortably alongside the near-normative conception of the title theme, which is mainly an exercise in democratic theory. Despite certain qualifications that are made in the text, the impression remains of a rather Panglossian view of the Anglo-American political culture being democratically superior to the others surveyed (West Germany, Italy and Mexico), and the model developed is not unlike those which appear in the writings of those more closely concerned with democratic and electoral theory (Lipset, Dahl, Berelson). Of much more lasting importance is the general model of political culture developed in the book, especially the assertion that 'the connecting link between micro- and macro-politics is political culture'.[27] Specific patterns of political culture will tend, if unhindered, to produce certain political structures and what Almond terms 'congruency' between them will result. In this respect, the 'civic culture' has relevance as the mix of character- istics (mainly participant but with dashes of the others) that results in a stable political democracy. The claims made for the micro–macro link are, however, not fully accepted by some commentators. Carole Pateman has argued that research into political culture has 'remained almost entirely focussed at the level of individual psychology' and has failed to explain many of the components of political change.[28] Since she has suggested some linkage herself, this may mean that this invaluable general concept still needs further refining if it is to have any predictive value in systems analysis.

In the larger framework that Gabriel Almond was elaborating at about the same time as the above work was being prepared, political culture appears as one aspect of the political system. This framework was outlined for the first time in an introductory section which has become far better known than the bulk of the study of the politics of 'developing areas' that it prefaced. It is a broadly functional categoric statement of the essential outline of the political system based on four characteristics which all political systems are said to have in common. These comprise the structure possessed by political systems, the belief that all systems share a similar range of functions, that structure is multi-functional and that all cultures are mixed, not fully modern nor completely primitive but somewhere in between. The core of the model has become one of the most noted—even most notorious— frameworks of the political system put forward by a writer in the last generation. It isolates seven functional categories shared by political systems the world over—three output, four input. The former indicate the 'separation of powers' entry-point into the model; rule-making, rule-application, rule-adjudication have obvious affinities with the tripartite division of, say, the American Constitution into legislative, executive and judicial branches. Transferring this division of basic functions to the input side of the political system, Almond produced the comparatively novel division of the political socialization and recruitment function, the separate articulation and then aggrega- tion of interests and, finally, the political communication function.

Certain conceptual difficulties are evident here. While the overall tendency for an input–output system is to show how an input originates, is gradually processed and finally appears as a finished output with some effect on the whole system (including a tendency for it to be 'fed back' to its originators), certain of Almond's 'categories' do not take this stage-like posture. 'Political communication' can be said to be everywhere in the system, since one part of a structure can only receive messages from another part via the communications network. Similarly, the way in which the political culture is perpetuated and altered by those who are socialized and recruited into it is a long-term process with indirect, though important, influences on the conversion machinery of the immediate 'throughput'. However, once we accept that the seven functions are *not* to be looked upon as equivalent stages in a continuous process, then the model is seen as an overall summary of the activity present in a political system.

In one of the best-known critiques of this seven-function analysis, Professor Mackenzie has argued not only that the output functions are no more than the separation of powers revisited but that the four input functions can be virtually equated with old-style formulations such as élites (for socialization and recruitment), pressure-groups (for interest articulation), parties (for interest aggregation) and public opinion (for communication).[29] He admits that Almond is attacking a real problem but argues that the new terms are no better than the old, for there is nothing to show how complete is the list, and he implies that a new basis for the comparison of political systems is needed but that this is not it: 'In fact, Almond attempted the right thing, possibly in the wrong way—but no one has yet improved on his analysis of the polity, old-fashioned though it is.'[30] Mackenzie is surely less than fair to Almond. For example, one of the vital points in the Almond model is the theory of multifunctionality which prevents any complete identification of the function with a structural section of the political system. Certainly, one thinks of the main pressure-groups in a political system as being the prime articulators of interests, but they are not the only ones, and Almond's classification of groups involved in interest articulation is wider than any pure pressure-group categorization would give us (his four types are: institutional, associational, non-associational, anomic).[31] Whatever else this set of analytical categories has given to the mainstream of political analysis, the acceptance of multifunctionality has probably made comparing political systems easier, for we are now more wary than hitherto about the contrast between the jobs carried on by named offices in one system as compared to another. Quite often, the functions in political systems appear in odd places:

> Thus it has shown that the courts not only adjudicate but also legislate: that the bureaucracy is one of the most important sources of legislation; that legislative bodies affect both administration and adjudication; that pressure groups initiate legislation and participate in administration; and that the media of communication represent interests and sometimes initiate legislation.[32]

Much of this was not especially new at the time that it was formulated by Gabriel Almond, but it is drawn together in his original paper and the book that later amplified the various categories in a manner which has provided half a generation of students of comparative politics with a useful general model. Its architect would be the first to agree that it was not perfect and we can see flaws in it at this remove. The checklist of functions may not be complete. Why not, for example, include a rule-administering function on the output side? This is supposedly subsumed under rule-application but certain bureaucratic tasks sit uneasily under this heading. Why does the model not give a clearer idea of the nerve-centre of the political process, the making of decisions? At the moment, the seven functions split like a watershed into inputs and outputs with a narrow razor's-edge between them. Complete models of the political systems should indicate clearly how inputs are converted into outputs. Almond's model is rather muddy in this area. But for what it sets out to do it is still something of a model of models, conventional as its terminology has now become.

One should remember that its main aim was to clear up certain misunderstandings in the comparisons being made between more and less developed parts of the world. An updated classificatory system of political systems has since been put forward by Almond and one of his colleagues (there is a danger in ignoring the work of the able colleagues that Almond seems to attract to himself). The criteria for the different stages of political development are based on the way in which roles become differentiated or specialized and the way in which the sub-systems develop a certain autonomy or independence from one another. There is a third important variable to be taken into account, that of secularization, which is defined as follows: 'Secularization is the process whereby men become increasingly rational, analytical and empirical in their political action.'[33] These three variables, differentiation, sub-system autonomy and secularization, allow a range of political systems to be isolated and classified according to the degree of maximization of each of the variables. Primitive systems, according to the classification, are low on all of these three variables, traditional systems begin to have a degree of differentiation in the governmental structure, while modern systems span a range from those still with limited differentiation and secularization (some African states), through those with high differentiation and secularization but low sub-system autonomy (Mexico) or virtually none (USSR, Nazi Germany), to those which score high marks on all three (Britain). Critics argue that there is a considerable amount of ethnocentrism about such a classification, favouring as it does the Western democratic yet capitalistic regimes rather than, say, countries claiming to have socialist or 'people's' democracy as their aim. The nub of the argument would appear to revolve around the nature of sub-system autonomy, whether it is correctly defined by the Almond and Powell book, whether the classification of systems according to it is correct, or whether it is relevant to the classification of political systems. As well as the ideological argument already hinted at, this discussion could be carried on within the pluralist–élitist debate so loved by many English-speaking political scientists. To some degree, the assumption of Western superiority indicates a normative content to the model (tending as it does to the preferred alternative of the 'civic culture'), and perhaps limits its usefulness for purposes of general analysis.

Perhaps the most valuable aspect of this type of thinking, though, is the emphasis that it lays in any general model of the political system being linked to development and political change. Although 'change' is self-explanatory, 'development' is not, and one of the key questions about the move to embrace 'development' as the vital point of study in the comparison of political systems is to try to define exactly what we mean by the term. In his more recent work Almond has put forward the idea that development is best seen as the overcoming of problems that systems meet as a part of internal change and the response to external change:

If one looks at the histories of specific political systems, it is quite clear that there are points in time which might be characterized as crisis periods, periods of greatly increased pressures for structural and cultural adaptation coming to bear on the political system, such as wars, revolutions, or threats of revolutions.[34]

This pattern of thought has now moved Almond's work away from the 'functional category' approach, although it is clear that he does not repudiate it in any way. Partially, this is due to the changing nature of the world at large. Europe and North America provide less of a general model for developing nations than a decade or two back and therefore the temptation to be 'ethnocentric' is less than it was then. Almond recognizes that there is nothing like complete agreement about the concept—'development' or 'modernization'—that he and a number of his contemporaries are trying to define and investigate. It is a pattern of change that seems to have something in common wherever it is found in the world, and the job of the political scientist is to find useful tools with which to study it: 'Concepts are intellectual instruments. Their test of utility lies in their ability to help us find our way in the real world.'[35]

In looking at the performance of political systems in the past and in trying to measure this performance in some way, Gabriel Almond is now in effect using an old discipline—history—to redress the balance in a new, behavioural political science. A set of case-studies recently published and produced by Almond with two new colleagues —Flanagan and Mundt—looks at critical periods in the history of certain political systems in the nineteenth and twentieth centuries, including the circumstances surrounding the 1832 Reform Act in Britain and the Meiji Restoration in Japan, to see how crises arise, how they are overcome and what consequences they have for the political systems in question. Using a range of method, the authors try to show how political change as an aspect of political development can be explained in terms of mobilization, choice and the exercize of leadership. To understand how nations develop, it is argued that one should look at those which are more as well as those that are less developed, study developmental problems and narrow these down especially to the crises that afflict most political communities from time to time. In the methodological construct, Almond arranges the four principal components of developmental theory—system–functional, rational choice–coalition, social mobilization, leadership—into a two-by-two matrix based on determinancy and choice (rows), stability and development (columns), all of these in his view being aspects of the developmental process.[36] Some continuity but a degree of change, the determining effect of certain variables but a limited range of choices which leaders can take, these are factors which are present in the majority of crisis situations. Therefore any general theory of development must be eclectic and only an approach which utilizes the sum total of our knowledge about development will be effective. Scott Flanagan criticizes one of the favoured mathematical models of recent years—game theory—by rejecting the use of minimum winning coalitions to predict coalition basis in crises—therefore the methodological eclecticism is not uncritically based; in Flanagan's view, something larger than the *minimum* winning coalitions favoured by game theorists is usually necessary in crisis situations.[37] Coalition analysis of a more flexible type, looking for effective combinations which can make choices that stick, is a vital part of this combined analysis; in the words of Almond and his other collaborator, 'coalition analysis alerts us to power-policy options in given crises'.[38] Functional analysis and mobilization theory provide the setting for the crises experienced by political systems, coalition theory the alternative choices open to the actors who in their turn depend on a degree of leadership to point up the options and to influence the outcomes. The authors admit that their approach to developmental analysis is complex and still unrefined, that it is weak on prediction of outcomes in some cases even though its explanatory power is, they believe, considerable. Frankly, this *is* its strong point and, in the state of present knowledge, a model that can provide a rich range of explanatory variables is as much as we can expect. The very eclecticism of the model is likely to make it suspect in the eyes of some but it is likely to have a considerable influence on developmental theory over the next few years.

Gabriel Almond has given flesh to the concept of development in a firmer way than any of his contemporaries. Most of the recent literature on comparative politics and many of the monographs that regularly appear on specific political systems embrace the ideas that he has put forward, such as the functional stages and the general approach to political culture; often this methodology has been tacitly combined with ideas culled from David Easton's work and the two sets of propositions do combine reasonably well. This means that current literature in these fields is often replete with references to 'input–output', 'feedback', 'interest articulation and aggregation', 'participant cultures', etc., with just a bare nod in the direction of the writing reviewed in this chapter. Perhaps this acceptance of at least the outline of systemic analysis is the greatest compliment to the work in question. However, when one looks at the wider context of developmental analysis it may seem unfair that so much writing which lies outside this systemic frame has been less widely recognized in secondary literature. One reason is that much of it tends to the piecemeal rather than being shaped into a grand strategy; nevertheless, a considerable interrelationship of material is now being built up, and one should appreciate the range of writing that examines the twin processes of modernization and development, much of it deriving from fieldwork carried on in developing areas by the writers themselves or their research associates.

Development and modernization

In *Crisis, Choice and Change* developmental theory was divided into four categories, according to its major theoretical tendency—functional, social mobilization, choice-coalition, leadership. It is possible to place much, though as Almond admits not all, theory explaining the modernization process into this fourfold category. It is useful to do this in a synthesizing effort but less useful if one is trying a general survey where residual categories are as important as these somewhat arbitrary ones. Most writers who have approached the examination of change and development in specific countries or a range of them have tended to produce concepts which, if at all valid, have been absorbed into later analyses as a matter of course. Just as structural functionalism has been modified into broader functional models and merged into a more general systemic view of the political system, the additions that one can pick out of a range of developmental literature are to be seen as providing pieces for the jigsaw which in time may indicate definitive models for overall analysis of the general process of change inside political systems.

One such concept—though one which has not been uncritically accepted—is the device put forward by Lucian Pye, best known perhaps for his study of Burmese political development. The question often posed by political scientists interested in development is 'development, towards what?' In other words, the very meaning of the term must imply something close to an end-state or at least a definitive stage where political systems will halt awhile before defining future goals in a way that we cannot conceive at the present time. Pye has put forward the idea of the 'world culture' as the state to which all political systems tend to gravitate in time. In order to head off the criticism that this is essentially an ethnocentric judgment because of the tendency of the world culture to look suspiciously like certain Western systems in its outlines, Pye points out that it was virtually fortuitous that the West elaborated this cultural approach first and that it can no longer be looked upon as tied to the one-way flow so long associated with Western colonialism: ' . . . by now the diffusion has reached such a point, and the culture has achieved such a dynamics of its own, that the culture can no longer be claimed entirely by the West.'[39] Even so, the shape that Pye gives to this substantive culture looks remarkably like the post-Enlightenment, in fact post-French Revolution, pattern of North Atlantic society:

> It is based on a secular rather than a sacred view of human relations, a rational outlook, an acceptance of the substance and spirit of the scientific approach, a vigorous application of an expanding technology, an industrialized organization of production, and a generally humanistic and popularistic set of values for political life.[40]

It is inevitable that there will be some similarity between the direction taken by political systems as they move from less to more developed patterns of social and political organization. Technology and an industrialized base are factors that most—though not all—developing nations wish to incorporate unto themselves, which means that two out of the six strands mentioned in the above quotation are of relevance in a considerable number of cases and will influence cultural configurations in their turn. What is less certain is whether the other four strands are clearly pointing along the same continuum, whether in fact one can think of development as 'converging', to use a popular term of recent years, to an eventual point where societies share a culture which is similar enough to be termed 'common'. Attitudes towards basic relationships between the individual and the state, towards say the Western standards of human dignity and inter-personal relationships, vary enormously and one cannot be certain that the values of transatlantic civilizations are those that will be readily acceptable in the newer nations as they reach more sophisticated forms of government. Brzezinski and Huntington, in their comparative study of the USA and USSR, tend to reject the 'convergence theory' as being oversimplified and placing too much stress on one or two factors out of many, especially the weight given to industrialization in its later stages as a conditioning factor: 'It is too simple to assume that the complexity of the human condition is reducible to a single social-economic or political mold. The evolution of the two systems, but not their convergence, seems to be the undramatic pattern for the future.'[41] Possibly, Pye would wish to disassociate the 'common culture' from convergence as such, but the one would seem to carry some implications of the other and, as we suggest, there is a great deal of evidence to indicate that cultural diversity will continue to be a powerful force in world affairs. Pye has made considerable contributions to the more descriptive side of the comparison of less developed with more developed political systems, and it is perhaps a pity that one cannot be more confident of this analytical tool, which seems so intrinsically attractive at first sight.

Much of the writing on political development has tended to detach institutional sections of developing polities—especially the military and the bureaucracy—in order to examine their significant contribution in a setting where there is a limited range of vehicles for the maintenance of sustained power and for the satisfaction of accumulating demands. In parenthesis here, one might note that there is some agreement on the point of view put forward by Morris Janowitz: 'In short, while it is relatively easy for the military to seize power in a new nation, it is much more difficult for it to govern.'[42]

Although the military and the bureaucracy have tended to play a significant role in modernizing polities, they tend to be inadequate by themselves to carry on the processes by which full-scale modernization of the political system can take place. Samuel Huntington has put forward the thesis that certain institutional developments are vital if the overall nature of political development is to proceed relatively smoothly. In particular, he isolates political organization through a party system as being the necessary vehicle for that degree of political participation which he considers essential for the eventual stability of a modernizing society. This could be an answer to those who query the 'modernity' of Marxist-based polities, for these seem to be able to combine an adaptation to a technological and industrial maturity with a lower level of individual freedom and weaker devotion to a liberal humanism than is claimed by Western democracies: 'The relative success of communist states in providing political order in large part derives from the priority they have given to the conscious act of political organization.'[43] Huntington insists that 'the stability of a modernizing political system depends on the strength of its political parties'.[44] He sees the process as one by which groups are absorbed into the party system instead of fighting each other, evolving from factionalism through stages to the mass party organizations found in a variety of forms from one-party states to multi-party systems where coalition government is the norm. Certainly, the political party has been a major feature of states which try to socialize their members into new roles; through the political party, the individual and the group can be taught the necessary adaptative techniques by which transition to a society which can be characterized as 'modern' can take place. Whether it can act in the way in which Huntington suggests without other supportive structures is open to doubt. There comes a time in the life of a developing society when even a maturing party system is inadequate if it is not supported by a diverse network of pressure-groups, for example, while participation in the fullest sense is not possible without forms of communication which are able to carry information and requests throughout the system. Modernization also relies eventually on a sophisticated cultural base; Huntington is aware of this, for he points out the dangers of corruption and how it can encourage decay rather than development. Whether, as he suggests, strong party systems alone will eliminate corruption seems dubious; this has not always been the case in the United States where strong local party systems have been eminently corruptible in the past.

Like many other writers, Huntington links modernization to that sister process known as 'social mobilization' already touched upon in the last chapter. Under this process, as Karl Deutsch has described it, 'major clusters of old social, economic and psychological commitments are eroded or broken and people become available for new patterns of socialization and behavior'.[45] The degree of social mobilization can be measured, in Deutsch's model, by seven sets of indicators (though the exact number is in fact arbitrary) such as literacy, urbanization and rise in *per capita* income. During gradual development the indicators tend to move upwards together and can be linked to other indicators, such as the increase in voting participation, to give a picture of a nation steadily moving over from traditional to modern political and economic forms. Even with this pattern the 'middle stages of development' may produce a 'cumulative strain on political stability'.[46] This strain is due to the increased demands that are made upon the government, especially because of the likelihood of an increasing gap, rather than a decreasing one, between rich and poor. This type of model as outlined here does allow some picture to be built up of the stresses that a developing nation is likely to undergo. Deutsch admits that it is 'crude'; one might go further and say that to some extent it states the obvious but, where statistical material is plentiful, it may well back up other methods of developmental analysis.

Karl Deutsch is possibly best known as a political scientist for the 'control' model that he outlined in his book *The Nerves of Government*. It emphasizes the shape of the political system as a communications network where goals are set, information is sought about the state of the entire system, feedback exercizes a control function on the decisions taken and new goals may be elaborated in the light of the effect of previous decisions. This is what Deutsch terms as 'government as a process of steering' or what elsewhere he calls the 'helmsman' concept.[47] It does not directly relate to development but, indirectly, one aspect of the model is relevant. He classifies systems into four categories according to the likelihood of their survival over time. Self-destroying systems, non-viable systems, viable systems, self-developing or self-enhancing systems comprise the range, and the further along this brief continuum a developing nation finds itself the greater is the probability that the 'mobilization' process will continue. Though Deutsch does not use the latter term in this context, his listing of a number of 'dimensions of growth' indicates how similar these are to the indicators used in the article cited above. Cybernetic models are now regarded as unnecessarily limiting in the amount of input material which they process; the emphasis on undigested information in particular seems less sharp than the demand/support distinction that Easton makes about inputs. However, Deutsch's elaborations of the patterns of growth under the mobilization process have been utilized considerably since he first helped to define it and, as we saw with the synthesis recently attempted by Almond and his colleagues, it can still be a fundamental part of a wider scheme.

David Apter makes use of the concept of mobilization in his survey of political modernization. He sees modernization essentially as that stage when a society has a government and, by implication, large numbers of people who understand the importance of making rational choices—'to be modern means to see life as alternatives, preferences and choices.'[48] Modernization can be effected by a whole range of political systems, that is, there is no one type of system which is essential to carry out the task, though some are more effective than others. The main variables used by Apter to delineate his authority types are information and coercion; all societies need as much information as they can obtain in order to make decisions which will further their aims and, at the same time, use anything from a little coercion to a great deal during the modernization process. In other words, information is a variable that governments will always try to maximize but the level of coercion will be dependent on other cultural constraints. These can be grouped especially along the consummatory–instrumental value spectrum with the former set of values involving certain ultimate ends, usually ones which could be said to be 'politically religious', all actions in the state being related to these. 'Instrumental' values are essentially more pragmatic and, in a society infected with them, many actions cannot be related to the long-term ends of the state. The authority types range from 'reconciliation systems', where the level of coercion is low and heed is paid to the wishes of the membership, through types like 'modernizing autocracies' (practically self-defining) to 'mobilization systems' with a relatively high degree of coercion, to totalitarian systems and eventually to the ideal type, a 'sacred-collectivity' model with perfect coercion and perfect information (the democratic ideal type is 'secular-libertarian' with no coercion and, once again, perfect information). Apter spends a great deal of time on the mobilization system, for he feels it is a prototype which is exceedingly common at certain stages in the modernization process. He argues that: 'Mobilization systems expand the modernization sector, alter the relationships of power and prestige between roles, and traditionalize the new through the manipulation of political religions. In order to accomplish these ends, they promote unrealistic industrialization goals and rely heavily on coercion.'[49]

Elsewhere, Apter has opted for a four-cell set of systems-types, using as axes the consummatory–instrumental dichotomy and the hierarchical–pyramidical differential for types of authority; the four cells on this occasion include the mobilization and reconciliation types but also bureaucratic (instrumental–hierarchical) and theocratic (consummatory–pyramidical).[50] All of these can be used at stages in the developmental process, and he argues that there is no perfect type but that each reaches a ceiling after which it is possible for there to be a change to another type of system. Although coercion is often high at specific stages of the modernization process, Apter appears to argue that, if modernization and industrialization go hand-in-hand as they have in Western systems, then there comes a time when the two processes have reached a point where coercion is dysfunctional and 'the long-term tendency is toward the reconciliation system'.[51] Once again, there are touches of ethnocentricity about this presentation of the Western cultural pattern as the stage which most, if not all, modernizing political systems must reach; there is rarely any estimation by any contemporary theorist of what might be beyond the liberal democracy. Yet Apter is conscious of the defects of his own society; not only the need to redress the balance inherent against the poor and the black community, but the problems of coherence in a society which is as lacking in consummatory values as is present-day America. Although there are places where Apter seems to believe that modernization itself is a form of consummatory value, he eventually settles back into a quasi-normative belief in a form of democracy as the ideal combination of the instrumental and consummatory goals of a society. The twin advantages of the democratic polity are, he would argue, relative freedom from coercion plus a ready flow of information on which something like rational choice can take place; what is needed is to marry this with the preservation of individual self-respect *and* welfare. In the last resort Apter is looking to a stronger moral basis for Western society to justify its road to modernization.

Conclusion

Like Thursday's child, general theory in political science still has 'far to go' before it can claim to have reached the explanatory power of other sciences and even some social sciences. Human behaviour, when taken in the large and unruly segments that are needed to encompass whole societies, is not predictable with any great accuracy and little more than general configurations of political action can be indicated. It is only when one looks back to the earlier attempts at explanation of how political systems operate that one can see that an amount of progress has been made in solving the problem of linking the many abstract and concrete elements of a polity in such a way that one can make at least a number of intelligent guesses at probable outcomes. The basic question about the present state of general theory is: to what degree is there agreement about the essential features of an overall model and, consequent upon this, what future progress is likely towards 'harder' general theory?

There is agreement—if only among those political scientists who came out of the behaviouralist movement—about the need to preserve a sense of the system as such, if only because no credible alternative has been put forward for examining the polity as a whole in other than systemic terms. It might be argued that this is tautological, and in one sense it is, but it has come to typify a way of looking at politics which emphasizes the interrelation of structures, behaviour and ideas in a dynamic context.

There is now another area of agreement, one which also commands some consensus at least. We tried to show in the later part of this chapter how the twin concepts of modernization and development offer one viable method of elaborating general theory. It is true that some writers criticize the 'entanglement of development theory with modernization' on the grounds that this leads to a 'spurious traditional–modern dichotomy'.[52] Yet development theory now rarely makes the mistake of equating modernization with the Western political process as such, and model-building is even less likely to tie itself in with a particular political system in the future as it did so often in the past. It is convenient to use the term 'modernization' at least as a staging-post on the developmental road and it would be almost impossible to abandon it now without considerable confusion. After all, it is not a firm or final condition as far as one can tell, perhaps more, as Kenneth Sherrill has suggested, a set of attitudes, a state of mind.[53] It is sometimes argued that modernization is synonymous with the general idea of change as being fundamental to political activity; in Dankwart Rustow's view, 'modernization, whatever else it may be, means social change'.[54] One would have to provide a highly sophisticated paradigm for this to be a total view. Barrington Moore's statement is relevant here; as much as change, patterns of cultural and social continuity have to be explained because 'both have to be recreated anew in each generation, often with great pain and suffering'.[55] If one included no change in a theory of change, it might sound like nonsense. Neither is development to be seen as unilinear; it is a favourite paradox to argue that where there can be development, there can also be decay. Therefore, general theory is likely to continue to embrace as many as possible of these concepts without becoming so eclectic that explanatory power is reduced to aimless generality. The recent set of case studies by Almond and his associates indicates that synthesis of a sort may be possible, and the next few years may well produce more sophisticated models which will provide a better 'fit' with the pragmatic accounts of the behaviour of actors in a political system with which we are familiar.

At the moment though, we must rest here with the examination of general theory and turn to the mass of partial theory which has grown up alongside the former and which many find more useful as an explanation of specific behaviour in political life.

CHAPTER 5

PARTIAL THEORY I: VOTING

The published literature purporting to explain the reasons why people vote as they do is substantial for one very good reason. The vote is eminently quantifiable, which is more than one can say for many of the phenomena of political life. Elections are regarded as the final sanction for government in most parts of the world. Even where democracy as many of us understand it is little more than nominal, elections are part of the system because of their value in terms of legitimation, mobilization and communication, a potpourri of reasons which carry weight, consciously and unconsciously, with the élites in the systems concerned. It is unlikely that there is much to be gained from the detailed study of elections in those systems where the free formation of parties or similar electoral groups is proscribed, although in general terms they may have a place. In what we like to think are the relatively 'democratic' states, some advance has been made towards an explanation of why people vote the way that they do, even if the development of a convincing general theory of voting behaviour is still further away than certain writers appear to believe. There is still a great deal of work needed to elucidate the basic motivation behind the vote in a situation of real choice, but there has been a considerable line of advance, one which has enlarged our understanding of this part of the political process.

In recent years the study of voting behaviour has expanded to take in the 'closed' groups that are so important in most political systems, such as the legislature or the multi-member high court with a political role, like the United States Supreme Court. The bulk of the analysis in all electoral study seems to have concentrated on sub-groups in the first instance, their behaviour and relationship one with another. This has now become quite sophisticated, but its origin was contingent on three factors. One, quite obviously, was the emergence of the mass electorate, a fairly recent phenomenon even in the most 'advanced' polities where, for example, female suffrage only followed the First World War. The second factor, comprehensive statistics, were becoming available by the same time, but the third, the elaboration of techniques capable of handling the data in terms of useful generalization, was not fully to develop until the late 1930s and 1940s. In particular, the reinforcement of gross data by the more acute weapon of sample survey techniques did not reach maturity until the latter date.

Polls and survey research

Interest in electoral behaviour has tended to settle on two levels which intertwine more than their respective practitioners would like to admit. Since this is one section of political analysis that produces a direct interest on the part of the public—perhaps because they participate directly in voting in a way that they rarely do in other parts of the political process—interest is high enough for newspapers and other organs of the mass media to attempt to explain the motivations of the mass electorate to the electorate itself. In the United States so-called 'straw polls' were in use long before academic analysis was applied to elections, and this tradition continued until the debacle of 1936 when the *Literary Digest* wrongly forecast Franklin Roosevelt's defeat at the hands of Alfred Landon, a prediction based on a sample of considerable size but of unreliable shape in that it depended on middle-class voters now known to be antipathetic to the incumbent president.[1] More accurate public opinion polling developed in the 1930s, based on statistically reliable sampling techniques; the work of Gallup, Roper and others is almost too well known to describe in detail, especially since newspapers came to rely on the work of these organizations to predict the likely outcome of important elections at national and local level. Occasional failure to recognize the limits of accurate prediction, such as the forecast of a Dewey victory in the 1948 presidential election by the major polling organizations in the United States, and a similar failure over the 1970 General Election in Great Britain, have only temporarily shaken the public faith in sample polls as a guide to election results. The raw material of these polls is invaluable to the political scientist interested in voting theory, and repositories like the Elmo Roper Center at Williams College in Massachusetts provide a convenient way of investigating a range of this material.

Peter H. Rossi, in a retrospective look at voting research from the standpoint of the late 1950s, picked out four landmarks, three of which were oriented towards specific presidential elections of the 1940s and 1950s, the Elmira and Erie County studies, associated with Paul Lazarsfeld and Bernard Berelson as the chief researchers, and the Michigan Survey Research Center study of the national response to the 1952 Eisenhower–Stevenson contest. His 'landmark' for the pre-1940s was a book by Stuart Rice published in 1928, which includes a review of the problems of measuring both political attitudes and the group bases of voting in public elections and inside legislatures. Rice used either published statistics or panel interviews with relatively accessible groups such as Dartmouth College undergraduates.[2] His interests were general ones in the application of quantitative methods to the expansion of political science methodology; voting behaviour lay to hand as the most convenient illustration of the viability of the quantitative approach:

> There are numerous forms of political behavior which might be measured, at least in theory. There is one, however that seems most easily available, that is characteristically associated with American politics, and that is clearly related to the underlying attitudes. This is the vote.'[3]

Much of the material explored tentatively in Rice's book was to become a basic approach for voting analysis for the next few decades, especially that which attempted to correlate geographic voting patterns with 'culture areas' drawn on the basis of shared characteristics or experience, that is, not only ethnicity, class and religion but such factors as the existence of state boundaries and the grouping of voters along lines of communication.[4] The eclectic nature of Rice's book is indicated by the fact that he also touches upon the value of making a quantitative analysis of legislatures and other politically authoritative bodies. Although he is able to predict one of the most useful lines of methodological analysis in such bodies—bloc analysis based on roll-call voting—he is pessimistic about the value of studying groups larger than twenty-five or thirty, a fear which has not prevented many useful studies being mounted on legislatures of several hundred members.[5]

The importance of Rice's book is that it was produced at all in 1928 rather than that it remains a definitive work in voting theory. However, it is difficult to underrate its pioneering quality as one of the first attempts to inject a degree of that quality Weber described as *'wertfrei'* to the study of politics. The lines that Rice suggested for research were still being followed by some academics in the 1960s, if in a more sophisticated manner. There are other writers from the 1920s who provide early indications of the way that voting theory would develop. For example, Walter Lippmann's observations on public opinion provide a vital prerequisite to an understanding of how voters decide between rival candidates, parties or ideologies when they are offered some freedom of choice. Like Rice, Lippmann saw the dependence on stereotypes as a barrier to the clear perception of men and events, for our images are largely preconceived with events often being rearranged to fit into them. This dichotomy, described by Lippmann as the contrast between 'the world outside and the pictures in our heads', must be understood by the student of opinion formation among the general public: 'The analyst of public opinion must begin then, by recognizing the triangular relationship between the scene of action, the human picture of that scene, and the human response to that picture working itself out upon the scene of action.'[6] Even fifty years after Lippmann wrote this, our understanding of this relationship is far from complete. Why is a succession of events, such as the various British bids to enter the European Economic Community, perceived so differently even by those of similar political persuasion? What are the characteristics of the 'glass' through which such a set of events is viewed? What part do personality, environment and other forms of conditioning play in producing the 'mix' that allows the same or a similar incident to be construed in a different way at a different point in time? We do know a little more about this than we did fifty years ago but our knowledge is still in great need of supplementation by fresh research.

One of the most interesting writers on voting behaviour of the pre-war era—his most important writing straddled the 1920s and 1930s—was the Chicago-based political scientist Harold Gosnell; his numerous books and articles took his own city in particular as a crucible for research.[7] From early attempts to understand the reasons for apathy among certain classes of voters—generally, he found, these were the ill-educated and underprivileged—and an attempt to prescribe remedies for this, he moved on to a correlation of the vote with reference group membership and the formulation of some general conclusion about voter motivation. He often had to fall back on imperfect data, like the unreliable *Literary Digest* polls, and an occasional lack of sophistication shows through, as when he suggests that Chicago newspapers must 'condition' their readers to vote for specific candidates. A mixture of shrewdness and naïveté is obvious in the following:

> The elections held in Chicago during the New Deal administration show that party tradition, as measured by previous voting behavior, is the most important variable explaining political attitudes. The main characteristics of party lines in Chicago, a typical American metropolitan community, were set long before the depression. The persons who first joined the ranks of the unemployed and who were the first to go on the relief rolls were, for the most part, members of the party which the economic crisis swept into power nationally.[8]

Though Gosnell obviously understood the importance of continuity across the generations in voting behaviour, he does not appear to have recognized the need to explain fairly sharp breaks (like the United States in the early 1930s) in the main outlines of a national or local vote. His appreciation of the way in which self-interest is perceived in terms of the vote is carried along by the wide knowledge he possessed of the political scene, especially in terms of the Chicagoan structure and the local actors. He can be seen as the first in a line of writers, later represented by men like the late V. O. Key and Duane Lockard, who used statistical data culled from the census tracts and elsewhere but supplemented it with a detailed examination of the basic political culture of a specific geographical area.

It was mentioned above that one of Gosnell's main preoccupations was the effects of newspapers on the vote; they were the main mass media of the day although, during the New Deal, when Roosevelt's 'fireside chats' were so influential, radio was gaining in importance. This preoccupation was reflected in the circumstances surrounding the first of the great voting studies, that mounted in Erie County, Ohio, in 1940. By this time, the broad, ecological approach, classifying whole districts as 'Irish' or 'Negro' and assuming that this was a uniform ethnic coloration, was often regarded as insufficient and newer techniques were sought. Public opinion polling, used commercially to test consumer goods as well as by political forecasters, seemed precise enough by this time to test hypotheses about the roots of voting behaviour. Mass media influence was a fashionable explanation for shifts in the popular vote and, together with the effects of social status and the effect of peer groups, was embodied in the general question that (for Erie County) ran: 'In short, how do votes develop? Why do people vote as they do?'[9] The 'panel' or sample survey used to try to answer these questions in 1940 proved to be a valuable new technique, if an expensive one, in the progress of research into basic motivation on the part of the voter.

One cliché of American–European comparison in the realm of political attitudes that was slightly damaged in this study was the view that class plays much less of a part in deciding voter intent in the New World than in the Old. Analysis of the successive waves of Erie County interviews showed that what the researchers defined as SES—socio-economic status—was a significant variable, and that social stratification and religion showed the strongest correlations with intent to vote Democrat or Republican, with both age and a place of residence along a rural–urban spectrum proving useful secondary correlations. The immigrant and working-class vote for the Democrats was probably at its height in the late 1930s (with some exceptions) and, compared certainly to the previous decade, one would expect it to be a feature of this study. As well as SES, Lazarsfeld and his associates coined another phrase which has survived—IPP, index of political predisposition—a summation of social characteristics which predisposes the voter to the Democrat or Republican camp. Where these characteristics clashed the voter was said to be 'cross-pressured', and this, especially when combined with a low level of political interest, tended to produce vacillation, lack of interest and a greater likelihood of abstention from voting than with voters whose 'pressures' ran the same way. Voters in this classification tend to be among the 'changers' or 'floaters' and help to swing elections one way or the other. Perhaps the most dramatic result of the Erie County survey, one that has rarely been challenged since, was the reversal it brought in the rating of the mass media as an influence on voting. Though the media could activate latent political attitudes and reinforce views already held, there was no evidence in the data that party propaganda or any other media coverage could convert the voter. The group theory of politics was reinforced by the conclusions: 'Repeatedly in this study we found indications that people vote "in groups" . . . voting is essentially a group experience. People who work or live or play together are likely to vote for the same candidate.'[10]

Erie County was not the first study to use interviewing to investigate the springs of voting behaviour, but it does seem to have been the first to use the technique of panel interviewing and reinterviewing for political research into the voting decision. Since 1940 the method has been widely used and, although techniques have become refined over thirty years, there is a direct link between much contemporary work and the 1940 inquiry in Ohio. The results of the study tended to rest heavily on the 'group' interpretation of political behaviour but it did also emphasize the need to understand the nature of individual choice. This component of voting behaviour remains the most difficult one to conceptualize. The book by Lazarsfeld and his colleagues finishes with the words, 'in the last analysis, more than anything else people can move other people'. This is true but it is at most only half the story.[11]

The complementary study to the one just described was carried out eight years later in a slightly larger community. This was Elmira, a town just to the north of the New York–Pennsylvania state line, close to Cornell University and to the Finger Lakes region. Dropping the question of mass media influence because of the way in which the previous study had seemingly demolished its effect, the team, including many of the same Columbia University affiliates, concentrate upon person-to-person influence and on the role of issues in the campaign. The extent to which voters were influenced by those around them had been one of the most profound and unexpected results to emerge from the 1940 data; for example, the role of issues in the voting decision was one that the team considered a 'puzzle' in need of clarification.[12] What the Elmira study did was to amplify and deepen the main conclusions of Erie County, and the picture built up of the voting process in that community in 1948 was summarized as follows when the study was eventually published: 'The individual's vote is the product of a number of social conditions or influences: his socio-economic and ethnic affiliations, his family tradition, his personal associations, his attitudes on the issues of the day, his membership in formal organizations.'[13] In examining this part of the process of motivation the study does not try to present the vote as something that is automatic, a Pavlovian reaction to external stumulus. However, the bases of the voting decision rest in the first place with the personal history of the individual voter, as indicated in the above quotation. It is a fact that voters who (through birth, environment and the nature of the life that they have made for themselves) have acquired predispositions towards a party or a set of candidates with some common cause will tend to vote in this ordained manner until something or someone moves them off course. The *Voting* team express this idea by relating the citizen to the stimulus of the campaign on the one hand and the basic dispositions held on the other, the outcome being a process of 'implementation': 'By this term we mean the way in which more or less vague dispositions, intentions and interests regarding a specific subject matter may lead, finally, to the performance of a specific act like buying a car, going on a trip, or voting for a candidate.'[14]

To put it into the simplest of terms, the basic interest here is to analyze the way in which the voting decision crystallizes. In the Elmira study, for example, some normally Democratic voters who were sympathetic towards Governor Dewey in the early stages of the campaign moved back to Truman by the end of it, not because they especially liked him but because he was the Democrats' standard-bearer. Group pressures help in this because they give guidance to a voter who feels confused when tempted away from what has been his 'natural' voting pattern in the past. This is part of what the authors term the 'social psychology of the voting decision', to which they devote one of their two final chapters, the other branching out into the even wider field of democratic theory. Although there is some evident nostalgia for the pure group theories of politics, one also detects the realization that it is necessary to supplement this with individual psychological processes which affect the voting decision, such as those which reactivate latent dispositions. Although the Elmira study is full of data confirming the influences of primary and secondary groups on the rates of voting for one party or the other and offers some new thoughts on the effects of waves or generations of voters on one another—the 'new voters' of the 1930s were obviously conditioned in a different manner to those of the previous generation—the core of the book would seem to lie in this realization that a more comprehensive analytical theory explaining voting behaviour was needed, one which would explain the actions of individuals and groups in this area.[15]

The two studies described above established something of a tradition in voting research, and they were copied elsewhere in the 1950s and 1960s in an attempt to provide a degree of comparative research and some check on the general conclusions reached in these two communities. In the same year that *Voting* was published another strand in the development of voting theory was established by the first national study to be published by the group of social scientists based on the Survey Research Center of the University of Michigan. From a fairly modest examination of the 1948 presidential election they had moved to a much more detailed assessment of the 1952 election, in an attempt to identify selected aspects of the national vote via a statistical sample of the whole. In an introduction to the book V. O. Key suggested that it compared to the 1936 Gallup Poll 'somewhat as the new Cadillac does to the first Model T', and this was true of its methodology since the results of a statistical sample in the vicinity of 2,000 were far more sophisticated than the mass sample of, say, the 1936 *Literary Digest* fiasco.[16] Yet there is little in this 1952 study that runs contrary to the earlier panel studies on a local scale, and perhaps the most useful feature of the first of these Michigan studies is that they confirmed that the local studies were not aberrants but at least represented the norms of American voting behaviour. Most of the fundamental problems were brought out and aired once again but not always in any manner that advanced understanding. The individual–group relationship was seen as 'exceedingly complex' for example, with only a tentative move towards the building of a model based on such dimensions as the ambiguity of the group's political position, how strongly the individual identified himself with the group, and whether his attitude to it was positive or negative.[17] These 'dimensions' could be seen as a statement of the obvious and therefore almost redundant in character.

For the all-American sample, the Michigan team were looking for the usual range of characteristics shared with other members of a 'group' and their correlation with the voting intent, the range of perception on the part of voters and the degree to which they participated in the political process. Some of the correlations of significance are far from surprising, though it is always useful in political science to have statistical confirmation of something that more casual observation has suggested to be true. Orientation to issues and/or to candidates tended to go along with a higher degree of participation

in the machinery of election rather than with apathy to this, and there
was, in the view of the writers, a causal connection here: ' . . . there
has been no crucial proof that issue orientation bears a direct causal
relationship to voting behavior, but all hypotheses compatible with
such a notion of causality have been firmly supported.'[18]

It may seem surprising that the writers view the phenomenon of
the voter's delay in making a firm decision a little differently from
Lazarsfeld and his colleagues, the authors of *The People's Choice*.
For Angus Campbell and his colleagues, reluctance to clarify which
way one will vote may not indicate indifference but instead 'a much
more dynamic process than simple lack of interest would imply'.[19] In
fact, the Erie County study had noted that hesitation in deciding who
to vote for was an especial result of 'cross-pressuring', a factor also
noted in the national sample.[20] Perhaps there is no great antithesis
between the two interpretations, although there is certainly a shift in
the emphasis, and one is attracted by an explanation which writes
voter vacillation into the democratic process as a useful and meaningful device. If 'changers' can be seen to be a critical component of the
electoral process, responding to personal influence and even to
propaganda, then democratic theory resting on the concept of free
elections once more becomes dynamic and not a mechanical or
deterministic device.

By 1960 the Michigan group were confident enough of their span
of research (primarily the presidential elections of 1948, 1952 and
1956) to publish a study, *The American Voter*. Panel interviewing
produced enough data, in the view of the team, to provide a profile
of the American voter over these years in terms of perception and
choice on the one hand and the determinants of these on the other.
Certainly, there is a vast amount of material contained between the
covers of this book and one must accord it a significant place in the
history of voting research, though in retrospect it seems to suffer to
some degree from the lack of one unifying mind. It is not clear, for
example, how much weight should be given to the electoral process
as part of the American political system. Most of the time its primacy
is stressed: 'Certainly few decisions in American government rival in
importance the choice of a President.'[21] Yet at the end of the book,
this assessment seems to have changed: ' . . . we do not arrogate to
voting a primary role in the political system.'[22] This may seem like a
mere haggling over the interpretation of key words, but it does reflect

an overall impression given by the book some years after its publication. Nevertheless, it contains a useful approach to the way in which voters are influenced to vote one way or the other—'We wish to account for a single behavior at a fixed point in time'[23]—and to do this the writers elaborate a model built on the concept of a 'funnel of causality'. The funnel terminates (at its narrow end) at the time when the vote is cast; to look to the wide end of the funnel is to go back in time to the many causal chains that lead to the voting decision. Inside the funnel lie the basic attitudes of the voter that impinge on the final vote decision and, set against the external events of the pre-vote period, tend to predetermine the way in which the vote will go.[24] Attitudes are the result of recent political history and the stances taken up by the political parties as a result of them, but the author's view is that this model enables one to isolate the relevant influences from the so-called 'exogenous' ones, for survey work allows the isolation of those factors that tell on the voting decision from those that are relatively superfluous.

For all this elaborate theoretical structure, much of the study still concentrates on the influence of such factors as social class and the membership of specific groups such as those based on ethnic or religious connotations. Where the formula does score is in the emphasis that it lays on the way that all external influences are interpreted by the voter, that is in stressing the importance of perception and how the 'cognitive map' of the individual voter is made up; this tends to refer back to the Walter Lippmann concept of 'the pictures in our heads' and the possibility that these may be based on an image of reality which was 'exceedingly ill-informed' or, at the best, may be once again formed by intangible reactions between the major events of recent history (like the Depression) and the predominant group membership of the voter.[25]

Even more than the authors of the Elmira study, the Michigan team appears to have realized that there are limitations to a theory of voting that depends almost solely on the concept that 'voters vote in groups'. It is true that a blue-collar worker who is a staunch supporter of his union and of Irish descent is highly likely to vote for the Democratic ticket, just as, in Britain, few Welsh coalminers vote for the Tory party regularly. Simple socio-economic interest and inherited predilections are responsible for this but, in voting theory, it is the aberrant, the highly cross-pressured voter, the 'changer' and the man who persistently misperceives the interests apparent to his peers who are of especial interest. If the analysis of voting is to contain a psychological plane as well as one that is sociologically orientated, some such initial approach as the separation out of attitudes indicated by this set of survey research seems to be indicated. The writers defined six 'elements of politics that seemed most clearly to be objects of popular attitude'.[26] Divorcing these from the specific context of the three presidential elections covered by the survey material, they prove to be based on the personal attributes of each of the two presidential candidates, the interests of specific groups, domestic and foreign-policy issues respectively and, lastly, the record of the major parties as 'managers' when in office. Yet this still tends to externalize the forces at work and not to explain how they are 'internalized' by certain voters. In the last resort, although this approach makes the influences in a specific election more apparent, it does not fully explain the problem that the authors had set themselves earlier: ' . . . voting is in the end an act of individuals, and the motives for this act must be sought in psychological forces on individual human beings.'[27]

The writers do, however, look at the object of the influences by trying to make a number of generalizations about the way in which personality factors operate in the voting decision. On the whole, the evidence supplied by the surveys carried out in these two election years fails to show up any dramatic correlations that tie in personality types with party or issue orientation. Yet surely this does not mean that the internalization of stimuli relating to elections is relatively unimportant? If the forces themselves are a key to this individual decision-making then the way in which the individual internalizes them must be of equal importance. One is driven to the conclusion that the type of interviewing carried out in the Michigan surveys of the 1950s was not adequate to uncover the deep motivations involved. This view seems to be borne out by an essay which predated the publication of *The American Voter* though not that of other surveys. The psychiatrist, C. W. Wahl, noted that the first of the Michigan studies ignored 'antecedent familial experience and presumably felt that it had little relevance to the problem of voting choice.'[28] The range of primary identification embodied within the family group could, according to Wahl, influence secondary identification of a political nature, yet it is true that survey research rarely throws up much hard information on this sector. The Michigan group themselves recognized some of the shortcomings of their approach and, in the 1960s, the essays produced by members of the group tried to investigate the interaction between personality and the external situation in which the voter finds himself; research into the degree of political involvement among voters and its relation to the concept of personal effectiveness (that is, how far individuals feel able to cope with the problems of everyday life) was one aspect.[29] Unfortunately, some of the early attempts of political science to ground political behaviour firmly into a limited series of personality types seem to have inhibited the Michigan theorists to a degree in following up this dimension of voter involvement.

In the 1966 collection of essays that these writers produced, the main emphasis is on 'aggregate properties of the electorate or with the party system' as the two main areas of their interest.[30] In *The American Voter* they had become intrigued with V. O. Key's famous classification of elections into those that realigned electoral forces and those that did not.[31] Amplifying Key's classification, they had produced three main types: elections that maintained the 'patterns of partisan attachments', those that deviated from the pattern due to short-term forces which defeat the majority party and, lastly, those that realigned electoral forces in such a way that majority and minority parties change places.[32] The essays assembled in 1966 tend to concentrate on fitting American elections into this set of categories and in developing the concept of the 'normal vote', that division of the vote which would normally be expected from a group in a period of time, for it is:

> . . . useful to consider any particular vote cast by any particular group—the nation as a whole or some subpopulation—as consisting of a long-term and short-term component. The long-term component is a simple reflection of the distribution of underlying loyalties . . . In any specific election the population may be influenced by short-term forces associated with peculiarities of that election.[33]

The essays cited indicate clearly the retreat into large numbers exemplified by the 'normal vote' concept. It has a definite use when considering, for instance, the way in which the 1960 presidential election proved to be a battleground between conflicting general forces, on the one side the post-Eisenhower tendency for the natural Democratic majority to reassert itself and, on the other, the effect of John

Kennedy's religion on those Catholic Republicans and Protestant Democrats who found a conflict between their religious faith and political predisposition. Survey research allowed some estimation of the effect of the first successful Catholic presidential candidacy on specific groups of voters and, if one is looking for a broad summary of the sort of people who reacted against Kennedy specifically because of his religion (rural voters and Southerners, for example), then this approach is a useful one.[34] Philip Converse, author of the paper on the 1960 election concludes: 'Bit by bit, as religiously innocuous information filled in, the Protestant Democrat could come to accept Kennedy primarily as a Democrat, his unfortunate religion notwithstanding. Vote intentions angled away from group lines toward party lines.'[35] This pattern of analysis is extremely useful as a verification of one's less structured observations on contemporary electoral history, but its drawback lies in the relative lack of progress it marks over the earlier waves of survey research. The Michigan studies are usually presented as a great step forward in the analysis of voting practices but, apart from their high viewpoint, surveying the broad strands of the vote at one electoral period as compared to another, it is difficult to accept that any great 'step forward' has been made. A friendly critic of the methodology of this wave of voting studies wrote in 1962 that 'the determinants of voting are by no means identified precisely; what is known is that a host of factors are related to the vote',[36] and it is still true that survey research, in particular, is still far from providing a precise and definitive identification of all of these factors.

Alternative approaches

The type of survey-research-based voting theory that we have described rests primarily on local or national samples that attempt to produce generalizations about the way in which the members of the universe in question approach the voting decision. Virtually all attempts to produce general theory to explain voting behaviour take their starting-point from statistical material, as one would expect, data culled either from voting returns or from sample surveys or both. Alternative approaches to the 'mainstream' of survey research have tended either to restrict the universe in some way other than geographic or to make generalizations that are based on gross statistics alone. For example, some quite remarkable predictions were made by Louis Bean in the 1940s by the latter method, must notably in the presidential election of 1948 when commercial polling organizations were confident in their expectation of a Dewey victory, while Bean forecast a Truman win. Bean, using the concept of the 'normal' vote before most of the more academic analysts, married it to the idea of a 'tide' in the American two-party system which ebbed and flowed in irregular patterns. Bean has been especially associated with the depiction of state voting patterns as they relate to the national, the discovery of 'bellwether' counties that show a rhythm in the variation of their vote for major parties that parallels the national trend, and an isolation of major factors like business prospects that influence the broad sweeps of voting victory and defeat.[37] The Bean approach is anything but pretentious, and does not attempt to analyze the 'why' of voting beyond the general noting of the more apparent political and social pressures on the voter.

Other approaches to the study of voting have taken restricted universes to observe, but since the limitation has been other than geographic they cannot usually be regarded as the system in microcosm. Studies of the way in which religious groups vote, chiefly carried out in the United States, do not tell one about the whole of the population but a part of it, for the United States is a country with a variety of religious groups. Inevitably, since the white American Protestant is regarded as the 'norm', providing the largest group based on religion and race, studies tend to focus on significant minorities, especially the Catholic and Negro voters. Apart from those relating to 1960 (and before it, 1928), an election which, as we saw earlier, did mark an incursion of religion as a major factor in a national election, studies tend to investigate the general adherence of religious groups to political points of view over a period of time. One study (made at the end of the 1950s) that was geographically centred but which focussed on the correlation between religion and politics affirmed the view that 'white Protestant *churchgoers*' (the noun is significant) tend to the Republican party and that this was true even when class values were held constant, that is, the white Protestant worker was much more likely to be a Republican if he was a churchgoer (in Detroit, where the survey was carried out) than if he did not attend church regularly.[38] The fact that religion influences political belief in the United States is indicated by the analysis of the seeming discrepancy between the Detroit Jewish community possessing both 'an affinity for certain classical capitalistic patterns of thought and action' and a sympathy for the ideals of the Welfare State. Gerhard Lenski, the author of the study, suggests two reasons for this. One involves the 'rational' approach that capitalism and welfare statism share in their separate fields of action, and the second rests on the fact that American capitalism has given the Jewish member of that society wealth but not status and that therefore the latter does not identify with the upper-class American and his suspicion of welfare politics.[39] This is a reasonable analytic conclusion for the period and place in question though it may now have become dated by the rising social status of the Jewish community (although Yankee social coolness remains to some degree) and, in particular, by a challenge from the socially deprived groups at the bottom of the pyramid, notably the black American, who refuses to take the liberalism and toleration of the Jew at its face value. Lenski's interpretation is essentially a group one, depending on the view that socio-religious groups assimilate a set of values from their churches and that this inevitably colours the view each holds of society regardless of the other motivating factors that undoubtedly exist, such as economic class. This essentially Weberian viewpoint is a sophisticated one even if, for the study noted, it concentrates on one dimension of motivation, for it presumes a complex and multi-dimensional set of factors motivating people's political views and their subsequent vote.

The 'ethno-religious' dimension of group voting is followed up by a number of writers, since it is a hotly disputed question. Unlike economic motivation, self-explanatory when labour votes for welfare-oriented politicians and business votes for those who support its ethos, ethnic voting often has to be explained in terms of history and more complex motivation than simple economics. For example, Laurence Fuchs, writing on the support given by American Jews to one or other of the American political parties at different times in the last two centuries, implicitly shows how a relatively liberal people, or at least one sensitive to discrimination, reacted in favour of the party of Jefferson and Jackson, then the party of Abraham Lincoln and, finally, the way being paved by Woodrow Wilson and Al Smith, the party of Franklin Roosevelt was embraced by the majority of American Jewry for more than a generation.[40] The political predilection of the Jewish community at different times can only be explained on the basis of Jewish values that embrace internationalism, toleration, admiration for learning, etc., all of these a direct result of the unique position that Jewry has been forced to take up in the many countries to which it was dispersed over eighteen centuries ago.[41]

The growth of popular interest in the 'Catholic vote' in this century has led to a degree of academic inquiry to see whether such a compact 'vote' exists. Just prior to the 1960 election, the most crucial of all presidential elections for those of the Catholic faith, John Fenton could elaborate three hypotheses concerning the Catholic as compared to the Protestant voter in the United States. The burden of these was that the Catholic voter, largely because of the strong cultural bonds that united the Catholic community, tended 'to discriminate in favor of Catholic candidates'[42] much more than Protestant voters, in the North at least, seemed to do in favour of Protestant candidates. It would seem that there is a difference between the types of conditioning that, say, Jewish and Catholic voters receive. The former have developed a set of political attitudes that result from their history since the Diaspora, rather than from assumptions that are inculcated by their religion, whereas the pressures on Catholics seem far more Church-centred. The influence of Church and ethnic background may be waning slightly as the Churches tend to relax their hold on issues which can form the stuff of political choice and candidate preference (such as the birth-control issue), yet it will be a long time before studies of the influence of race and religion become superfluous in American voting behaviour. Key, Moynihan, Glazer and others have insisted on the retention of ethnic influences on the vote; Wolfinger summed it up thus: 'It seems plausible that this will be the legacy of ethnic politics: when national origins are forgotten, the political allegiances formed in the old days of ethnic salience will be reflected in the partisan choices of totally assimilated descendants of the old immigrants.'[43]

Some approaches to the study of the vote involve complex techniques rather than an emphasis on one approach rather than another. For example, simulation techniques which caused a certain ripple of popular interest in the United States in the early 1960s, owe an obvious debt to the mainstream of survey-based theory which was described above. The authors of the Simulmatics Corporation inquiry into the probable result of the 1960 and 1964 presidential elections emphasized that they owed a debt to both the 'Lazarsfeld–Berelson studies' and to the mass of data made available by the public opinion surveys of George Gallup and Elmo Roper.[44] Ithiel Pool and his colleagues were forecasting the result of the election before it took place, something that the commercial pollsters did with reservations and which many academic writers on politics would regard with the utmost suspicion. The project rested on the ability of computers to handle a vast amount of data and produce a 'simulation' in advance of the likely outcome of the election. Crucial to the organization of the data was its elaboration in 1960 into fifty-two 'issue-clusters', indicators of public opinion based on questions in domestic and foreign policy, images of the parties and so on, and 480 voter-types, each defined by socio-economic characteristics (hence the title of the Eugene Burdick novel based on this project, *The 480*).[45] The advantage of the method was that, using data that was of 1958 vintage in the 1960 simulation, it gave a fairly accurate forecast of the result with one or two allowances that had to be made, especially in the South, where state-by-state idiosyncrasy was considerable as far as party organization was concerned. The advance value of such a prediction for a politician is considerable where, as in this case, it indicates why a candidate is leading or losing and thus allows concentration on areas where performance is significant to the voter. For the political scientist, the value of such a process lies more in the explanatory nature of the prediction, the subsequent postdiction, and the way in which these related issues, group loyalties and other stimuli persuade the voter to vote for one candidate or another. The 1964 follow-up showed one remarkable feature to be the salience of issues in the campaign, a trend which could make group-centred voting analyses inadequate.

It may be inferred from some comments made earlier in this chapter that there are some shortcomings in the dependence of most voting theory on group behaviour. Even when the socio-economic approach is circumvented, typologies tend to be the order of the day, and it must be admitted that to a degree this is inevitable given the considerable problems involved in providing exact answers to the questions concerning motivation and the vote. Those studies that have tended more towards an emphasis on the personality of the voter, on the lines of Heinz Eulau's dictum that 'political behaviour is personal behaviour', have encountered their own difficulties in handling material and have fallen back on the elaboration of types; it is obviously impossible to handle data on elections in large political systems by enumerating the precise idiosyncrasies of each individual voter. A certain amount of basic investigation has been done on the way in which voters are conditioned by their early life, how in fact they are 'socialized' into the political system, and this will probably throw more light on personal motivation in the act of voting when a wider range pf research is available.[46] The most widely disseminated of the 'personal behaviour' concepts has probably been the type known as the 'alienated voter', a term which has had a certain currency among journalists and is therefore used in a manner which is loose and not entirely consistent with the patterns of behaviour described by the academic writers who first coined the phrase.

'Alienation', in the way that it is used by the principal architect of this thesis, Murray Levin, describes a state of mind in which the voter believes himself to possess no power as compared to the politicians and therefore he concludes that he is to all intents and purposes excluded from the political process. The alienated voter notes the dichotomy between the world as he knows it, in which powerful and often corrupt politicians operate almost unhindered, and the world of democratic theory where the voter is deemed to be the puppet-master in the last resort, controlling the politician via the ballot box. From this dichotomy arises frustration, scepticism and a general hostility towards the whole democratic process, expressed in the pithy comments about the politicians or 'pols' being 'all crooks' that one occasionally sees attributed to American voters and, in fact, to the voter in many a supposedly democratic polity.[47] Levin's summation arising from a study of the 1959 Boston mayoral election is as follows: 'Political alienation is the feeling of an individual that he is not a part of the political process. The politically alienated believe that their vote makes no difference. . . . Political alienation may be expressed in feelings of political powerlessness, meaninglessness, estrangement from political activity and normlessness.'[48] The rough-and-tumble of Massachusetts politics, especially Democratic party politics as practiced in that state, might lead to a degree of cynicism among some voters, and Levin's studies used as the basis of his principal books are illustrated with many pungent remarks quoted from voters that reflect a considerable suspicion of the political process. Yet the fairly high degree of interest in politics that is noticeable in the state in question, the fact that some of the evidence gathered was statistically suspect, and the distinct impression which is left with any student of state politics in the north-east of the United States that the pattern of 'voting against' rather than 'voting for' a candidate is a reasonably healthy attitude leaves the theory based on voter alienation more than a little suspect.[49] Perhaps the game is given away by the passing comment in the article which introduced this concept: 'Given this condition of extreme skepticism and hostility, *or perhaps in some instances extreme sophistication*, the traditional vote-getting techniques and the customary political rhetoric are likely to backfire.' (our emphasis)[50]

Voters in urbanized, comparatively developed societies are 'sophisticated' and, where party discipline is low, will be more interested in a candidate's integrity than in his programme, for only the former can ensure the latter. In short, 'alienation' is incomplete, at the very least, as an explanation of voting patterns in the type of society used as the model in the relevant literature.

'Alienation' leads one inevitably to that more common psychological classification (more common that is in social science literature), the phenomenon of 'anomy' or 'anomie' (both spellings are used). Following Durkheim, Merton and others, the term is now used to describe individuals who have completely lost their relationship to the norms of society and, through external conditions and a resultant state of mind, lose all sense of responsibility to the society which claims them as a member. McClosky and Schaar have tried to show that the intervening variable of the individual personality is as important as the socio-cultural setting and that certain psychological types will react differently to a set of external circumstances that can produce anomie in some of them.[51] They echo the findings of other researchers who have found anomie to be highest among certain groups, including the old, the socially isolated or disadvantaged, and the American Negro.[52] Although little of this area of research has been concentrated to date on the vote as an indicator of the degree of alienation of individual or group, survey research shows that, for example, low turn-out often stems from the same types of voter who are most susceptible to anomie. The external variables are much easier to handle than the classification of individual psychological difference. The connection between the disadvantaged condition of a group such as the American Negro and a resulting tendency to anomie is as obvious as anything ever can be in social science. Black voters in the

United States, though 'ethnic' to some degree, differ from other ethnic blocs in the intensity with which they have reacted both to discrimination and to barriers to the privilege of voting. Research into Negro voting in the South has inevitably come up against what has been termed 'the psychological characteristics instilled by decades of subordination' and the coiners of this phrase go on to suggest that: 'Segregation's greatest triumph has been its impact on Negro minds. For some the scars are permanent: nothing short of death will eliminate their crippled psyches from the political scene. For others the scars will respond but slowly to the salve of objective equality.'[53] It may be, as Dwaine Marvick has suggested, that the American Negro has never become detached from the main body of American political life for the simple reason that he never became fully socialized into it in early life.[54] The rapid change in the expectations of the black American in the last decade, automatically increasing the gulf between these and the performance of society, is beginning to produce a new pattern of voter in the black community, looking for rapid change but uncertain whether the indirect method of the ballot-box is an adequate means to the end. Further research into the behaviour of the black voter may help to provide us with the answers to the relationship between the interior and the exterior causes of anomie and alienation, as far as these concepts can be validated inside a general theory of voting behaviour. It is likely that, even where social factors are held constant, variation in strength of commitment to the vote as a means of achieving community goals will vary and can only be assessed by some form of individual psychological investigation.

Once one moves away from the survey research pattern, work done seems to be episodic and isolated from much in the way of a general theme. It is often the case that research into voting patterns forms a part of a larger design which attempts to describe the way in which political life is changing over an area like the American state, region or the whole country. The work of the late V. O. Key on the American South, Duane Lockard on New England, and Samuel Lubell's books on changes in American political life in general are three examples of this tendency.[55] All three of these men, two academic and one a reporter, interweave the statistics of the vote with demographic factors, group loyalties and the residues of history that lie upon voting patterns in many parts of the United States, often managing to throw new light and even explode old myths by intensive study of this interaction; Lubell's analysis of the 'isolationist vote' and its relation to the density of German-speakers in specific areas is a good illustration of this.[56] Interesting, though less vital, is a technique like 'friends and neighbours' voting as described in Key's and Lockard's books for, although it shows how factionalism can be tied to locality in primaries where party designation is suppressed, it provides little insight into the deeper springs of voting behaviour.[57] On the other hand, V. O. Key's overall contribution to voting theory is considerable for, in addition to the 'critical election' theory mentioned earlier, he was working at the time of his death in 1963 on a riposte to those who had argued that voters who changed their votes from one election to the next were essentially disinterested and apathetic as compared to party regulars. Key argued in his posthumous book defending 'the responsible electorate' that 'switchers' were more numerous than had been supposed (often cancelling each other out) and, secondly, that they were swayed by real policy preference to make a change. The evidence, drawn from public opinion polls, is not entirely conclusive because of the small sub-samples taken, but the argument is eloquent and one that we would like to believe if further research bears it out.[58]

The European voter

Virtually all the examples to date have been taken from American experience; like so much of modern analytical theory, generalizations about the voter have chiefly come from American writers. Not entirely though; there is now a respectable body of writing from European sources which to some degree charts the behaviour of voters on this side of the Atlantic. It is worth looking at the attempts to examine European elections to see whether they add anything to the American research.

It is a truism that the study of politics in Europe has been either a normative one or essentially a descriptive exercise and that, until recently, little attempt had been made to emulate the American styles of political analysis, despite the fact that some of the latter's inspiration came from European sources, notably from the work of Max Weber. In the examination of elections this tendency is gainsaid to some degree and there is a tradition of electoral analysis that stretches back at least to the end of the Second World War. In France, Britain and Scandinavia especially, elections have come under scrutiny, originally as exercises in contemporary history or political ecology, but more recently such study has been infected by the approaches from across the Atlantic. Both the extra data and the contrast in approach, where it exists, provide some supplementation of the American material.

In Britain, 1945 is an especially key date in electoral history because of the installation of the first Labour government with an overall majority in the House of Commons, following their dramatic General Election victory. It also saw the beginning of a long series of electoral studies of General Elections, mounted by academics associated with the new Nuffield College in the University of Oxford. From 1945 to February 1974, nine elections have been followed by nine accounts of the campaign, issues, candidates, etc., and these have become as familiar a part of British political bibliography as, say, the highly personalized accounts of Theodore White have done in the United States since 1960. In fact, the emphasis in the Nuffield studies lies somewhere between the White approach and the Michigan one, although there were signs of a veering away from the former and towards the latter by the 1970s. The early Nuffield studies almost ignored electoral analysis in favour of political reportage. In the account of 1945, which was the trail-blazer that set the style, the only tentative reason for the Labour victory was that it was 'the fruit of twenty years' expanding secondary education', and the only theoretical references in the 1950 study are to the statistical curio of the 'cube law' and a genuflection in the direction of the 'mandate theory'.[59] In 1951, and again in 1955, David Butler was firm in his insistence that the books described the elections and did not analyze them: 'It is not a work of sociology, and it cannot pretend to offer any definite explanation of why the voters behaved as they did. . . . The 1955 election offered ample evidence of the general ignorance of politicians, journalists and academic students about the motivation of the British voter.'[60] As a result of the 1959 election, the British Labour party found its number of seats declining for the fourth successive time in a General Election, and the writers of the 1959 survey put forward the beginnings of a 'cohorts' theory as a possible explanation. The suggestion was of a general weakening of class consciousness among younger voters as a result of the relative prosperity of the late 1950s and that 'a predominantly prosperous people is unlikely to welcome major changes'.[61]

The 1959 study having almost written off the Labour party as a force attracting the British voter, there had to be some explanation of the Labour victories of 1964 and 1966. 'Guesswork' in 1964 seems to arrive at a 'plague on both their houses' theory to explain the inconclusive result[62] but, by 1966, the cohorts theory was being brushed up again as the long-term explanation, although this time the younger voters were to be the saviours of the Labour party, since they replaced the gradually dwindling band of those who remembered politics at a time when the Labour party was young and barely an alternative government.[63] Admittedly, these snippets of analysis do less than justice to the mass of raw material in these studies, notably the latest ones, which have copious statistical appendices.[64] Yet even here there is virtually no attempt to dig into the motivation of an electorate that wobbled as conspicuously as did the British vote in 1970, a year which, for example, ranks with 1936 and 1948 as one where the public opinion polls were caught with their predictive pants down. One reason for the reluctance to analyze the results at all intensively seems to have been the production in 1969 of a large volume attempting to show how political change comes about in British voting patterns, one which involved the senior author of the Nuffield studies and one of the team from the University of Michigan which had tried to delineate the motives behind electoral choice in the United States presidential elections of recent years.

Before assessing this volume, one should not lose sight of the alternate stream of voting research in England, one which paralleled the previous American studies of elections on a local rather than national scale. A number of the early post-war General Elections produced the by-product of constituency surveys, trying to isolate reasons for voting behaviour at a particular place—one constituency—at the time of a General Election. Genuflection in the direction of the pioneer American studies, especially Erie County, is common, and there are some similarities in the conclusions of the studies made in both countries. Voting 'in groups' was the general conclusion drawn from the English constituencies examined, as it was in the United States. There is some difference in emphasis; religion and ethnicity are rarely mentioned as root causes of voting intention in Britain while the emphasis on the socio-economic group is persistent, the 'class issue' in British politics showing its predominance here.[65] The approach to this concept in the studies made in British constituencies in the early 1950s was not entirely consistent. Whereas the report on the 1951 'fight' in Bristol North-East drew a difference between the American and British voter: ' . . . the voting behaviour of the British elector appears to be more of a product of his social background, whether viewed objectively or subjectively, than of the American elector, which is more closely related to his personal estimation of himself,'[66] a study of Greenwich took the parenthesis in the above as being much more central to voting behaviour and perhaps closer to the American's 'personal estimation': 'Voting Conservative may be a cause as well as an effect of thinking oneself as middle class and voting Labour may be a reason for thinking oneself as working class.'[67] The observers of these elections are agreed on the broad outlines of British voting behaviour within the fairly elementary frames of reference used—on concepts like voter identification with party 'images' for example—and often look forward to a build-up of research which will throw more light on vexed questions like the character of 'changers' or 'the floating vote' in British terminology. Greenwich in 1951 produced a five-part classification of voters which included a group of 8% of the registered voters labelled as 'converts', who switched between elections, and found a very low percentage (1%) of complete 'indifferents'.[68] The Bristol studies concentrated much effort on examining 'floaters', producing some evidence to suggest that this category was not as disinterested as sometimes alleged: ' . . . in a larger sample might it not be possible to identify "illiterate" floaters, "intellectual" floaters and perhaps even other clearly defined groups.'[69] It was obvious that more sophisticated frames of reference would be needed to clarify problems such as this.

In the late 1950s and early 1960s, few really new devices were apparent in British voting theory or methodology. The sample survey was refined and, as in the United States, a common interest developed between academics on the one hand and political activists on the other, which was aimed at finding out the 'why' of voting intent, if for different reasons. The best-known British example of this trend was the post-election survey carried out at the request of the magazine *Socialist Commentary* following the 1959 General Election, the cause of so much contemporary gloom in the Labour party. The survey, later incorporated into a paperback book, was based on multiple-choice questions and answers, a method which involves those who draft the questions in a process by which they prejudge the alternative answers, and one which can be dangerous in the hands of the relatively unskilled pollster. The survey in question was in fact drawn up by one of the most competent of survey research experts on this side of the Atlantic and, given the confines of multiple choice, it was as sophisticated as one would expect in that period. It must be remembered that the 1959 election took place against a backdrop of seeming prosperity in Britain, spurious perhaps but evidently felt by the voters, and true enough for many groups who compared war-time austerity and pre-war depression with the full employment and the availability of consumer goods of the late 1950s. The survey especially concerned itself with the 'image' that the two main parties in Britain projected to the voter and also the 'image' presented by the respective party leaders, Macmillan and Gaitskell. The Conservatives appealed to the ethos of the day, one which accentuated the possibilities for prosperity spreading among the young and the middle class in particular, and to all the working population to some degree, while the Labour party was seen as the party of the lower working class with little ambition to improve its economic lot. Similarly, the image of the party leaders differed, Macmillan appearing strong, able and even with 'some qualities of greatness' (to 40% of total sample), while Gaitskell scored only by being practical and in touch with the masses.[70]

In the analysis attached to this survey, Richard Rose also saw the 'image' as a significant unit of assessment on the part of the voter. Rose claimed that: 'Elections are decided by three interrelated influences—the material and social environment, individual values, and party activities.'[71] Values are supposed to relate to three separate images, of society, of the voter himself and of the party that the voter embraces or rejects. In trying to line up all three of these, patterns of voting emerge, such as the voter who sees society in class terms, and identifies himself with either the middle or working class and votes accordingly, Conservative or Labour. Conservative voters include those who follow the party out of deferential motives or out of social pressure from their peers; Labour supporters are those who are altruistic, believing that Labour government produces the good society or, at the other extreme, those who believe that Labour means more return, in the form of social welfare for example, when it is in power.[72]

Alas, the only general conclusion from this is that 'politics is continually in a state of flux'.[73] Although this model is an intelligent way of trying to simplify the complexity of the large numbers of a General Election, it still tends to produce relatively few categories into which voters must fit and tells us little about the reasons why they find their way into certain of them—deference and altruism, for example, allow more investigation and have proved fruitful grounds for inquiry in recent years.[74] The social survey tends to whittle large numbers down to small ones yet, in the form described here, it lacks enough clarity to make us understand the real springs of motivation when people vote.

The brief duration of the complacent public attitudes that predominated in this 1959 survey is apparent to anyone who has followed the fortunes of the British political parties in the 1960s and early 1970s, and once more indicates the need to understand the nature of that section of the voting population which can shift its allegiance fairly abruptly; Mark Abrams, following up his 1959 inquiry before the subsequent General Election, managed to pinpoint it a little more exactly than hitherto: 'For it is efficiency, more than anything else, that the floating voters demand from the political parties. . . . The floater wants a Government which will be competent and expert, and he will vote for whichever party seems currently to produce the better "managerial" performance.'[75] Therefore, even if the voter who switches easily is not well informed about political affairs, he is still sophisticated enough to know what he wants from the politicians and to set about getting it. Yet during the 1960s much voting analysis in Britain still centred on so-called 'psephology' and arid mathematical arguments about 'swing', etc. A high-level discussion in 1964 at the Royal Statistical Society bears this out, for the author of a paper on the 1964 election commented: ' . . . as Mr Steed admits it is impossible to measure the size of the floating vote. Nor is it very easy to define it.'[76] The more recent local studies have been rather more effective in advancing knowledge about the British voter. In Birch's study of Glossop in the late 1950s, for example, one can detect the beginnings of the 'cohorts' theory mentioned earlier.[77] Both this study and a later one by other academics on Newcastle-under-Lyme try to dig deeper than hitherto into the social composition of the electorate, the reasons why voters develop certain group characteristics, and points of interest such as the importance of self-assigned class or the occasional relevance of religion to voting behaviour (in a context where Anglicanism—the 'Conservative Party at prayer' as someone once commented—is strong among the working class).[78] There is still an air of quiet frustration about these studies, brought about by the barrier that seemed to exist to a deeper understanding of the springs of voting behaviour. Yet, as in the United States, elections were being slotted into larger concepts of the polity as an action system. A sample taken in Stockport in 1964 formed the basis of a 'functional analysis' of voting and elections and, in the views of the two authors (of American origin incidentally), the replies show that the British voter tends to view voting as 'a necessary but not particularly pleasurable duty', unlike the United States where voting seems to provide rather more of an emotional outlet and satisfaction for the participant.[79] Voting, on the basis of this argument, is merely a democratic norm, giving the citizen a mild sense of gratification and involving him momentarily in the political process; some misinterpretation of Easton indirectly leads these writers to downgrade the act of voting to the status of a minor response mechanism, a view which may have been fleeting, for it seems unlikely to stand up to intense scrutiny.[80]

On occasion, the study of a particular constituency or constituencies is motivated by the desire to isolate some unique influence on the voting process. This was the case when a study was made of two Northern constituencies, West Leeds and Pudsey, which adjoin each other in the West Riding of Yorkshire. A team from Leeds University tried to assess the impact of electoral television on the images of parties and leaders in the General Elections of 1959 and 1964. This 'unknown factor', as they originally termed it, was tested by the usual technique of a series of panel interviews to see whether any correlation could be detected between changes in political attitude and the rate of exposure to the mass media, especially television. As with the American studies, mainly carried out in pre-television times, little correlation could be found, particularly in the 1959 election; there was only 'a small measure of association between political change and exposure to propaganda'.[81] Television did appear to increase the voter's store of knowledge about the campaign but it did not seem to influence his decision in any decisive way. To some extent, this was qualified by the 1964 findings, which suggested that special factors intervened in that year and that the 'new Liberal voters of 1964 were weaned from the ranks of former supporters of the major parties and that television facilitated the severing of their old ties'.[82] The erratic nature of the Liberal vote nationally since then, down in 1970 and up again in February 1974, seems to suggest that television has only a marginal effect on Liberal fortunes overall.

To date, the most extensive examination of the English voter is probably the study mounted by cross-fertilization between the 'Michigan School' and the main author of the continuing saga from Nuffield College. The 1969 book by Butler and Stokes purports to examine 'political change' in this country as seen through the eyes of statistical samples of the adult population carried out between 1963 and 1966. The authors recognize that certain limitations still exist in the analysis of data of this type. Motivation must often be inferred from the broad movement of groups of voters and no suitable methodology has yet been developed to link the deeper springs of the individual personality to voting intent. This is made clear by their plain statement: 'We shall not probe very far into the realms of personality in this book, but we have no doubt that such factors supply part of the motives of electors who find intrinsic values in supporting a given party.'[83] Instead, the writers concentrate on charting political change by tracing the way in which the electorate is altered by the natural rhythm of birth, coming-of-age and death; they also consider the real changes in long-term and short-term alignment of the electorate brought about by external influence. They argue, using the 'cohorts' theory, that the key date for any elector is the date that he is first able to vote and that the impressions made on him by the political parties at that time are likely to remain with him for life. Their view of party support at any one time is therefore partially dependent on what they term 'the procession of cohorts through the electorate'.[84] At the same time, the traditional view of English voting as class-based is allowed for, although they argue that class alignment is tending to weaken, with less perceived difference between the two major parties than there used to be. This generalization does show up one of the weaknesses in the design—its dependence on intensive study and interviewing carried on over a relatively short space of time. Only a few years after the book was published, the pattern of events at the time of the Edward Heath Conservative administration might suggest that some class-consciousness was creeping back into British politics, just as religious difference has obliquely slid back into British political consciousness because of the Northern Ireland troubles of the late

1960s and early 1970s.[85]

If what Butler and Stokes term 'the individual's social ambience'—not only class but the general social environment in which the voter finds himself—is likely to dominate the direction in which voting habits are formed, what are the forces that cause the sort of short-term deviation which, for example, raised the Liberal vote in the early 1960s, depressed it by 1966 and raised it again by 1974? The evidence put forward from the samples taken seems to invalidate what has sometimes been a popular explanation for the maintenance and occasional sharp increase in the Liberal vote. This is the 'halfway house' concept; party changers (from Conservative to Labour or vice versa) may use the Liberals as a temporary stopping-place before making the full transition. The Butler–Stokes samples showed little or no sign of this.[86] The tendency was to move back to the party of origin, usually the Conservatives, for this is where the Liberals had picked up the greater part of their gains in the 1959–63 period.[87] Since the samples taken did not go beyond 1966, it is impossible to say whether the 'Liberals' favourable exchange with the Conservatives' had any counterpart with the Labour party in the later 1960s, though the evidence of declining Liberal fortunes in this period suggests that it would be very small. Overall, one is hesitant to accept the explanation of the circulation of Liberal votes as a universal one, for the character of a third party is that it may take up different roles at different times and any repeat of the Liberal 'revival', such as that of the 1970s, could show quite different characteristics to that of the early 1960s.

The 1960s were ripe with short-term issues that caused a swing which may have been short-term only and by early 1974 the two major parties seemed evenly matched. It could be that long-term changes in the electorate will benefit the Labour party, but certain of the short-term issues listed by these two writers may not be repeated in the near future, for example, those referring to the 'modern' and 'exciting' character of Labour policy in the middle of the decade.[88] Where the Labour party scored in the 1960s, and will perhaps again, is on social welfare, which was salient in 1964 but beginning to recede by 1966.[89] On the whole, the general picture of the movements between the two major parties in the period covered by the sample surveys supports the interpretation offered by a 'valence' model with: ' . . . the Government of the day, whichever party is in power, being rewarded for good times and being disapproved of for bad times'.[90]

Although the Butler and Stokes book is replete with complex diagrams and awash with statistics, its message is ultimately a relatively simple one, balancing up the changes that take place in the electorate with the effects of contemporary economic and social history on each election. If the sampling had been taken in a different period of years, it is tempting to agree with the late Iain MacLeod that some of the conclusions would have been different (although MacLeod was anything but an impartial observer).[91] It is an important source-book for the early 1960s and the voting attitudes that were prevalent at that time, and it also sheds some light on a number of areas related to voting in Britain such as press influence (if any) and the part played by the unions in party loyalty. It does not provide a universal model for the depiction of political change because of its self-imposed restrictions; the view is an aerial one and not sufficiently analytic about the root causes of individual attitude towards politics and parties. Much time, energy and money would be needed to fulfil the authors' ambition to present us with a comprehensive picture of the 'forces shaping electoral choice' as their subtitle puts it. In time we may be the fortunate recipients of their more comprehensive attempts at electoral model-building but, until then, the 1969 book remains simply a great storehouse of raw material about electoral attitudes at a key point in British political history.

At least the British electoral system has remained a constant during the twentieth century with virtually the only dramatic disturbances coming from the changing alignment of parties, in particular the substitution of the Conservative–Labour for the Conservative–Liberal dialogue. Looking at the French Republic, now in its fifth reincarnation, the situation is more complex, not only because of the changing selection of parties available to the voter, but also because of the alterations that have taken place from time to time in the electoral system itself. Even in the comparatively brief historical period since the end of the Second World War, the French electoral system has changed several times; Roy Pierce, writing in 1968, summarizes it:

> The eight postwar elections to the National Assembly were held under three different kinds of electoral system. The first three elections were held under a system of proportional representation. The next two were held under a hybrid system. . . . The elections of 1958, 1962 and 1967 were held under a system which the French refer to as the 'scrutin uninominal à deux tours' (single-member district system with two ballots).[92]

Despite these changes, which have spanned the century that has elapsed since the Third Republic was created, there is a tradition of analysis of the vote in France. In the main, it can be described as 'electoral geography', since the tendency is to concentrate on the correlation of variables with the basic variable of the vote in each geographical area. André Siegfried, the principal pioneer of this technique, opened his 1913 study of western France with the following statement: 'J'ai remarqué souvent, dans les élections, que les opinions politiques sont sujettes à une repartition géographique' (I have often noticed that political opinion at election-time divides along geographical lines).[93] Siegfried suggested that just as there were clear climatic and geological regions in the country, it was possible to distinguish clear divisions in the political 'climate' between one region and another. Siegfried's approach is highly eclectic and not unlike that used later by V. O. Key when he examined voting patterns in the American South. Each region separated out by Siegfried is shown to have a set of climatic and geographic characteristics; these influence the economic base and the distribution of population, even the class structure of the area. Add in factors like the possible significance of religious division and historical persistence of old loyalties such as those to the 'Bonapartist' tradition and the observer will begin to detect correlations that have meaning and which will explain, or help to explain, the political divisions of the area. When Siegfried wrote, such self-contained political regions were undoubtedly more discrete than they are today. Moving from one part of La Vendée to another a few miles north, he noted: 'Tout change subitement: c'est un autre pays et, à plusiers égards, un autre siècle.' (It all changes unexpectedly: it's another country, and, in many ways, another century.)[94] Thirty-six years later Siegfried was still detecting sharp boundaries of electoral opinion inside the large geographic regions of France—this time in the Ardèche area immediately to the west of the Rhône valley: 'Le primaire, d'une part, est plus à Droite que le calcaire . . . il est intéressant de rappeler qu'en Vendée il en est de même quand on passe de la plaine au bocage.' (The primary rock area is, on the whole, more right-wing than the limestone belt . . . it is interesting to compare it with the Vendée where much the same thing happens when one leaves the plain for the wooded area.)[95] This pattern of analysis has tended to pervade French electoral studies, although now it is being overladen with those transatlantic techniques that we have examined at length. A writer such as Francois Goguel seems to carry on the style of Siegfried well into the electoral history of the Fifth Republic, with studies of individual elections slotted into the general geographical and historical trends that form the basis of this approach. Of the 1965 presidential election, for example, Goguel notes that the support given to de Gaulle's principal opponent, that is, the one who survived until the second ballot, was concentrated in specific areas that tended toward the left: 'Le support essentiel de la candidature Mitterand réside moins dans l'existence de facteurs d'ordre économique ou social que dans la persistance d'une tradition historique ancienne et solidement enracinée. . . .' (The main support for Mitterand can be related less to economic and social factors than to the persistence of a historical tradition and a deeply rooted tendency. . . .)[96] The French polling organization SOFRES provides French political scientists with the sort of data that has long been available in the United States and this has allowed some refinement of the traditional approach described above.[97] However, electoral analysis in France is still heavily influenced by the work of Siegfried and Goguel, even though cross-fertilization is generally making the styles of electoral research more international.

Apart from France, Scandinavia is probably the other area of Continental Europe with a tradition of electoral research, even though a much shorter one. Mogens N. Pedersen has suggested that his country, Denmark, is a 'dull country' for voting research, but other Danish political scientists argue that the 'lack of marked cleavage' in the social structure has not prevented the elections of the 1960s marking an abrupt end to a period of 'maintenance' in electoral pattern with the Socialist group, in particular, in the Danish Parliament producing a short-lived majority in a series of dramatic results.[98] Research into elections to the Norwegian Storting has been similar to that carried out in America, and some comparative work indicates the sort of contrast one would expect with the post-war Norwegian parties showing more of a class basis in electoral terms than the American ones of that period.[99] Outside of France and possibly Britain, the influence of American models for electoral research seems almost overpowering. Each of the major Western European countries is now armed with organizations which, for commercial or academic purposes, collect data that can be used to further electoral analysis, and the import of American techniques of processing this data means that a relatively sophisticated understanding of electoral support in the European democracies is becoming possible. One example is Klaus Liepelt's comparison of the nature of party support in Austria and West Germany, using data from social research organizations in the two countries plus a 'branching tree' pattern of analysis of voter types to indicate that class polarization is reflected to a greater degree in Austrian than in German parties.[100]

Although European political scientists have not been slavish copiers of the American pioneers in voting research, it is evident that the major direction of influence has been from the United States to Europe rather than vice versa. This was inevitable to some extent because of a number of factors—the early development of sample survey work in the United States and the sheer numbers of the American political science profession as compared to Europe are two obvious ones. Because European political characteristics differ from American, styles of analysis are beginning to diverge to some degree—for example in the need to clarify the nature of social stratification, a vital line of cleavage in most patterns of voting in Europe—yet it is still true that there is little of a dramatic nature that has originated in Europe. Even the French tradition of electoral geography has long been paralleled by studies in the American states. What is now evident is that increasing co-operation between political scientists on both sides of the Atlantic is leading to a general increase in international comparison between political systems where voting is free and significant (which limits the number of polities in any world-wide comparison). This is a valuable development in that contrast inevitably highlights features of voting that might otherwise remain clouded. However, in Europe and in the United States, the conclusion remains the same. One is now aware of the crucible in which voting takes place, the forces that appear to operate on the voter as an individual and, even more, as a member of a series of groups. We are still appallingly ignorant of the way in which these influences are internalized and why some voters appear to swim against the tide of influence which should carry them one way. Inevitably, one is driven back on to the realization that the often discredited cries for some understanding of the psychological processes by which political choice is made may have contained the key to this problem after all. Unfortunately, the amount of fieldwork needed to make any impact on voter motivation is likely to be enormous—possibly based on extensive depth interviewing—and the resources are not likely to be available for such projects in the foreseeable future. Yet until there is an extension of our knowledge in this way, or until there are clearer frames of reference in which to slot our present range of information, voting research is doomed to retain the comparatively blinkered outlook that it presents at this time.

Voting in decision-making groups

As a postscript to this chapter—and reasons of space will prevent it being much more than this—one should refer to the range of writing on voting in legislatures and multi-member courts that has appeared in the last few years. That this is a fairly recent line of research is attested to by Heinz Eulau, who in 1962 suggested that judicial behaviour research barely existed prior to 1957![101] Yet, on the face of it, there are good reasons for posing the question that Glendon Schubert phrases: 'The question to which I address myself is this: When men (and, at least in principle, women) play political roles, to what extent are their public acts influenced by their personal beliefs?'[102] Where judges play political roles their behaviour can be, and should be, studied. Further to this, multi-member courts are relatively small, certainly as compared to the voting universe in public elections, and even to legislatures. On the other hand, there are contrasts between, say, voting in the Supreme Court and voting as an exercise of the public at large which make comparison of doubtful value. Justices are trying to interpret the basic law of the land rather than express preferences for one set of policies or ideologies rather than another. However, it is true that distinct correlations have been found between personal belief and votes cast in the Court. Glendon Schubert's major study of the Court produced axes of attitude with the help of statistical techniques, such as Louis Guttman's cumulative scaling, and suggested that judges brought their inherent attitudes to bear on their interpretation of cases. The main axis, in Schubert's view, was a liberal–conservative one but not of a straightforward character:

> There is both a liberal ideology and a liberal attitude, and there is a conservative ideology but there is no conservative attitude . . . we find that the conservative ideology spans two quite disparate

conservative attitudes: a conservative attitude toward political issues, and a conservative attitude toward economic issues. Thus, the eighteen justices who constituted my sample are partitioned, by their attitudes, into three groups of approximately equal size: liberals, pragmatic (economic) conservatives, and dogmatic (political) conservatives.[103]

The work of Schubert and others indicates that, in the Court, blocs emerge which remain relatively static over time, that leadership can be detected in these and that external stimulus only occasionally changes the direction of the Court (as it did in the late 1930s).[104] If the Supreme Court is insulated to some small degree from external pressure—one reason for this is that appointment is for life and while of good behaviour, another is that few justices go back into politics after resigning from the Court—other American courts are progressively more influenced by politics the lower one reaches into the various strata. In Louisiana, for example, Kenneth Vines has noted that: 'The dominance of localism in the selection of judges suggests that local interests and local political structures may be important in judicial decision-making.'[105] Bloc analysis and simple matrix formation have been used in state supreme courts to show that leadership patterns are detectable, and the reasons for indulging in the exercize are summed up in Sidney Ulmer's comment: 'If such leaders are successfully identified, their ideological and legal positions acquire added meaning.'[106] What the studies of judicial behaviour do indicate is that the powers of acquired attitudes and the pressures of group membership are almost as powerful in a closed quasi-political universe of small dimension as in the large amorphous universe of the voting public. There are constraints and opportunities that do not exist among opinion leaders in the general public. The opportunity to 'be oneself' on the United States Supreme Court, for example, has never been better illustrated than by the definite shift made by Earl Warren during the first few years of his tenure as Chief Justice, when he moved from the relatively conservative political position he had shown in his pre-Court days to a much more liberal one.

The study of legislatures has produced much the same conclusions as those produced by the investigations into judicial behaviour. Of necessity, it is a somewhat wider field than the latter, since the relationship between the legislator and his constituent must be added to such factors as the internal cohesion of voting groups inside the legislature. Although research suggests that perception of a legislator's stand on specific issues by his constituents is, to say the least of it, limited, Miller and Stokes have pointed out that, for Congressmen: 'Although the conditions of constituency influence are not equally satisfied, they are met well enough to give the local constituency a measure of control over the actions of its Representatives.'[107] Guttman scaling, bloc analysis and other statistical devices have been used to illustrate the expectations and perceptions of legislators inside their respective legislatures.[108] Roll calls are the raw material for such analysis and are now used in a highly sophisticated mathematical manner to determine, for example, the degree of cohesion and partisanship within specific groups and within political parties. Even a relatively simple pattern of analysis (in mathematical terms) can be effective, such as David Mayhew's approach to the relation between party affiliation and issue areas in the first eight Congresses elected after the Second World War. From this examination of the way in which each of the two main parties reacted to four areas of policy— the farmer, the city, the worker and the West—Mayhew was able to point out a difference between the cohesion of the Congressional Republicans and Democrats; the former were prepared only to cleave to a narrow interpretation of their main interests (the 'exclusive' compromise), while the Democrats were prepared to be 'inclusive' and support causes in these specific areas which only concerned directly a minority of their members in the two houses.[109] For a much more complex pattern of analysis, one can instance the tendency to use factor and cluster analyses, especially now the latter which, as Duncan MacRae points out: ' . . . together with precision scale scoring will exploit the data as fully and accurately as any other available method. This approach makes fewer assumptions than factor analysis, stays close to the data, and requires little mathematical preparation to learn.'[110] MacRae admits that all methods which attempt to measure partisanship in legislative systems have drawbacks and it would seem that, for all the appearance of relative mathematical sophistication that these methods give, roll-call data has to be used with care if it is to produce reliable models of legislative behaviour. The tendency is for sophistication to centre on the methodology, however, and the interpretation of results is still highly tentative.

Legislators—and judges, for that matter—are different animals to the general run of voters. By their very nature, they are highly politicized and tend to react to a wider variety of inputs than does the average voter, whose contacts with the central material of politics may be minimal. Because of this, the legislator accepts roles which tend to be foreign to the citizen who confines his political participation to such a limited role as that of the voter in public elections. This is well summed up, as far as the legislator is concerned, in one of the key books on legislative behaviour:

> The analytical distinction between clientele, representational and purposive roles is helpful in dissecting the legislator's total role. Actual behaviour, however, is not a function of discrete roles, but of a system of roles. It is the network of interpenetrating roles which gives structure and coherence to the legislative process.[111]

Role-playing for the non-activist in the political process is a simpler affair than this, as far as the political system is concerned. Therefore, although the research into the behaviour of the more activist members of the system has value in terms of tracing influence on the voting decision (summarized by the above mentioned writers as 'their prior experiences, attitudes, and predispositions; . . . their current perspectives and goals; and . . . their anticipations of the future'[112]), the frame of reference is bound to differ from that of the relatively non-activist participant. Since all research in political analysis does tend to reinforce other research, it is reasonable to expect that work done on voting in these small decision-making groups will shed light on voting behaviour in general, but it would be unreasonable to expect too much. The manner in which all of those involved in voting situations rationalize their prior experience into a predisposition to vote one way or another is an area which has been better covered by the judicial and legislative studies than the general ones on voting. This is because of the ease with which a small voting universe can be comprehended as against a large, amorphous one. In other aspects, though, the activist's experience may shed little light on what motivates the voting public.

Conclusion

There may seem to be a strain of frustration running through this chapter. This is because the writer feels that there has been some over-selling of the conclusions of voting behaviour research in the recent past. This evident complacency stems from the tendency to feel that a field which is so replete with statistics and methodology must have produced definitive answers to the basic questions of motivation on the part of the individual voter. Although a great deal is known about the probable movement of groups, whether their point of reference is geographic, class-based or whatever, little is understood of the basic motivation of 'the voter' as such. Voting research must take a new turn before the mass of data that is available from the survey work of the last few decades takes on a new meaning and allows a clearer answer to the question 'why do people vote the way that they do?'

CHAPTER 6
PARTIAL THEORY II: DEMOCRACY

There are few more value-laden words in the political scientist's repertoire than 'democracy'. In the last generation especially, the dispute between the main ideological factions in different parts of the world has often centred around the values implied by the term, and how they can be translated into concrete political relationships. In political science, as we know it on both sides of the Atlantic, discussion has turned less on questions such as the issue of 'people's democracy' versus 'liberal democracy' and has tended to concentrate on the problem of making anything meaningful of the 'role of the many'. Yet one needs to look, very briefly, at the history of the term before tracing the series of disputes which has bedevilled attempts to operate a general theory of democracy which would be of relevance to non-Marxist states at least.

Aristotle's classifications of democracy and oligarchy are well known to students of government as are his suspicions of extreme forms of any 'type' of government drawn from the basic classifications. Since he equated 'democracy' in its known forms with the predominance of the poorer classes in society at a time before outright condemnation of riches was widespread, Aristotle favoured systems which, in his view, would protect all classes in society. Kingship, aristocracy or a 'mixed' system would provide this; the last, or 'polity', has some of the elements of what we would term democracy.[1] In view of his dislike of pure democracy as an aberrant form of government, it is difficult to see Aristotle as a true founder of democratic theory.

One has to jump forward to the Enlightenment to isolate the real beginnings of democratic theory in the ideas which led eventually to the American and French Revolutions. It is not possible to identify the ideas of political liberalism with a developed theory of democracy though there is a great deal of common ground between the two. Since political liberalism could lead to economic servitude, there is something in the argument that democracy is barely viable in a society with vast inequalities of wealth. Rousseau rediscovered the common people and was far more influential in his propagation of the community as a political ethos than were the odd, utopian schemes that had cropped up in the centuries since the initial decay of medieval institutions. Both Rousseau and Locke before him elaborated concepts of the community at large which suggested that it possessed a repository of power which it could assert in the last resort. Rousseau's paraphrase of Grotius's suggestion that 'each man can renounce his membership of his own state' complements Locke's allegation that power can revert to the people on 'miscarriage of authority', and both give some basis to the concept of a 'popular will' on which wider concepts of democracy could be based.[2]

Since the French Revolution led to the creation of a general principle rather than a permanent form of government, the American Republic came to be the chief example of democratic government in the fullest sense of the term in the nineteenth century. It was certainly the example that Alexis de Tocqueville used when he wanted to discuss how and what the European could learn from democratic experiments in America. What Tocqueville called 'equality of conditions' seemed to have come earlier to the United States than to the post-French Revolution era of Europe.[3] Yet it is debatable how far the original American Constitution of 1786 was designed to be 'democratic' even in the way in which Tocqueville envisaged in the 1830s. *The Federalist Papers*, perhaps as exemplified by Madison's famed No. 10, set out eloquently the difference between 'pure democracy' and the proposed constitutional republic. Unlike the European theorists, especially Rousseau, Madison felt that delegation of government 'to a small number of citizens elected by the rest' was, with certain safeguards, the best protection for the type of limited democracy that could establish itself in the North American subcontinent.[4] This Madisonian model, with its distrust of pure majority rule, is one of the three that Robert Dahl concentrates upon in his 'Essay' with which we must deal a little later on.

Tocqueville saw America in the Jacksonian period (and Jacksonian Democracy is the second of Dahl's models), when the country was

closer to a nominal democracy with the disappearing barriers
against participation for white Americans, such as the property
qualifications which restricted the franchise in the early Republic.
John Stuart Mill, writing a few years before the war which tested
American institutions, also felt that the United States was the country
'where both society and the government are most democratic'.[5]

Like Tocqueville, whose book had impressed him greatly on its
first publication, Mill saw the spread of democratic institutions as
inevitable (and perhaps even more desirable than Tocqueville, who
had been quick to spot the defects of a democratic system such as the
envy of the governed for the governors). Mill is the great mid-
nineteenth-century advocate of democratic institutions and the
principle of majority rule, yet he too saw some dangers in a democratic
society, the intellectual poverty of the majority and the danger that
they will therefore produce bad, class-biased legislation.[6] Since their
faults could be checked by such a device as proportional representation
(which could bypass superficial local popularity), Mill could fall back
on self-evident advantages of representative government, that of a
highly modified utilitarian approach, 'self-protecting' and 'self-
dependent' as he puts it.[6] To Mill, representative government was the
great liberator of the Protestant ethic—though he was far from being
profoundly religious—the force which makes people want to improve
their lot and that of the society in which they live.[7] Mill takes a
societal view of democracy, implying that it is not only institutions,
important as they are, but the whole tenor of a society that make it
democratic. It is sometimes suggested that there *is* an inherent
contradiction in his view of democracy for although democracy is
desirable, it presents a new danger to the existence of liberty in the
shape of the 'tyranny of the majority'. However, as Richard Friedman
pointed out in a perceptive essay, Mill in fact offers a complex, almost
Platonic, defence of democracy. It includes an argument which can be
'sold' to the majority to persuade them that they should favour rule
by an enlightened and able minority for this is the only way in which
'progress' may be made, something which almost all members of the
society will desire.[8]

This brief glance at some of the best-known of the pre-twentieth-
century commentators on democracy indicates some of the dilemmas
which were passed on to this century. Democracy was first envisaged
as something applicable to relatively small communities—such as the

Greek *polis*—and its assumption by some modern industrializing states raised inevitable problems of the type subsumed under 'mass society' questions in recent years. Democracy implied mass or majority control, yet the administrative and decision-making processes of a modern state could not stand still while the whole population were polled on a specific issue. How can the popular will be brought to bear in decision-making? Should an élite party, as the Marxist–Leninist thesis propounded, take power in the name of the people and take decisions for them as the CPSU élite claims to do? This question may be academic if one takes a non-Marxist line, but a workable set of propositions in democratic theory should take the economic–political boundary into account when discussing the distribution of power. Much of twentieth-century democratic theory has tried to clarify the relationships between rulers, however nominal, and the ruled, to see what each expects of each other (and what they receive) in political situations where a degree of majority rule is said to exist. It is this corpus of material which one needs to unravel.

The élitist thesis

At the turn of the century a 'progressive' democrat could either believe in an inevitable drift to a 'traditional' form of participatory democracy in developed countries, or he could adopt the more messianic conclusions of Marxism with its emphasis on class conflict and the eventual domination of the working class in industrialized societies as explained in the dialectical process. In contrast to these two pictures of society, both of which genuflected towards the ability of the masses to exercize power, there emerged the 'Machiavellian' doctrines of a range of writers who threw doubt on the capacity of the mass of the people to exercize power under any political system. Chief among these were Mosca and Pareto, with Michels as another contributor to the overall shape of the élitist thesis.

To some, the elaboration of élitist theory is a symbol of reaction against the range of socialist doctrine prevalent in the intellectual circles of the period. James Meisel summed it up: 'Elitism is a defensive doctrine, a new Dismal Science aimed at the naive optimism of eighteenth-century enlightenment.'[9] At the same time it is an attempt to describe an existing situation and is therefore the very reverse of normative theory; rather, it can be seen as a strain in the development of behavioural theory of a type. The point at issue is whether the distribution of power in a political system is *essentially* élitist as a matter of course.

The term 'élite' was popularized by Pareto but a clearer formulation of the concept is probably Mosca's idea of a 'political class' or 'ruling class'. He argues that, whatever the outward show of political form—monarchy, oligarchy, democracy—a limited range of persons will eventually exercize power (one-man rule being as ridiculous as mass rule). His argument is that 'the predominant criterion . . . to the formulation of a ruling class is the ability to rule'.[10] The ruling class is not inviolate and it can disintegrate if powerful forces attack it successfully. A regime will persist over time when the liberal and autocratic elements are well-balanced and where the ruling class gradually renews itself from talent existing elsewhere in the system. Curiously, Mosca sets this within a less than conservative frame, emphasizing the necessity for the secularization of the state and for a firm limit to political coercion; though he—and Pareto—are often regarded as 'counter-revolutionaries'.

Pareto's schema is more academic, as befits a pioneer sociologist who believed that one could discover 'natural laws' (*not* natural law) expressed in abstract terms. Rather like Plato, he writes of the need for 'guardians' who, by providing 'public tutelage', increase the utility factor in society and provide an overall increase in the satisfaction of wants. Like Mosca, he claims to be describing fact and not offering prescriptions for the way in which society is to be run. The division of society into two strata, a 'higher' and a 'lower', is, in his view, 'so obvious that it has always forced itself even upon the most casual observation'.[11] Like Mosca, he does not suggest that élites—in class terms—are self-perpetuating. Hence his comment that 'history is a graveyard of aristocracies'.[12] However, he did develop the concept of the 'circulation of élites', the idea that individuals and groups are continually rising out of the non-élite and replenishing the élite which would otherwise decay or disappear. To a limited degree, he accepts the concept of the 'class struggle', but not in the strict Marxist sense with the working class inevitably conquering and ruling indefinitely. 'Isms', in Pareto's view, 'spring directly from an incomplete observation of the laws of social science.'[13] New élites arise, old ones wither, depending on the culture patterns of a particular society. This can happen slowly, or very rapidly as in a revolutionary situation.

Elitist theory is often seen as a defence of the status quo in a given society and little more. It is equally tempting to see it as a tautological view of the world, a statement of the obvious in that if everyone spent the majority of his time attempting to participate in government, there would be no one to carry out the essential tasks of keeping life going by producing food, goods, services found essential by mankind—no butcher, no baker, no candlestick-maker. Robert Dahl, who became the severest critic of élitism as applied to modern political systems, provided the *reductio ad absurdum* with his simplified version of the élitist view: 'If a ruling élite hypothesis says anything, surely it asserts that within some specific political system there exists a group of people who to some degree exercise power or influence over other actors in the system.'[14] Therefore, unless one believes that political systems can be operated without the exercise of 'power' or direction of some sort, then it is inevitable that there will be some separation in a political system between those who exercize and those who are the recipients of power.

In one form or another, the concept of élite rule has remained a feature of political thought in the twentieth century. The thesis has been widened somewhat to include an enlarged class of those who can be considered as members of the élite. Harold Lasswell, in possibly the most important of his books, described it as follows, though he writes in terms of politicians in the main: 'The influential are those who get the most of what there is to get. . . . Those who get the most are *elite*: the rest are *mass*.'[15] If there is any agreement on this issue now, and, as we shall see, it is a highly limited one, it is that élites must be defined in such a way as to bring in all the activist elements in a polity, that is all of those who have an effect on the decisions taken in the political arena (this might exempt some 'activists' who do not impinge on political decision-taking such as non-violent extremists). The 'people' are regarded as the 'mass', in Lasswell's terminology, and can never exercize power in any continuous sense although, in democratic societies, they exercize some long-term control by the use of the ballot-box. To see the exercize of power, one primarily looks to the élite for, as Plamenatz has stated: 'They are the people that matter, the politically active, the articulate, who between them run the whole life of the community.'[16] One might expect that, if élites are accepted as an essential concomitant of political life, then the picture would be alleviated by a degree of egalitarianism inside the institutions which provide the core of the élite framework. Yet it was the thesis of Robert Michels, for example, that the political party itself was essentially an élitist organization with power flowing from the top of the hierarchy only. Organization was an indispensable feature of party development and, in Michels' view, it led inevitably to a high degree of bureaucratization and then to oligarchy. This 'iron law', a phrase firmly associated with Michels' major book, is another formulation of élite rule and, to quote from one of his chapter headings, an illustration of the 'mechanical and technical impossibility of direct government by the masses'.[17]

The concept that 'élites rule' has remained a distinct feature of contemporary political science, and the writers mentioned above had their successors in the 1950s and 1960s. One of the most famous of these was C. Wright Mills, whose book *The Power Elite* influenced generations of the radical young in the United States; his main thesis even entered the consciousness of President Eisenhower if the 'farewell' address at the end of his administration is any guide (it included a reference to the potentially dangerous influence of the 'military–industrial complex'). Mills extended the 'mass society' argument becoming fashionable in post-war America with the corollary that mass society involves control and direction by a balancing yet remote élite. He felt that certain societal traits of the America in which he lived were conducive to the maintenance of power by such an élite; the lack of an independent Civil Service such as those found in Europe for example was one such cause, while the inability of professional party politicians to infiltrate the highest posts (presumably another contrast with Western Europe) was an additional one. The effect is summarized in the following paragraph:

> As a result, the political directorate, the corporate rich, and the ascendant military have come together as the power elite, and the expanded and centralized hierarchies which they head have encroached upon the old balances and have now relegated them to the middle levels of power. Now the balancing society is a conception that pertains accurately to the middle levels, and on that level the balance has become more often an affair of entrenched provincial and nationally irresponsible forces and demands than a center of power and national decision.[18]

Mills was not alone in perceiving a degree of élite or class rule in modern American society. Marxists take it for granted of course but non-Marxists often echo it, drawing their data and their theory from an eclectic range of sources. A good example of this approach is the work of William Domhoff who, in a mild way, updated Mills' thesis, drawing not only from the master but from the Marxist writer Paul Sweezy and non-Marxists such as Digby Baltzell (and even Robert Dahl). With some modifications, he defends Wright Mills' thesis from its detractors, such as those who claim that it is a managerial, not an upper, class that rules America. The military are downgraded to an extent from their position in Mills' view of the hierarchy, Domhoff's concentration being on a social élite which, largely due to its power base inside the economic system, dominates the federal government. His final summary rests on his mentors heavily, but the attempt is to reconcile them into a uniform theory which will explain who directs, rules and leads the national political system (he explicitly excludes subnational units in the general thesis):

> For ourselves, we conclude that the income, wealth, and institutional leadership of what Baltzell calls the 'American business aristocracy' are more than sufficient to earn it the designation 'governing class'. As Sweezy would say, this 'ruling class' is based upon the national corporate economy and the institutions that economy nourishes. It manifests itself through what the late C. Wright Mills called the power elite.[19]

Even this recent writing does not overcome the suspicion that élite theory lacks an essential element of political analysis—that of providing an 'isomorphic' model which explains how a sector of the political system works and which conforms to the configuration of that sector. Of course, there is *some* explanatory power in élite theory but it tends to be that of stating the relatively obvious. As we observed earlier, it borders on the tautological. However, it is not the only set of theories which revolves around the way in which power is distributed in so-called democratic societies. 'Pluralism' is one alternative to élite theory and both, in their turn, have provided ammunition for several generations of argument about the way in which power is distributed in civic communities—towns and cities mainly in the United States though with an increasing range of examples in Europe. It should go without saying that the élitist–pluralist dichotomy does not exhaust the range of options open to a viable theory of the democratic process, and other alternatives are available, but this quarrel has tended to be dominant especially for much of the last two decades.

Pluralist theory

The arch-critic of élitist theory as it was restated in the 1950s was the Yale political scientist, Robert A. Dahl. It is doubtful whether Dahl has ever wished to dismiss élite theory as completely unfounded—or to argue that élites never exist in political systems. What he did in his writing in the latter half of the 1950s and the 1960s was to question the evidence for élite rule as 'given' in certain political systems at a local or national level. From this query he developed an interpretation of the power distribution which is an alternative to the élitist model and which, by direct implication, would replace the élitist model at certain levels; for instance, the model replaces the Wright Mills concept of a power élite dominating the United States. This is fairly clear in the conclusion of his early article attacking the inevitability of ruling élites:

> For the whole point of this paper is that the evidence for a ruling elite, either in the United States or in any specific community, has not yet been properly examined so far as I know. And the evidence has not been properly examined, I have tried to argue, because the examination has not employed satisfactory criteria to determine what constitutes a fair test of the basic hypothesis.[20]

Dahl has tackled the problem of the distribution of power at the two distinct levels of the 'national' political system and the local community. The latter argument has become a part of the general 'community power' controversy, itself a reflection of the élitist–pluralist dichotomy to a great degree, and this is examined in the following section. Therefore, it seems advisable to look at the pluralist thesis as a general theory at this stage and, in particular, to see how it can apply to the grand·community that is usually termed a nation or state.

Dahl has followed the general thesis of pluralism—or polyarchy, his alternative title—through a number of studies, the first of which asked the basic question about popular sovereignty in the United States—what model explains it best? American democratic theory had long been torn between the two models associated with Madison and populism, the latter emphasizing the right of the majority to rule, the former alive to the danger of 'majority tyranny'. In Dahl's view, both theories were incomplete—his answer to the basic dilemma between defending the rights of the majority to rule and the minority to be protected is to suggest that such a crude contrast is unreal:

> If majorities in a democracy nearly always govern in the broad meaning of the term, they rarely rule in Madison's terms: for as we have seen, specific policies tend to be products of 'minorities rule'. In the sense in which Madison was concerned with the problem then, majority rule is mostly a myth.[21]

In America and similar democracies, Dahl sees a series of what in effect are shifting coalitions which produce effective decisions and on which the remaining groups in the system have a good chance of exerting some influence. From this stems his well-known dictum about the 'normal' political process in the United States as 'one in which there is a high probability that an active and legitimate group . . . can make itself heard effectively at some crucial stage in the process of decision'.[22] This has often been attacked as an unrealistic assessment of the way in which groups achieve access to decision-making centres in American life. It is true that Dahl protects himself to some extent by admitting that different groups have a different range of chances of influencing decision-making at a political level. However, this now seems a little simplistic. It is no accident that the later 1950s, which saw the birth of pluralistic theory, was also the period when group conflict seemed to have abated in American society—it was the so-called 'end of ideology' period. Today, it seems more obvious to us that one basic problem of modern political systems is the degree of differential participation that exists from group to group. 'Incremental change' now comes too slowly for the more disadvantaged groups in society—racial or economic—and their frustration at their lack of participation is likely to flare up into intermittent violence. Dahl's 1956 definition of what is to be considered 'active and legitimate' seems too restricted for present-day purposes; he commented: 'In the South, Negroes were not until recently an active group. Evidently, Communists are not now a legitimate group. As compared with what one would expect from the normal system, Negroes were relatively defenseless in the past, just as the Communists are now.'[23] Despite the artificial fears of the McCarthy period, it is doubtful whether American Communists were ever a 'significant' group in the country at large, but a system which excluded such a sizeable minority as the black population certainly falls short of a true democratic model of a descriptive, let alone a normative type. The question that is begged here is surely why the Southern blacks—and the Northern blacks to almost as great an extent—were relatively inactive politically and the answer, which would include the element of coercion, does tend to modify the model itself, not just its application to one historical and geographical setting.

Other aspects of pluralistic theory seem less objectionable. In the 1967 text which tries to adapt the pluralist analysis to the national political system as it appeared at that time, Dahl emphasizes that there exist 'multiple centers of power, none of which is or can be wholly sovereign'.[24] In that there are certain checks and balances in most democratic polities, and even in many that are not usually considered democratic, this statement seems as nearly accurate as a generalization can be, especially if one takes the term 'wholly' literally. Further, in one of his latest expositions of the pluralist thesis, Dahl is more careful with his explanation of the way in which subdued and disadvantaged groups fit into the democratic process. He admits that the American Negro has not, until very recently, been a member of a pluralist society but a 'hegemonic' one and that it is eminently possible for a duality to exist in a state between two forms of political society, one pluralist and the other non-pluralist: ' . . . historically it has been possible to develop and even to sustain over a very long period a dual system that is competitive with respect to the dominant group and hegemonic with respect to a deprived minority.'[25] In this book Dahl produces an overall model which indicates the range of conditions favouring polyarchy and those that are least favourable to it. It resembles many other analyses of the preconditions for the Western pattern of democratic society that have been framed by political scientists in the last twenty years.[26] It is evident that what Dahl has produced is an 'ideal type' brand of theory, one which sets the ideal type of polyarchy as against, for example, the ideal type of hegemony. Neither is likely to be found in pure form but, with the refinements and sophistication of his latest writing, it is now more likely than before that Dahl had made a major contribution to democratic theory. Yet it is a pity that he does not throw more weight behind this interpretation. It might deter the tempting criticism that he presents us with an ethnocentric view of democracy, one that is so heavily biased with American values—and possibly American middle-class conventional values at that—that the analytical potential of the theory is still severely limited. In a book published just before *Polyarchy*

Dahl defines polyarchy as 'representative democracy as *we* know it in practice' (our emphasis) and here he seems to recognize the degree to which this is an 'ideal type' theory: 'Using the term polyarchy for systems of this kind has the advantage of keeping open the question of how closely polyarchy actually approximates representative democracy as an ideal.'[27] In fact, he suggests later that the ideal type is actually a form of 'primary democracy', but this overlooks the fact that the conditions originally laid down in his model of polyarchy in 1956 (for instance, that all voters have identical information about the alternatives offered by political parties) are themselves 'ideal' if a true polyarchy is to allow for their maximization. It seems therefore preferable to see polyarchy itself as an ideal to be maximized if one agrees with it as a concept of how a democracy should be organized and this will depend in turn on the values which one wishes to maximize.

Dahl remains one of the liveliest theorists of the democratic process and one can only touch upon the main points of his argument, brushing by the many side-issues that he illuminates on the way. In his antithesis to élitist theory, he not only provided a strong counter-explanation to the belief that élites inevitably rule—Dahl tends to the view that sometimes they do and sometimes they do not—but also provided another set of counter-arguments when the élitist–pluralist thesis was argued out in terms of 'community power'. Since it is easier to pinpoint the centres of power on a local than on a national scale, the study of 'community power' in the last twenty years has been riven with a basic argument about whether élites inevitably rule in local communities, or whether the pluralist alternative is applicable. It is worth looking at this controversy to see whether it clarifies a basic problem in democratic theory.

Community power

Although studies of communities, their social, economic and political structures, were fashionable forty years ago,[28] it was particularly in the 1950s, with Floyd Hunter's study of Atlanta, Georgia, that a more methodological approach was used to analyze the way in which power distributed itself in a discrete community. Hunter's title, *Community Power Structure*, makes this clear. Unfortunately, the book eventually became the first round of a long dispute over the 'correct' methodological approach to the analysis of power relationships in a specific community. Shibboleths were created and the tag in medicine that to 'choose the doctor is to choose the diagnosis' soon seemed even more appropriate to the study of community power. However, this should not be allowed to obscure two fairly obvious facts, one that the study of specific communities does illuminate the political process in a community with certain social and economic characteristics, secondly that community power studies generally isolate and suggest some solutions to the central problems of democratic theory.

Many community studies try to hide the identity of the town or city under scrutiny but inevitably it soon becomes common knowledge. Atlanta, Georgia was Floyd Hunter's 'Regional City' and the methodology used came to be known as the 'reputational' one. Hunter's belief was that power could be represented spatially with lists of apparent leaders, that is, those who had held appropriate office, given rank order by 'judges'—'persons who had lived in the community for some years and who had a knowledge of community affairs'.[29] Interviewing them gave a fleshing-out of the spatial pattern and showed the interrelationship among the 'top leadership'.

It must be emphasized that Hunter's study does give us an intimate picture of relationships between certain active community leaders in Atlanta *circa* 1950. It also emphasizes the segregation in a Southern community between white and black, rich and poor—this is very much a stratified society. Yet the doubt remains. Have the issues and the decision-makers been clearly selected by the methodology used? The writer is dependent on decisions made by his panel, dependent on their identification of top community leaders, dependent on the lists of community leaders drawn up by the civic organization in the first place. Issues of the day were what the 'leadership' said they were and little attempt was made to take an issue and trace its lengthy passage from inception or germination to consensus, decision or other settlement. Hunter's study is a little more than an examination of élite rule but it does assume that 'policy is controlled by a relatively small group of the citizenry'.[30] The overall emphasis of the methodology is on a sociometric map of the leadership as it is interpreted for the observer by a somewhat arbitrarily selected group of participants.

Reacting against the élitist thesis which springs fully armed from a study such as Hunter's, the 'pluralist' thesis implies that power is more widely distributed than in his community controlled by a few. Robert Dahl tried to show that New Haven (he does not use a disguise for his choice of community) had moved from 'a system in which resources of influence were highly concentrated to a system in which they are highly dispersed'.[31] To illustrate this, Dahl chose a small number of issues—political nominations, urban redevelopment and public education—to trace the major influences on decision-making in the political arena. While the political executive and party leaders exercized evident power, Dahl attempted to prove that their power was dependent on other groups in the city; difference in influence between leaders and the rest was evident but a matter of degree not of kind, leaders being unable to follow policy lines without a measure of general support. 'Coalition-building' is thus a necessity to obtain support for policies put forward by leaders, competition among the latter allowing room for alternatives to be voted upon.

Dahl's picture of New Haven is, in effect, an extrapolation of his view of the 'American hybrid' presented in his 1956 book on democratic theory. As it describes political life in New Haven it is reasonably convincing, but doubt remains when he infers that this pattern is universal in the United States: 'I should like to advance the hypothesis that the political system we have just been supposing corresponds closely to the facts of New Haven, and in all probability to the United States.'[32] To be scrupulously fair, this quotation need not imply that exceptions are not possible among the gamut of American cities. In fact, a careful reading of Hunter and Dahl, the two archetypes of élitism and pluralism in community power, indicates that the contrast between their approach is not quite as emphatic as some of their supporters would have us believe: even Hunter admits that 'community attitudes' or public opinion must be taken into account by the élite. Dahl recognizes that New Haven was more élitist in the past than when he carried out his study, and the obvious inference from this is that different communities at different times may have power structures on differing places on the élitist–pluralist continuum (due, for example, to their differing rates of economic development).

Other representative samples of the war between pluralist and élitist reflect the degree of ambivalence at which we have already hinted. Vidich and Bensman, in their study of 'Springdale', in New York

State, assume a degree of élitism in the community with a small coterie of leaders who attempt to maintain, and largely succeed in maintaining, control over the directions the local community chooses to take. Yet there are severe constraints on the power of the clique at the top as the authors readily admit. These include the property-owners who 'constitute an important and easily mobilized electorate in town elections'.[33] Further, they confess that 'no simple or general theory of politics is sufficient to exhaust the concrete and detached data which make up the political life of Springdale'.[34] This would seem to be a retreat from the cruder pretensions of élitist theory. As a final quotation from the modified thesis put forward here, one notes that local affairs are essentially of limited importance to Springdalers and that 'the opposition to the local leadership does not consist of dissident groups within the community but rather the whole trend of mass society which impinges on the local arena'.[35] Without trying to detract from the élitist core of the Vidich and Bensman thesis, it is so qualified as to make the community, assuming their analysis to be correct, as an élitist-tending sliver of a larger world which could be moving in either direction.

Similarly, if one looks at Nelson Polsby's follow-up to Dahl on New Haven, it is not as purist for pluralism supreme as one might suppose. It is, of course, a virulent attack on the stratification thesis as such, that which presumes that economic power in the community in particular equates with political power. Yet even this book recognizes that there is some 'pyramiding' of power in the American situation, while fighting the 'conspiratorial élite' thesis at the same time:

> One of the most common patterns of behavior to be observed in American community life is that participation in the making of decisions is concentrated in the hands of a few. But this does not mean that American communities are ruled by a single all-purpose élite, after the fashion suggested by stratification theory.[36]

It is the 'single all-purpose élite' concept, associated nationally with C. Wright Mills especially and in community-power analysis with Hunter, that Polsby finds unacceptable. In its place, he suggests the 'issue-area' as the one which defines the group making the decision and, by implication, no issue, no decision, no decision-making group. Linked to a theory of 'inertia' this produces a primitively functional view of actors; that is, bankers primarily bank, city officials have power because they are officials and have decisions to make. There is much that is attractive about this gloss on the pluralistic approach generally but also a certain naïveté. Inertia exists but so do ambition and the drive towards the acquisition of power. Therefore, in communities as with nations at large, it is doubtful whether preconceived ideas of élitism or pluralism act as any more than a guide to potential patterns of power.

. In the 1960s the debate on community power, far from dying down, tended to increase in intensity, the 'élitist–pluralist' argument tending to be supplemented with rebuttal and support from 'neo-élitists' and 'neo-pluralists', while less committed political scientists looked for some middle ground or perhaps a new approach entirely which would remove what had come to seem a degree of sterility from the examination of a social phenomenon. The latter alternative seemed often to be more logical in that it avoided the dialectic between the two 'classical' approaches. One of the best-known of the more eclectic studies was indeed multi-faceted in that it stemmed from three writers (Agger, Goldrich and Swanson), and involved the study of four separate communities in two regions (Western and Southern United States) over a period of several years, four potential types of regime (oligarchy, guided democracy, underdeveloped democracy, developed democracy), four potential types of power structure (competitive élite, consensual élite, competitive mass, consensual mass), and a range of political ideology for the leadership cliques studied in the four communities (conservatives, community conservationists, liberals, with sub-groups inside these broad categories). This is certainly a richer panoply than either pluralist or élitist has to offer even though the 'developed democracy' type of regime and the 'community conservationists' leadership, both of which were the most typical feature of the communities studied by the early 1960s, seem to be closer to the pluralist than the élitist model. To be fully pluralist, the 'consensual mass' type of power structure should have been more evident, but the writers found this undermined by competition from the radical right at the time when they ended their study. Other constraints on the pluralist model seem to have included the fear of illegitimate sanctions or force, though on the other hand there was some permeability of the power structure from the bottom to the top, unlike the élitist assumptions of a closed-off peak of power.[37]

The above study deliberately used a time dimension to denote the changes that are possible in the power structure of a community, and it seems obvious now that these studies should be 'movie-like' rather than 'snapshots' of a moment when the dispersion of power is frozen for examination. Robert Presthus, in another eclectic study, pinpointed this problem: 'With rare exceptions . . . community analysis has been a historical, a slice of discontinuous material, which may be valid for one point of time, but fails to provide the depth and understanding made possible by a historical perspective.'[38] Presthus studied two communities within easy reach of Cornell University, over a decade. Both 'decisional' and 'reputational' methods were used and found to be 'mutually supportive' in his words.[39] In fact, the reputational method, which has received much criticism, 'will identify something over half . . . of the most powerful active leaders' but, by implication, the second-level leaders (often in active and apparent roles) are best isolated by the decisional method.[40] Certainly, Presthus's methodology uncovered the relative balance between the two main leadership groups, economic and 'political', in the two communities, economic dominance being the major characteristic of 'Edgewood', political of 'Riverview'. He seems to have started the research on these two communities with a slight bias towards the decisional approach and therefore an expectation of a high degree of pluralism appearing in each community, especially in the way in which participation in decision-making was spread in each community. The divergences noted between the two communities were so marked, however, that no one generalization sufficed, apart from the fact that an élitist–pluralist continuum provided an overall explanation, one of the communities being farther along the road to pluralism than the other. Therefore, if pluralism in communities is to be regarded as a desirable state of affairs, it seems to follow from the Presthus research that American (and probably other Western) communities are likely to be dotted along a continuum according to the degree of participation of groups in the decision-making process. Presthus makes his points more concisely than the somewhat ponderous trio of Agger, Goldrich and Swanson. He indicates that the future may not lead to an increase in pluralistic practice, as Dahl seemed to suggest, but that a more significant fact is that economic and political decision-making is beginning to remove itself from local communities to larger units (since so many problems now straddle large geographic areas), even for those issues where localities were once paramount, and that this immediately cuts the chances of meaningful participation.

One would have thought that the 'synthetic' school of community power analysis would have by now swept the board, with its emphasis on eclecticism, variety of expected results and avoidance of preconception, but this is not so. There are still narrower disputes between 'neo-élitist' and 'neo-pluralist' writers. Of the former, one can cite the Bachrach and Baratz emphasis on 'non-decision-making', which claims that it is not as important to study *what* is decided in a community but to see what is prevented from reaching the decision-making stage.[41] They insist that some of the printed studies, such as that by Vidich and Bensman, support this, and that although it is difficult to study a non-event, the conditions surrounding it, such as the 'latent issue' and the 'mobilization of bias', are subject to analysis.[42] Richard Merelman, attacking from what one might term the neo-pluralist position, alleges that the federal structure of the United States breaks down the conditions necessary for the imposition of a 'false concensus' by an élite on a non-élite and that American communities are not self-contained enough for this type of concensus to be common.[43] 'Neo-élitism' does appear to be a line of argument which is likely to be less true in the present and the future than in the past, when transport and mass communications had not yet demolished the relative isolation of many communities. Further, the Bachrach and Baratz arguments seem to postulate inherently unstable situations in the modern world, where, if enough people feel strongly about something for long enough, only an amount of force unacceptable in most Western eyes is necessary to restrain that feeling.

There are few subjects which have caused more dissent than the field of community power. However, it is noticeable that British entry into the research area of local community politics has been more cautious than the American when it comes to establishing models of democratic participation and the distribution of power.[44] The controversy in the United States has been overlaid in recent years with the rise of a radical movement inside the political science profession and the consequent attempts to contain it. In particular, there has been an intensification of the counter-pluralist attitude on the part of the radicals, many of whom organized themselves into the Caucus for a New Political Science. It used to be said that America needed an ideology. The view of Caucus members (most of whom tend to the radical left end of the ideological spectrum) and some non-Caucus political scientists is that pluralism itself *is* an ideology or, as Darryl Baskin put it, 'Pluralist theory is reduced to the status of partisan apologetics at worst and ideology at best'.[15] Over the last few years the position of 'disadvantaged groups' in the American political system (blacks, chicanos, Indians, even women) has been put forward as a proof that any pluralistic interpretation of American democracy is absurd. Typical of this style of criticism is the following from the dustjacket of *The Caucus Papers*: 'How real, for example, are the pluralist assumptions that still dominate our political science textbooks when viewed from the bottom up—say, as a poor black in Newark, New Jersey?'[46] At the same time, one can see some move away from the evident sterility of the community-power debate into a wider context where local and national dimensions of the distribution of power, economic and political, are seen to be interrelated so closely that it is difficult to isolate the local strand, even for purposes of study. This would certainly allow for a more complex framework than some of the more simplistic explanations have suggested and, as well as a variety of potential power structures at local level, it leaves considerable room for debate about the extent to which the United States— and other Western political systems—are 'democracies'. Duane Lockard has pointed out how unreliable are pluralist and élitist explanations if one wants to explain the distribution of power in an American city such as Newark, which is perhaps the epitome of the debased and depressed condition of life in an inner city in the United States. In its stead, he notes that:

> A more likely explanation of the conditions of Newark and its companion cities around the country is that they are the dumping grounds of an economic system that is grandly successful for most people but miserably unresponsive to those who get left outside the upward spiral of economic growth.[47]

It is likely that any new theories that are developed about community power will attempt to avoid certain of the past errors, particularly the dangers of preconception and of compartmentalized views of that power structure which distributes valued things to members of a specific geographical area. Neither conspiracy theories nor complacent pluralist solutions are sufficient explanations for the diversity, complexity or the occasional sheer muddle that tends to bedevil attempts at democracy in Western societies.

In this crowded field of research and opinion, one has tried to indicate both the main lines of argument and the main protagonists, although inevitably a degree of vigorous selection has been necessary —more than in other fields—to avoid being swamped with material.[48] Democratic theory has tended to be dominated in recent years by the debates arising from power analyses, although there is more to it than the question of whether political systems look like pyramids, diamonds or some other geometrical shape. For example, the writers who have borrowed from economic theory to illustrate aspects of democracy have successfully sidestepped the 'tree of power' question and have concentrated on the voter–politician relationship, one that is a key to the understanding of democracy in any society where elections are meaningful in the distribution of power and not merely decorative or ceremonial.

The 'economic' theory of democracy

Students of social science theory are often fascinated by the dichotomy between the pretensions of economics as compared to the inadequacies of political science, especially when the latter tries to define the relationships of actors in the political system. It is probably for this reason that approaches to political theory involving the transference of an economic mode of thought to the political world have often seemed attractive. Economic theory is reasonably rigorous in its methodology and the chain of reasoning based on general principles is often more isomorphic to actual economic situations than is the sister science of political theory to real-life political situations. In addition, there are certain concepts used in economic reasoning which have applicability in political thought and it is especially in democratic theory that one can see this application.[49]

A basic concept that is often transferred from economic to political thought—though it is almost as likely to originate in the latter field— is that of 'rationality', in general the use of reason to reach goals, or, more particularly, the use of the most economical means to reach desired ends. To some extent, rationality has been downgraded in the behaviour of economic man but nowhere near as far as in that of political man. Schumpeter's contrast is well known: 'Thus the typical citizen drops down to a lower level of mental performance as soon as he enters the political field. He argues and analyses in a way which he would readily recognise as infantile within the sphere of his real interests.'[50] In making political decisions, Schumpeter argues, the citizen has no yardstick as he has in the decisions he makes in his everyday personal life and therefore prejudice, impulse and other 'irrational' forces tend to dominate his decision-making. This is a persuasive theory and it is followed by many who discuss contemporary democracy and the place of the voter within it.

Alternatively, there are those who believe that the concept of rationality can be transferred to political science with only a minimum of modification; inherent in this attitude is the feeling that economic choice and political choice are not so radically dissimilar. Dahl and Lindblom were obviously of this opinion when they tried to plot the maximization of goal attainment in a politico-economic environment. For them, rationality is virtually synonymous with efficiency:

> The more rational action is also the more efficient action. The two terms can be used interchangeably. Stripped of prejudicial inferences, efficiency is the ratio between valued input and valued output. An action is rational . . . to the extent that it is correctly designed to maximize net goal satisfaction, given the goals in question and the real world as it exists.[51]

This concept is at the very root of many of the analytical approaches to political behaviour. As we indicate elsewhere (Chapters Five and Seven), questions of rationality enter into the behaviour problems of administrators, voters and indeed any actor in the political system. The general problem revolves around questions of the individual's power of perception, comprehension, awareness and ability in forecasting outcomes. Opinions differ over the degree to which the actors in a democratic or quasi-democratic setting can exercize a degree of rationality—it is not even as easy to define 'rationality' in political as in economic terms for the setting is so much wider. In economic models, a comparatively narrow dimension is apparent; political models are prone to involve more variables and therefore their predictive value is more limited. Rational thinking, with its need to measure up the parsimonious use of means against desired ends, is therefore more suited to economic than political models.

Despite this tendency, an 'economic' model like that of Anthony Downs has generated a considerable interest and has produced a range of propositions worthy of examination and research. As one would expect, Downs starts from 'rationality', identifying a 'political man' who is a 'rational citizen', one who balances costs against expected gains not unlike economic man. Irrationality is recognized but his view is that 'a high degree of political rationality is necessary in every large-sized society if it is to solve its problems successfully'.[52]

The shape of Downs' general theory has often come under fire. He starts from two basic assumptions (this term is important). One is that of voter-rationality—that citizens tend to behave rationally in politics; the second is based on vote-maximization by political parties which will promulgate policies to achieve this end. It is important to recognize that these are assumptions and not, for example, 'axioms' as one of Downs' critics, Haywood Rogers, insisted; the difference is vital for Downs is only assuming their truth as part of the model and not for all time or even in the world at large.[53]

From the 'basic hypotheses', a whole string of 'testable propositions' are generated, all built on the producer–consumer relation that Downs makes the centre of his thesis. Voters tend to make comparisons of the utility income expected from each party operating in the system and this preference governs their vote at election time, although the technique of voting depends on the number of parties and the expected chances of specific parties—especially minor parties—winning control of the government.[54] Similarly, government strategy is to garner votes by welfare spending, or indeed any expenditure that attracts voting support from large blocs. The thesis seems to be that spending (balanced against taxes) should be aimed at maximizing voting support to the point where a majority is created, something that is easier in a two-party system with clear divisions over issues than, say, a multi-party system with viewpoints on key issues split into well-separated minorities.[55] Ideology and the nature of political leadership are integrated into the model by the inclusion of the ingredient of 'uncertainty' on the part of the voter, for both tend to clarify the position of competing parties in the minds of potential voters.[56]

The competitive nature of political parties, expressed at least partially by competing ideology, is stressed by Downs, and he tends to illuminate the contest by recourse to the theory of spatial competition and its best-known depiction by Harold Hotelling (in an article dating back to 1929). Hotelling, in fact, though mainly concerned with economic competition as such, believed that he had lighted upon 'an observation of wide generality' and transferred it to politics:

The competition for votes between the Republican and Democratic parties does not lead to a clear drawing of issues, an adoption of two strongly contrasted positions between which the voter may choose. Instead, each party strives to make its platform as much like the other's as possible.[57]

Downs refines the Hotelling approach by introducing other possible distributions of voters along the linear scale. Hotelling's two-party convergence system occurs where the spatial distribution is unimodal; multi-party systems reflect an electorate much more divergent in its views with a tendency to produce parties which base themselves on 'idealogical purity'.[58] Yet most of Downs' model flows directly from either the voter-rationality or voter-maximization precepts. For example, the theorem which concludes that 'democratic governments tend to redistribute income from the rich to the poor' is based on the numerically large groups of 'poor' voters in a democracy who are grateful enough for income redistribution to vote for the government which ensures it.[59]

One of the main criticisms involved in transferring classical economic theory to political situations is the nature of the political world, where alternatives are often wide-ranging and information at a premium. In the Downs model, a 'rational information system' is a vital component and he believes that the marginal cost-return principle operates much as it does in economics. 'Rational behaviour' encourages only a minimum investment in political information on the part of the electorate at large, for the marginal value of one vote is small and the voter can usually get by on the amount of information that comes his way without great effort on his part. Downs points out the paradox that exists between the 'traditional ethical' models of democracy and his, particularly over this question of the well-informed citizen, a necessity according to the civics books, much less so in Downs' eyes. As well as information-gathering, voting itself is costly —in time at least—but a general 'economic' theory of citizen participation is possible, based on the citizen balancing costs and returns; in turn, his assessment of these is influenced by factors such as his interest in democracy, his expectations about the election and his loyalty to a party.[60] Ends–means rationality is the key to the whole model—it is a limited econo-political form of rationality and precludes much of the socio-psychological aspects of motivation in a democratic setting.

Despite this latter factor, and the comparative lack of substantive research work directly based on the Downsian theorems, the book remains one of the richest and most enticing examinations of the central relationships of the democratic process that one has seen in the last twenty years. As a model, it is not always truly isomorphic for one can often cite points at which political life seems to depart from it. The dependence on even a limited amount of 'rationality' on the part of non-activist members of the political system is a contentious issue and a great amount of argument still rages over whether any substantive degree of 'rationality' can exist in this context. As we note in Chapter Five, voting research still tells us little about the motivations of voters—the 'why' of voting—yet until voter-motivation is more perfectly understood, exchange theories of democracy will remain suspect.

Brian Barry, in his exhaustive survey of the work of Downs and Mancur Olson, has pointed out that the 'economic' theories of democracy do try to explain observed phenomena and that these theories ' . . . have a built-in pressure toward, and possibility of correction, whereas nothing forces one to change a conceptual scheme such as that of Parsons'.[61] One would agree with Barry's contention that Downsian theory explains at least part of the voter–party relationship which is central to the working of democracy. We noted above that it is not truly isomorphic but then models rarely are, for they inevitably simplify the complexities of real life. Although there are, for example, emotional values in election campaigns which it is not always possible to place into what one may term 'issue form', survey research often indicates *some* reference to past performance and future expectation on the part of voters (as Barry shows, this could be expressed in an argument between the V. O. Key approach and the Michigan School).[62]

Messrs Buchanan and Tullock, in their attempt to provide an economics-inspired theory of democratic politics, also stress what they term 'the limitations that any single explanation must embody'.[63] Like Downs, they firmly believe that, if the natural world and the world of economic organization is open to the deductions of scientific method, then political life in a democracy must be almost as accessible to such theorizing. Utility-maximization in economic choice and in political choice provide generalizations which relate to the real world. Buchanan and Tullock try to overcome the problem hitherto found in 'economic' theories of democracy, that is, that the vote has no value unless it is sold corruptly and this is held to destroy the basis of rational choice. They see the time element as an essential part of the model, voters grouping together at one time to gain what they want by creating a majority. Not all members of the majority may be interested in the issue or at least not with the same intensity, but they 'go along' so that they can call on those who do feel strongly when another issue turns up, one which the erstwhile apathetic members of the coalition now wish to see supported. This 'log-rolling' or 'vote-trading' is regarded as being a perfectly acceptable practice when it allows for collective actions over time which otherwise would not occur at all.[64] It can be seen that the Buchanan–Tullock thesis bears a resemblance to minimum winning coalitions in game theory (which they cite) and even to the pluralist thesis. It gives a clear economic value to the vote and explains, what is perhaps self-evident, why votes are 'bought' in varying degrees and not necessarily corruptly, though it even makes corrupt practice more explicit in motivation if not in ethical terms.

'Economic' theories of democracy are among the coolest—some would say most cold-blooded—examinations of the democratic process. They do suffer from a somewhat narrow frame of reference, both in terms of ethical norms and in terms of the actors cited; the former may not be very important in a descriptive model (one which is light on normative considerations). They also tend to be rather stark in terms of voter–élite relations, with little place given to the many intermediate organizations and channels that tend in practice to soften the exchange element in political relationships. However, the logical approach afforded by this set of theories provides a sense of parsimony which encourages a degree of clarity when defining the relationships which make democracy work.

Conclusion

Democratic theories range widely and take surprising forms at times; rarely has a definable set of relationships produced such a number of interpretations which, Rashomon-like, present the same actors in such differing guises. Much of this depends on the emotive content of the word 'democracy'. James Bryce attempted to show that it was a universal concept but that it changed its style from country to country because of what we would now term cultural difference; he alleged that:

> The term Democracy has in recent years been loosely used to denote sometimes a state of society, sometimes a state of mind, sometimes a quality in manners. . . . But Democracy really means nothing more or less than the rule of the whole people expressing their sovereign will by their votes.[65]

Would that it were as simple as the second sentence suggests! As we can see from the variety of theses touched upon in this chapter, democracy, as seen by Western theorists, can appear to range from a seeming conspiracy to a relative utopia. Any form of government which would find general acceptance as being 'democratic' is inevitably complex, just because it allows for a variety of pressures and opinions to be exercized and to influence the governmental process. Even a system tending to 'élite domination' will be far from simple if replenishment of the élite is to be a vital part of the plan, and a relatively 'open' form of democracy will contain numerous channels if anything akin to a 'sovereign will' is visible.

It is particularly difficult to analyze 'democracy' without being normative—without saying that society ought to be organized in such-and-such a way if the 'whole people' are to be given a sense of participation in the making of political decisions. Even a discursive look at classical theory such as that provided by Giovanni Sartori plumps for something close to one of our models—the polyarchy: 'Democracy ought to be a selective system of competing elected minorities.'[66]

This type of definition does prejudge the issue to some degree. Almost all theorists of the democratic process agree that maximum participation is desirable and that the main balancing factor required is the effective running of the state by government; for instance, that instant referenda are impractical and that the public can only lay down broad lines of direction for a government to take. The quarrel seems to lie with the *degree* of participation that already exists in specific societies (hence the pluralist–élitist controversy) and how this incidence of participation can be increased. Like so many key areas of analysis, we need more case-study work on greater and lesser political communities before these two vital questions can be answered. Most of the allegations about the existence or absence of a democratic content to current society still lie in the category of 'not proven'. It is very easy for democratic theory to stray over the border from description to prescription, from analysis to polemic. By its very nature, attempting to maximize what is to some extent an abstraction, it requires delicate application to specific contexts. However, the existence of the concept of democracy as the most devout political belief of Western society will ensure that men will continue to describe and prescribe for it until a convincing general theory makes its appearance.

CHAPTER 7
PARTIAL THEORY III: BUREAUCRACY

Like the term 'politician', 'bureaucrat' has come to have distinct pejorative associations; successful and popular national politicians often become 'statesmen' and, presumably, those who feel benevolent towards senior bureaucrats would suggest that they are 'administrators' carrying on a vital and important task in government. Most writing on the place of the bureaucrat or administrator in modern government tends to reflect this tension between the seeming inevitability of large-scale administration as a part of the political systems of the more 'developed' nations and the supposed evils of impersonal bureaucracy on this scale. The process of administering the decisions of the legal authorities sits very uneasily in most of the classical theories of politics and even in much modern theory; in few other areas is there such a dichotomy between what a group of political actors do in fact and in theory. Are bureaucrats a completely neutral agency in the political process or do they have a profound influence on its outcome? Few would hold to the first alternative today. In fact, a corpus of theory about administration and about bureaucracy has evolved over the last few decades, one which attempts to explain the behaviour of a set of 'actors', individuals with distinct 'roles' whose performance can be isolated to some degree from others in the political system. In the English-speaking countries these men are known as 'civil servants', but the generic term of 'bureaucrat' is one which commands almost universal acceptance. The only disadvantage of the term is that it is often extended to cover the work of those who take the decisions and cope with the paper-work in any large-scale organization, whether it be a commercial enterprise, a trade union, an armed service or, of course, a governmental organization, yet behaviour patterns are similar in certain respects in the administration of all big organizations so that research into one type can be usefully used to investigate the workings of another. In practice, confusion rarely arises, and the cross-fertilization of the hypotheses drawn from viewing the actions of administrators in purely political and nominally non-political organizations is useful, for the latter often have some influence on the political process.

The study of bureaucratic behaviour can be viewed as part of the overall increase in interest in political behaviour in general, but it is also indicative of the vast increase in the size of governmental (or for that matter all) bureaucracy during the twentieth century. This is not to say that there was no interest in the performance of governmental administration before the present century. J. S. Mill was critical of the education and selection of potential civil servants, while Walter Bagehot struck a gloomy note about their behaviour, commenting that: 'It is an inevitable defect, that bureaucrats will care more for routine than for results.'[1] The observations of British and American writers on government gradually widened in scope by the early twentieth century; A. L. Lowell (writing during the First World War) contrasted that period with fifty years previously when 'the public was not aware of civil servants' and was quite sure that the bureaucrats had become wielders of 'great power' in the course of the half-century.[2] By the middle of the twentieth century the sheer size of the bureaucracies that underpin the governments of most modern nations, amounting often to something like 3% of the labour force even at a conservative estimate, has led to the many attempts to distinguish between the conventional and the observed patterns of behaviour inside this branch of government.

Max Weber

Max Weber's commanding position in the early development of political sociology was outlined in an earlier chapter when we looked briefly at his three 'ideal types' of legitimate authority; it was in the setting of one of these, the 'rational–legal' type, that Weber evolved an outline theory which describes the nature of modern bureaucracy and its characteristic patterns of behaviour. The scattered nature of much of Weber's early writing—in essays and the transcripts of lectures—was alluded to at that time but, fortunately, he summarized his views on bureaucracy in the extensive work (*Wirtschaft und Gesellschaft*) that he was preparing in the years before his relatively early death in 1920 and the relevant extracts have been available in translation for some years now.[3] For Weber, as for many more recent writers, bureaucracy was an organizational arrangement which combined great advantage with potential danger, an asset to the modern state that could soon cease to be one if it was not properly controlled. Its very existence seemed to be inevitable, given the economic and political complexity of the modern political system, for how could such a state survive without a large body of men to mediate between the rulers and the ruled at a time when law-making was becoming so detailed and all-pervasive?

Weber's model for his analysis of the bureaucracy was close to hand, for Germany and its principal territorial precursor, the kingdom of Prussia, provides the archetype of a modern civil service. By the time Weber reached manhood the Prussian bureaucracy was about two centuries old as an organized arm of the state and 'administrative science' had been taught in German universities as early as the eighteenth century. It presented most of the features that Weber and many of his successors have described as the hallmarks of the civil service—professionalism, hierarchy, rigidity—in fact a general picture of a technically efficient but somewhat soulless organization. For the evolution of Prussia, this bureaucratic machine may well have been a necessity, as Weber recognized, but nonetheless he was critical of the extent to which the bureaucracy could operate without higher control. While Karl Loewenstein may be exaggerating when he contends that 'if Max Weber identified any single factor as Political Enemy Number 1, it was the untrammeled rule of a bureaucracy',[4] his writing leaves no doubt that he viewed it as a *potential* Frankenstein's monster, in need of firm checks on its power.

For Weber the essence of bureaucracy was its 'rational' character; it was governed by a set of rules that were easily discernible. He commented that 'rules, means, ends, and matter-of-factness dominate its bearing'.[5] Inside this frame, the structure of 'modern officialdom' could be accurately delineated according to a list of characteristics which are expressed in terms of the 'functions' of the organism. The first of these flows directly from this concept of the observance of a set of rules; this is the principle of 'fixed and official jurisdictional areas' wherein the hierarchical pattern operates between the officials who are in the position in the hierarchy for which they are suited by their training and qualifications. Another strand in the pattern is the dependence of the 'bureau' or 'office' on the written record which provides the continuity of purpose in the organization; from this, Weber also deduces that there must be a basis of management involved which, once again, is dependent on discernible rules that govern the bureau. Finally, there is the characteristic of what we might term 'professionalization'—the official pursues his job as the main activity of his working day; implicit in this is the concept of the upkeep of professional standards expected from each official and, of course, the career of the official depends on a pattern of promotion where examinations play at least some part.[6]

Weber's main concern after describing the characteristics of the bureaucracy was to show how it related to human society at certain stages of its development in different parts of the world. His encyclopaedic knowledge and breadth of understanding of world history made this a particularly useful exercize. There is certainly an awareness of the positive advantages of bureaucratic organization and also of its relative permanence once it is established in a society:

> The decisive reason for the advance of bureaucratic organisation has always been its purely technical superiority over any other form of organisation. The fully developed bureaucratic mechanism compares with other organisations exactly as does the machine with the non-mechanical modes of production.[7]

Societies that demand this level of technical superiority, mainly those that are more advanced economically, inevitably tend to support a bureaucratic structure sooner or later. Its durability is illustrated by the contrast between the bureaucratic content of the 'rational–legal' ideal type (of authority) and the more unstable world of the 'charismatic' leader. The only comparable form of legitimate authority to the 'rational–legal' model is that in which 'patriarchal' power flourishes, for bureaucracy is the 'counter-image' of patriarchal authority.[8] Both provide a certain amount of routine and satisfy the need of a society for a degree of continuity in the dispensation of authority, but only bureaucracy with its aura of professionalization and specialization, its reliance on precedence and the written record, can cope with the constant onrush of rule-making that can be observed in, say, Western European countries since Weber's day.

Although Weber saw the increase of bureaucracy among the major nations of the world as an inevitable process, he was unsure whether or not this implied the inevitable increase of the power of the bureaucracy within the individual polity; but it is difficult not to believe that this was what he suspected. He states that its position and its potential for power is normally 'overtowering'.[9] Since Weber was opposed to despotic control from any man or group—despite his occasional emphasis on the significance of individual, virtually Caesaristic, leadership—he insisted on the power of the bureaucracy being balanced by some form of check or control and, since his death, this issue has been debated as much as any aspect of his outline theory of bureaucracy. Weber's medium for the control of possible bureaucratic excess was parliamentarianism and one at least of his main followers, Reinhard Bendix, is satisfied with the power of a popularly elected legislature to curb the administrators. In discussing parliamentary committees, he states the following: 'The contact with administrators they provide has the twofold function of controlling the bureaucracy through public disclosure and of providing both leaders and followers with the necessary political training and education.'[10] Karl Loewenstein, on the other hand, feels that: 'The parliaments have proved unequal to the task of curbing bureaucracy, but the courts have stepped into the breach.'[11] In truth, both have been used to 'curb bureaucracy'. The French appear to have preferred legal curbs; the Americans use the Congressional committee as one of their main checks on the administration right up to members of the presidential Cabinet. In Britain, both varieties have been attempted. Of late, interest has centred on the parliamentary specialist select committee, which seems to be a weapon of legislative control conceived within the Weberian mould; its comparative effectiveness is indicated by the reluctance of the Labour government of the later 1960s to extend the area of inquiry to more than two or three fields at any one time, and it would be reasonable to suppose that the close liaison between senior civil servants and Cabinet members was at least the partial cause of this. Obviously, parliamentary control over the bureaucracy *is* possible; because it did not work under the Weimar Republic this is no reason to suppose that it could not be effective where parliamentary rule is deep-rooted. There are other ways than these to check the bureaucracy and any contemporary list of possible devices would undoubtedly include the power of the mass media, especially the press, to do this or at least to provide the necessary pressures and publicity to ensure that governmental organs provided the appropriate remedies.

Max Weber provided a first-rate introduction to the shape and characteristics of bureaucracy and its relation to society. He does not spend much time on the inner workings of the bureaucracy, apart from a minor discussion on the propensity of administrators to indulge in secrecy while carrying on their work; this is highly relevant to the above comments on parliamentary control for most modern research tends to confirm Weber's contention that: 'In facing a parliament, the bureaucracy, out of a sure power instinct, fights every attempt of the parliament to gain knowledge by means of its own experts or from interest groups.'[12] This lack of analysis of the inner decision-making processes of the bureaucracy would be a major criticism of the Weber model if it was intended to be an exhaustive analysis. In fact, the main interest groups.'[12] This lack of analysis of the inner decision-making of modern society and in the historical development of bureaucracy as a modernizing influence in specific polities. It would be unfair therefore to criticize Weber for not examining something that he did not intend to investigate and to call him to account for not being more exhaustive than he was. Bureaucracy is introduced as being archetypal of the legal–rational form of authority, and Weber is more concerned to review the interrelation of the differing patterns of authority and how one can evolve into the other rather than to set up case-studies of the individual bureaucrat in action. Most of his historical examples tend to reinforce the general shape of the bureaucracy as a means of exercising authority rather than illuminating the nature of the decision-making process; this was left to his successors to analyze, often by means of specific studies which provide evidence on which to base general theory about bureaucratic behaviour.

Post-Weberian theory

Once Weber's writings began to be diffused through the Western world, particularly that part which is English-speaking, they influenced a number of different areas of social scientific thought, including the growing interest in the analysis of administration as practised in government. In fact, most references to bureaucracy were based on the Weber typology, a tendency which still persists though now there is a mass of later work to compare with it. Much of the behavioural theory that could be of interest to students of this subject was being produced by men who counted Weber as one of their chief influences, such as Karl Mannheim and Talcott Parsons. Mannheim, one of the many intellectual refugees from Hitler's Germany, took the 'ideal-type' concept as a way of showing that interpretations of political situations were inevitably coloured by the political position of the observer. One member of his typology was described as 'bureaucratic conservatism' and, like Weber, much of the generalization about bureaucracy under this heading is based on observation of the part that bureaucrats had played in the development of the Prussian state and the German Empire. Mannheim commented that 'the majority of books on politics in the history of German political science are *de facto* treatises on administration'.[13] Bureaucrats fail to see political problems as anything more than administrative ones, for they are taught to confine their appreciation of a given situation to the application of the rules or laws that govern the society to which they belong. Mannheim was concerned with the way in which a specific group developed its own '*Weltanschauung*' in political terms; class position could decide this but some groups, such as intellectuals, lacked a fixed class position and could in theory make a choice or even a synthesis of viewpoints.[14] It is evident that bureaucrats looked at the world specifically in terms of their own position as administrators of a set of rules, regarding any aberration from the ordered pattern of events in the political systems, such as political revolution, as something to be removed as soon as possible.[15] Mannheim's analysis thus goes a little further than Weber's, in that he begins to enter the bureaucratic mind and looks briefly at their pattern of behaviour, although his material on bureaucracy is otherwise much less extensive than that found in Weber. Mannheim, like Weber, realized that bureaucracy had its positive side and that the good inherent in this type of organization could outweigh the potential evil. For example, it allowed the development of 'impersonal and classless justice' which was not present in earlier societies more dependent on personal rule exercized from the apex of a hierarchy.[16] It should be possible to develop the inherent benefits of bureaucratic organization in government—efficiency and objectivity in particular—while restraining the inherent dangers, chief of which was its potential for dehumanizing situations that called for justice tempered with mercy, administration tempered with sympathy for the cause of those who are being administered.[17] With its emphasis on rationality and modernity, Mannheim's analysis is clearly in the first wave of the Weberian tradition, if one can call it such, but its development, though not extensive, does indicate the direction that was likely to ensue in the 1940s and 1950s.

Talcott Parsons, as was made clear in the third chapter, used Weber as one of his models for the construction of his 'theory of action'. He was also one of the first 'popularizers' of Weber's ideas in the English-speaking world as a translator and editor of parts of the posthumous work alluded to above. Much earlier than this, he had included Weber among the writers around whom he built his major book of the 1930s, *The Structure of Social Action*. Parsons did not extend Weber's theory of the bureaucratic component of rational–legal authority to any great degree although he does offer some new emphases. For example, Parsons stresses what seems to be a passing note in Weber that 'in a rational bureaucratic structure there must always be a source of the legality of its order which is, in the last analysis, charismatic'.[18] Since most glosses on Weber emphasize the tendency to polar opposition in the concepts of bureaucracy and charisma, it is worth noting this point, one which of course tends to support the 'ideal-type' nature of these concepts, that is, the fact that they are extracted from reality for heuristic purposes and that authority always implies a degree of faith in leadership that could be described as charismatic.

As the writings of Max Weber became more widely known and the ingredients of the Weberian model became established as a means of examining the bureaucracy, it was inevitable that some criticism of the character of Weber's analysis would appear. Carl Friedrich, for example, while recognizing that Weberian analysis is a vital starting-point for bureaucratic theory, claims to have found its application of limited value because of its dependence on 'ideal types' and on Weber's belief in the almost inevitable transition of all societies towards a state of rationalization. In several text-books and in some shorter pieces, Friedrich has given in passing a brief picture of the way in which bureaucracy operates in modern society.[19] It would be too presumptuous to terms this a 'model', for it is couched in rather general terms, but it does claim to be based on 'an empirical and comparative enquiry',[20] itself stemming from Friedrich's general interest in what we would today call comparative government. From his study of bureaucratic behaviour in such countries as Britain, the United States and Brandenburg–Prussia, Friedrich concludes that one can isolate six elements contained in a bureaucratic structure. Three of these are organizational in aspect—centralization of control and supervision, which implies a distinct hierarchy present in the structure; differentiation of functions or, more simply, specialization; and qualification for office.[21]

These three characteristics are not dissimilar to the observed phenomena described by Weber, since the latter emphasized the need for training and for a visible hierarchy, therefore there does not appear to be anything that is novel about these initial characteristics put forward by Friedrich. Even the three so-called 'behavioural' characteristics detailed below are not entirely new and it is difficult to see why he thought that they were such an advance over what Weber had written, although they do tend to amplify the Weberian pattern to a marginal degree.

'Objectivity' is an ideal to which the administrative structure aspires and, in practice, there is usually some falling-away from the ideal. The expert or professional—here one is looking back at one of the organizational characteristics, that of 'qualification for office'—can be objective and suppress his personal views or feelings in a given situation much more easily than the 'layman' or administrator, who lacks the necessary training or conditioning. 'Precision and consistency' make up another 'element' but one can distinguish between them. The former is perhaps self-evident since it is essential to the communication of decisions to those who are closely affected by them, usually the general public. 'Consistency' is important because legal or quasi-legal precedent is a key to the fair-play aspect that underpins the acceptance of much of what the bureaucracy imposes on this latter group. Perhaps the most contentious of these behavioural traits is that of 'discretion', which in this context is a polite way of pointing out that bureaucracy works best when its main activities are cloaked in a degree of secrecy. The degree of secrecy is open to question though, for while it is reasonable to use it to protect the legitimate rights of clients and even to see that unnecessary embarrassment is not caused to colleagues in the administration process, it is surely necessary on occasion to let a certain amount of publicity into the administrative processes, if only to provide a check on the political effects of decisions made in the bureaucracy.[22]

Friedrich attacks Weber's 'intuitional ideal type of bureaucracy' for its failure to recognize that a strong normative element is present at the same time as he is claiming the type to be illustrative of a *'wertfreie Wissenschaft'* or value-free social science. According to Friedrich, the phenomena regarded as absolute by Weber are in fact 'the real tasks of empirical enquiry' and he illustrates this with the example of responsibility, an aspect which he claims to find absent in the perfectly developed bureaucracy of Weber's model. Since Weber was concerned with the problem of control, this seems to be an over-statement, but it does lead Friedrich to enlarge on the internal organization of responsibility in a way not seen in Weber; in particular, there is a useful categorization of five ways of encouraging the bureaucrat to be responsible. The first two are essentially carrot-and-stick disciplinary measures for those who err, promotion for those who are responsible to the hierarchy above them. Two of the others imply eventual sanctions—financial audit and judicial measures—while a fifth suggests that the encouragement of a spirit of craftsmanship will make the administrator take a legitimate pride in the task at hand. Presumably, these categories provide a way of assessing how respon-sible a particular bureaucracy is to control from above. They are not absolute but comparative, and do provide a method of internal analysis more typical of the post-Weberian development of administrative theory than that of the master himself.[23]

Most post-Weberian theory still bases itself on broad impressions of the place of the bureaucracy in the modern state; the emphasis is distinctly on the few well-developed Western bureaucracies that have existed in the nineteenth and twentieth centuries. There has been some movement towards clearer concepts of behavioural study in this area in that the post-Weberians have tended to recognize that one key to the study of administration is an understanding of the patterns of behaviour inside the bureaucracy. However, this was not really a practicable proposition if, like Friedrich, one tended to confine oneself to general comprehension of national bureaucracies. What was needed was more knowledge about how bureaucracy worked in a relatively small units, whether or not it was part of a larger administrative set-up. One or two pioneer studies appeared in this vein by the late 1930s and in the two following decades a much wider range of case-studies became available, allowing the existing theory a chance of enrichment by cross-reference to actual cases of small-scale organizational behaviour.

The 'case-study' approach

One of the best-known discoveries of modern social science is the so-called 'Hawthorne effect', associated with a series of studies that were carried out at the Hawthorne Works of the Western Electric Company during the last years of the 1920s. It describes the tendency for work groups to react to the very fact that they are being studied, rather than to any material alteration in their conditions of work. The tendency for this phenomenon to be picked out of the considerable amount of evidence assembled by the principal observers conducting the Hawthorne experiments has almost overshadowed the basic discovery emphasized by the operation of the 'effect', that is, that work groups are social organizations and that they will develop norms and patterns of behaviour like any other human organization. In the final codification of the conclusions of the Hawthorne experiments, published nearly ten years after the last of them took place, the authors drew a clear line between the former tendency to treat the member of an organization as a 'physiological machine' and the more sophisticated approach suggested by the experiments. For example, the significance of increasing the number and duration of rest pauses allowed could be appreciated only in this context:

> As long as the investigators conceived of rest pauses as having only physical effects, it was, of course, difficult to explain their beneficial results other than in terms of a reduction of fatigue. But once the social meaning to the worker of his environment was appreciated, it became clear that the beneficial effect of rest pauses could be explained equally well in terms of their social function.[24]

From this flows the general idea of the importance of 'informal organization' as a key to the behaviour of the members of any large-scale organization. We can study the formal layout of an organization by examining its constitution, organization chart or any other documentation which sets out the chain of command and the levels of authority showing who is responsible for what and to whom. Alongside this formal pattern a more informal one tends to develop, especially inside the small sub-units where the bulk of the work is carried on. This cannot entirely replace the formal pattern except in extreme cases, but any examination of the way in which a specific organization works ignores this aspect at the risk of giving an incomplete and inexact picture of the working of the organization. An example of this phenomenon in the Hawthorne Works was the self-regulation of output—not too fast a rate, not too slow—which was observed in the Bank Wiring Observation Room study and the emergence of one or two natural leaders who mediated between the group and the supervisory staff.[25]

Since the dissemination of the Hawthorne material, informal patterns have been looked for in most case-studies of specific organizations, including those with a high bureaucratic content. Chester Barnard, in his Lowell Institute lectures of 1937 (later put into book form), lays a great deal of stress on the primacy of informal over formal organization as when he states that 'informal association is rather obviously a condition which necessarily *precedes* formal organisation'.[26] Formal organization does usually require a degree of informal organization to set it up and the need for formal organization is often seen when a loose, informal one proves to be inadequate. This is not of much import for administrative theory though; what is more important is the juxtaposition of the formal and informal structures in the same organization. Barnard's contention is that the function of informal-inside-formal organization is threefold and this is a key to the great importance of noting and studying this pattern; the three functions are those of maintenance of cohesiveness, personal integrity and self-respect.[27] The common claim that large-scale organization encourages depersonalization—the 'soulless bureaucrat' of popular belief—is to some extent offset by the presence of informal organization inside most bureaucracies and other large formal organizations. It produces what Barnard terms 'vitality' in the organization and this is to its credit.[28] The problems of informal organization are, however, lightly glossed over by Barnard. What happens when the norms of the informal clash with the norms of the formal organization? For example, informal groups within a bureaucratic structure may tend to restrict output against the wishes of supervisory or senior personnel rather in the way seen in the Hawthorne Bank Wiring Observation Room. Since one of the great advantages of a bureaucracy or a similar organizational pattern is supposed to be the pursuance of the ends of the organization by the most efficient means, the possible clash of norms can be seen to be dysfunctional to the organization; it remains one of the problems of the efficient organization of a bureaucracy.

In practice, this tendency occurs much less often in the bureaucratic situation than it does in the sort of work situation found in, say, the factory type of structure. This was well illustrated by another of the classic case-studies, that carried out by Peter Blau in 1948–9 in two American government agencies, one in the federal government and the other in a state government. Informal organization was easily detectable in both of these agencies but the 'unofficial practices' that resulted from this, even where they violated explicit rules of the agency concerned, tended, more often than not, to contribute to overall efficiency rather than detract from it. The reason for this lies in the position of the bureaucrat compared to the factory worker. The latter relies on group solidarity to protect him both from possible exploitation by the management and from the impersonal and anomic tendencies of large-scale industrial organization. The bureaucrat, except for some of those at the bottom of the structure, tends to see himself as rather more of a craftsman with a definite code of conduct. Supervision is rarely as direct as in an industrial concern and, to a degree, the middle-range bureaucrat is left to get on with his work without continual checks being made on his actions. Blau suggests that bureaucracies possess a high degree of vertical social cohesion rather than the tendency to pronounced horizontal social cohesion that is found in industrial organizations.[29] This is undoubtedly true of the middle-range bureaucrats predominant in the agencies that he studied. Whether it is true of those members of an administrative organization who are at the bottom of the heap is much more debatable. There seems in fact to have been little vertical social cohesion in the case of a file-clerk cited by Blau, who was ordered to implement the department head's memo to use an unsuitable colour coding for tabbing applicant's records, a process that the supervisor realized was inefficient but one that the supervisor insisted should be carried out rather than taking the responsibility for countermanding it. The sense of hierarchy and what Blau terms 'inefficient rigidity' can supersede a sense of vertical social cohesion, especially when the situation is viewed from the position of a junior member. This illustrates the problem of viewing bureaucracies as a cohesive whole; the lowest ranks inevitably have a different 'world-view' from senior officials who have more independence, suffer less direct regulation and pursue a career rather than a job. Most generalizations about the personnel of bureaucracies are therefore more valid for the latter than the former, since the file-clerks and their like are often more akin to the operatives of a factory, or at least to the lowliest clerks of a commercial organization (with some differences such as in the area of job security).

The Blau case-study also claimed to refute one of the classic generalizations about bureaucratic behaviour, that which states that bureaucrats are highly unlikely to be innovators and that bureaucracies are usually resistant to change. Blau cites, for example, von Mises and Michels as two of his authorities for this point of view and it is probably the latter who is best-known for a thoroughgoing attack on bureaucracy for these faults. In his book on oligarchical tendencies in party politics, Michels uses terms such as 'petty, narrow, rigid and illiberal' to describe the defects of large-scale organization such as that found in governmental structures, and indeed in the political parties that were attempting to extend social democracy in Western Europe in the early years of the twentieth century.[30] Michels' formulation of this theory is best seen in the formula set out near the end of his book: 'Who says organization says oligarchy.'[31] It is this oligarchy at the top of the organizational tree which, in Michels' view, resists change and stifles democracy. Blau's observations of governmental agencies led him to modify this pessimistic conclusion and to suggest that bureaucracies can be more flexible than Michels believed.

The occurrence of 'inefficient rigidity' mentioned above is one area where there is a resistance to change inside the bureaucracy. Yet in Blau's two agencies (a state employment, and a federal enforcement, agency), his observations suggested that this phenomenon was over-shadowed by many instances of a free acceptance of change if that change made it more likely that the long-term aims of the organization would be reached. It must be remembered that the federal agency studied was a child of the New Deal and in its early days it had possessed a pioneer quality which provided a high level of satisfaction for officials in sympathy with the reforms implemented by the agency. Even though those days had gone by the time that Blau's study was under way, many agents still looked for new ways in which they could improve working conditions in the factories that their agency regulated. Therefore the agency pressed for new laws and Blau puts this forward as a peculiarity of this rather specialized type of bureaucracy: 'The succession of organizational goals is more conspicuous in innovating organizations, since some of their initial objectives tend to become obsolete, but it is not confined to them.'[32] One could turn Blau's argument on its head and ask whether the agency was not more concerned with its own continuance than the pursuance of those general goals with which its birth was associated. If this was true then the one strand of the Michels argument that emphasized the semi-permanence of oligarchies once they were set up seems to have some support. The other type of innovation mentioned by Blau, that which removed procedural irritants, appears less important and more of an adjustment than an innovation. However, Blau does tend to open up an important issue and indicate that there is a more 'dynamic' aspect to bureaucratic structures than had previously been maintained. If one can argue that, given certain preconditions, bureaucracies will be innovators rather than merely instruments of policy, then it must change their whole relationship to the rest of the political system.

Blau's study is one of the few case-studies that focusses on a bureaucracy pure and simple rather than on an organization which shows elements of bureaucratic behaviour. For example, the Michels argument that organization inevitably leads to oligarchy was shown to be a rule with certain exceptions by the study mounted on the International Typographical Union by Lipset and his associates. Trade unions have been highly prone to bureaucratization, as Michels argued by extension, since they are voluntary organizations like the political parties that he examined. Yet the ITU in the first half of the twentieth century was marked by a resilient two-party system not unlike the system that allows the alternation of two political parties in office in a number of Western and British Commonwealth polities. The general argument put forward is perhaps more interesting to the student of democratic theory than of bureaucracy, but the thesis demonstrated here is that bureaucracy in voluntary organizations can be balanced by a considerable degree of democratic control if the conditions are right. The ITU is, however, shown to be peculiar in that it combines a literate, almost professional membership with a comparatively small status gap between officials and rank-and-file and has had a history which has encouraged left–right cleavages over many issues. The authors of the study put forward twenty-two propositions which attempt to describe the way in which the ITU presents this unique face to the world.[33] The absence of many of these in other unions leads the authors to fear that many voluntary organizations do lack that most important feature of many full-scale political systems, the check of parliamentarian and pressure group on officials who are freely voted into office but, once in, are difficult to remove without something akin to palace revolt.

Other case-studies of formal organizations tended to accent the presence of informal organization alongside the formal and the tendency for 'unintended consequences' to occur which often influenced the way in which the organization developed. Selznick's examination of the way in which this happened in the Tennessee Valley Authority is important for the light it sheds on the 'clientele' relationship that is a part of many bureaucratic structures. The TVA became keyed into the local networks in the areas in which it operated and came to oppose other governmental agencies—such as the departments of Agriculture and the Interior—where their policies ran counter to what the locals believed was in their best interests. The Authority practiced what Selznick termed 'co-optation' as a way of ensuring the legitimacy of its authority among the local communities; this is defined as: 'The process of absorbing new elements into the leader-ship or policy-determining structure of an organization as a means of averting threats to its stability or existence.'[34] Political bureaucracies always have the problem of balancing up the interests of the different groups to which, in some degree or another, they are accountable. Executive and legislative leadership will call the organization to account, so will its specific clientele if it has one, and almost certainly pressure groups and other opinion leaders among the public at large will be critical from time to time. Occasionally, a case is documented where an agency manages to keep all interested parties happy; probably Jesse Jones and the Reconstruction Finance Corporation as described by Richard Fenno comprise the best-known example of this.[35] In the TVA case the decision seems to have been made that the clientele were all-important although, even in so doing, the TVA appears to have practiced a sort of benevolent paternalism in cases where the locals were not able to keep up with the officials in knowledge and application to the inevitable technical problems that arose in the early years of the TVA experiment.

Selznick's choice of an organization to study is almost a model of what we traditionally think of as a bureaucracy since the TVA was, in part at least, an organization set up to carry out a specific set of governmental policies. Its mode of operation, resting heavily on its work with individuals and groups in the locality in which it was centred, suggests a functional need for a certain style of operation. Students of bureaucracy who are looking for cases to study tend to choose non-governmental organizations (government departments are often difficult of access) and issues of this kind emphasizing external relationships are frequently neglected. The tendency with the case-studies carried out up to the 1950s was to take the early models as starting-points, Weber or perhaps Michels, and to test them against their observation of the specific organization concerned.

When (in 1948–51) Alvin Gouldner took an industrial complex involving a factory and a gypsum mine as his 'case', he was also examining the functional necessity of a pattern of bureaucracy, one which became embedded in the organizational structure of the plant. Since 'bureaucratization' was increasing in this case, there had to be a reason for this, and the most compelling seemed to be the need to legitimize succession when a new manager took over. On the basis that the past is always beautiful, new managers needed to intensify the observance of formal rules by employees if they were to receive the same degree of co-operation that their immediate predecessor had enjoyed.[36] (Gouldner terms this the 'Rebecca myth', an analogy derived from the romantic novel of Daphne du Maurier!) Since intensification of bureaucracy increases tension within the organization it was possible to distinguish different patterns of bureaucracy in action, in this case by subdividing the phenomenon into three types— 'mock', 'representative' and 'punishment-centred'. The first can be quickly brushed aside since it was rarely effective—probably because it was imposed from outside—but the other two more effective patterns differed in the degree of mutual acceptance, representative bureaucracy being accepted by both sides, punishment-centred imposed by one only. Gouldner states quite clearly that the true bureaucrat—the 'generalist' rather than the expert in some technology—will operate inside the punishment-centred rather than the representative frame-work: 'There are grounds, therefore, for expecting that punishment-centred patterns, the sphere of the true bureaucrat, may have more than an equal share in the conduct of organizational affairs.'[37] It would seem more reasonable though to see these two patterns as two faces of the large-scale bureaucracies with which we are more familiar than with the bureaucratic tendencies in relatively small industrial and commercial concerns. For any large-scale bureaucracy to exist for any length of time in the modern world, it must contain a high degree of legitimacy of the type that, in Gouldner's view, exists within the representative rather than the punishment-centred type of bureaucracy. The latter's dependence on sanctions is echoed by the need of virtually all bureaucracies to implement decisions and see that they are carried out with the imposition of sanctions if necessary. Therefore the two sides tend to be balanced off; long-term legitimacy and short-term pressure or coercion on specific issues. To be fair to Gouldner, he does present his patterns as coexistent in bureaucratic behaviour but he does not appear to stress the possibilities of the one complementing the other; orders for the sake of giving orders surely represent bad administration in the great majority of cases that one can envisage in civilian bureaucracy.

The majority of case-studies in the field of bureaucracy and organizations have been conducted in the United States; this leads one to the suspicion that theory derived from them is likely to be ethnocentric to a considerable degree. It is therefore somewhat refreshing to turn to one of the best-known studies of recent years, which, in this case, was carried out in France, a country with cultural roots that are quite different from those of North America (with perhaps the sole exception of the French Canadian enclaves of the north-east edge of that subcontinent). Michel Crozier, a Frenchman familiar with the relevant literature from both sides of the Atlantic, took two organizations for analysis, a Parisian clerical agency and an industrial monopoly, in an attempt to isolate what he terms the 'bureaucratic phenomenon'. Crozier presents us with a harsh and unsympathetic picture of both organizations, one that shows them as being heavily stratified and dependent on the strict application of rules with, especially in the clerical agency, a low degree of informal organization or even social contact between the members of specific work groups. The amount of rigidity present in these organizations made them highly resistant to change, yet change is necessary in any modern organization and therefore often takes place in an atmosphere of crisis since it occurs only when inevitable. There are obvious contrasts between the French model and the American if these two organizations are typical of the former; Crozier links the French model of bureaucracy with the values of traditional France:

Resistance to participation, and preference for centralised authority and the stability and rigidity of a bureaucratic system of organisation, by preserving for each member a minimum of autonomy and individual discretion, proceed from the same values which peasants, craftsmen and noblemen embodied in the delicate balance of human relations that characterised the *art de vivre* of traditional France.[38]

Crozier is suggesting here that the pattern of bureaucratic activity in a country is directly dependent on the cultural content of that society. French society is based on the balance between a hierarchical system of authority and a high degree of individual liberty within the range of each of the strata. In the French bureaucratic model individuals were constrained to accept the 'militaristic structure' but the power of those at the top was essentially limited; this is why change was so difficult to bring about. Crozier draws the perhaps obvious parallels with French political life, the highly regulated structure and the occasional anomic outburst that disturbs the equilibrium.[39] Since he wrote this account, the events of May 1968 make the parallel even more appropriate. Yet France has changed dramatically in many respects, particularly economically, since 1945, and this suggests a certain flexibility in the national administrative process that was not present in earlier times. It is a pity that Crozier will insist on using 'bureaucratic' in its pejorative sense, emphasizing the dysfunctional aspects of certain bureaucratic traits. That he is well able to distinguish the functional from the dysfunctional consequences of the presence of formal organizations is evident by the closing pages of the book where, for example, he looks again at the Weberian model and foresees that '. . . the elimination of the "bureaucratic systems of organization" in the dysfunctional sense is the condition for the growth of "bureaucratization" in the Weberian sense.'[40]

The development of bureaucratic theory would have been a much slower process without the evidence supplied by the leading case-studies, and their worth is reflective of some of the best empirical trends in modern social science. The early models could be tested and refined; it is noticeable though that they were rarely superseded. What the case-studies did well was to flesh out our knowledge of the way in which organizations worked and a direct result was to make it essential to widen the range of model-building. Even in the United States, because of the diversity of American society it could be seen that bureaucratic organization, where it was discrete and relatively self-contained, could take on many patterns. When one introduced the variation in national cultures, it was evident that the variety was increased. This latter point was to be invaluable when later observers started to consider the relevance of bureaucracy to political development in the non-Western world. 'Fleshing-out' the earlier models also meant that, for example, the importance of understanding the relationship of informal to formal organization would form part of any future picture of the bureaucratic process.

But the case-study method did have its drawbacks. For reasons of convenience of access, it often concentrated on non-governmental organizations and, although this told those interested in organizational theories a great deal, the specialist in bureaucratic theory tended to wish for a greater insight into administrative, especially governmental, organization. There was little general theory derived directly from the case-studies because of their episodic nature. Two great questions remained. What was the exact and unique nature of the bureaucracy that distinguished it from other human groups? How could one give an intimate and detailed analysis of the relationship of governmental or other specifically political bureaucracies with the remaining parts of the political system? Much of the general theory developed in the last twenty years or so has tended to concentrate on these questions and to try to give a clear picture of the internal working and the external relations of a bureaucracy.

'Decision-making'

One of the fundamental problems in the attempt to produce a more exact means of analyzing politics and political behaviour is the definition of what politics comprises in terms of subject-matter. Similarly, when one discusses 'bureaucracy' as part of the political system, there is a structure–function problem in that the term is used interchangeably to describe *either* a group of actors *or* a set of attitudes and roles among groups that might not necessarily be seen as 'bureaucrats' pure and simple. This confusion goes back to Weber at least and has only begun to be resolved in the years since the end of the Second World War; interest now is especially directed towards the behaviour of those who take decisions in the administrative context of government.

In the immediate post-war years the man who was most successful in giving point to the behavioural side of the bureaucracy at a theoretical level was Herbert Simon, whose fairly brief examination of administrative behaviour is still relevant today. In Martin Landau's words, Simon ' . . . was trying to redefine public administration so as to give it a "solid center", a standard of relevance, a set of operating concepts—to make it, in short, a "field" of enquiry'.[41] To do this, Simon had to define exactly what divided administrative behaviour from other types of behaviour that might be termed social; his conclusion was that the essence of administration was the act of taking decisions, not just the long-term or general policy decisions but those that went on all the time. Therefore, if one understood the way in which decisions were taken and implemented in an administrative body, then one would understand the basic nature of the organization and its main function. Implementation was also of importance but this was not completely separate from decision-making in an administrative organization—the one was predicated upon the other. The focus of attention should be the individual decision-maker, from whom one can work outwards to the organization as a whole. As Simon summarizes this: 'Insight into the structure and function of an organization can best be gained by analyzing the manner in which the decisions and behaviour of such employees are influenced within and by the organization.'[42] Simon strays onto one or two highly controversial issues in trying to delineate the area within which administrations operate as, for example, when he tries to disentangle the fact–value dichotomy in decision-making. Although there is a reasonably acceptable logic in his identification of value questions as being the main concern of (elected) policy-makers and fact analysis as being the main concern of administrators, accepting the inevitability that the two can never be completely disentangled in practice, this is a thesis which has been bitterly attacked by many other writers.[43]

The core of Simon's model is the examination of the sort of decision-making that is the particular province of the administrator, and he does this by approaching the problem through a concept of rationality, rational decision-making being the reaching of desired ends by appropriate means. The yardstick is chosen from the actors in the economic system, Simon assuming a high degree of 'rationality' from economic man. Rationality implies knowledge of all the possible solutions to a problem and the consequences that follow from them.

'Economic man' has got closer to this concept of rationality than has 'administrative man' although even Simon would agree that the former has only approximated to this position. The latter is not able to 'maximise' satisfaction in the way that his economic counterpart can do, for the world that economic man operates inside is closer to the real world than that in which administrative man operates. The world of the administrator is, in Simon's view, denuded of most of the heterogeneity of the world at large and therefore he cannot come at all close to maximizing; what he can do is to 'satisfice', that is to select the best alternative from those that face him.[44]

This depiction of the administrator as someone who moves in a world where rational decision-making is limited may be thought to accord with views of bureaucrats as being essentially limited and blinkered, unable to take any long view of their actions and the decisions that they take. However, Simon's picture of the administrative process is not too dissimilar from the classical one which emphasizes the difference between the establishment of policy in broad outlines and its implementation by administrators. Simon's goal seems to be a process by which the values of the individual in the organization will broadly accord with those of the group in the form of the organization as a whole: ' . . . the organization must be so constructed that a decision which is (subjectively) rational from the standpoint of the deciding individual, will remain rational when reassessed from the standpoint of the group.'[45] Since there is no direct explanation of the method of achieving this, one is left with the suspicion that, by implication, this process would lead to the 'organization man' pattern of corporate executive which has been attacked by popularizing social science books and articles in the United States since the 1950s. Yet elsewhere Simon appreciates that administration is not a mechanistic process, that it is essentially operated by human beings 'whose behavior is influenced by knowledge, memory and expectation'.[46] Therefore, it may be that what Simon is emphasizing are the essential limitations of the administrative process, dependent as it is on the limitations of individual behaviour patterns and the physiological impossibility of assessing all the alternative courses of action. Without a doubt though, Simon has produced a focus for the analysis of bureaucracy which still has relevance by its concentration on one of the main functions, if not *the* main function, of the administrator—the taking of decisions, not in a vacuum of course but as a vital link between the basic aims of the organization and their implementation.

From Simon's book has come a whole generation of writing on the organization as a decision-making process; this has proved an incisive way to analyze bureaucracy even though it is not a complete answer to the nature of the administration in all its complexity.[47] Since the decisions that are analyzed via this approach are assumed to be authoritative and policy-centred ones, the value of a decision-making approach is that it emphasizes the part that bureaucrats play in making policy at the highest level. Senior bureaucrats are now presumed to be among that select group dubbed as 'proximate' or immediate policy-makers, that is, unlike, say, the general public which only has a tenuous relationship with the direct making of policy. Charles Lindblom, in coining the phrase 'proximate policy-maker', argues that:

> It was once a common doctrine in political science that administrators, even high-level ones, only administered policies elsewhere determined in the political system—usually in the legislature. We have come to understand, however, that in high enough levels of the administrative system, administrators inevitably *make* policy.[48]

In placing the senior administrators, the bureau chiefs or top civil servants in this category, Lindblom points out that they form part of a network with the other groups of actors in the political process; in the American context, for example, the president and his immediate advisers, the Congress, the bureau's clientele and the general public. In making decisions, senior administrators are constrained by prior decisions made in the two institutional branches and by pressures mounted by all four. I have argued elsewhere that major change in the administrative structure of American, and by implication most democratic, government is only likely to occur when there is a high degree of congruency between these various 'interests' that are at work.[49]

Analyses of the inner workings of the bureaucracy have tended to proliferate in the last decade or so; like Simon's model, economic behaviour is often used to contrast with administrative behaviour and also to suggest that similar 'laws' should be developed to explain the behaviour patterns of the bureaucrat. Another feature of much of this literature is the preoccupation that one finds with the role of the bureaucrat. Is it functional or dysfunctional for the achievement of individual and group goals respectively? There is still a tendency to see large-scale organization as inherently dysfunctional and destructive of individual initiative, creativity and the general development of the individual personality. In what one would assess as an extreme form, this is expressed, for example, by Robert Presthus:

> This analysis . . . seeks . . . to raise questions about the social and psychological impact of big organizations and, by implication, to suggest greater discrimination in their use. It maintains that their impersonal, long-range objectives, patent control mechanisms, size, and tendency towards absolutism may have dysfunctional anxiety-producing results for their members.[50]

From the early days of administrative theory and organizational analysis, these doubts have been well voiced and it is accepted that there are dangers of this type inherent in large organizations. Yet, Presthus, though paying lip-service to the belief that one cannot return to a 'rural utopia', emphasizes the demerits and dysfunctional aspects of bureaucracy without recognizing that the Weberian concept of the bureaucracy as an essential prerequisite of the modern rational–legal society has never been convincingly refuted. Any model of the administrative structure that dwells on its shortcomings without providing some room for the patent advantages that organization has brought to government in particular seems to be an incomplete one.

What one would concede is that not only are there demerits and some dysfunctions in specific bureaucracies but that there is some limitation of the general capacity of a system of large-scale organization to carry out certain of the necessary functions of a modern state. Moving away from the rather negative model supplied by Presthus, one finds a slightly more satisfactory one in that provided by another writer in this general vein, Gordon Tullock. Like his work with James Buchanan on constitutional theory which is viewed through methodology largely derived from economics, Tullock's 'bureaucracy' model is based on the assumption that the actors behave 'rationally' and attempt to 'maximize their utilities' in a given situation. He examines a political organization, distinguishing little between those members of the hierarchy who are appointed and those who are elected. For Tullock, the essential ingredient appears to be the hierarchy itself and the classification of the actors inside it. All-important is the difference between the 'sovereigns', the authoritative superiors of the reference politician, the 'peers' who are his equals and the various subordinates

on the ranks below him. Techniques adopted by the politician allowing him to rise in the hierarchy are said to be similar in many cases
to those adopted in the feudal hierarchy of medieval Europe, as when
a baron with independent power is promoted to a position where he
is dependent on his sovereign and therefore becomes a courtier.[51]
Bureaucracies grow in size through the addition of subordinates and
this in effect is a form of power maximization on the part of the
sovereign. The latter's job will consist of co-ordinating the employees
in their tasks, but the greater the distance between top and bottom in
the hierarchy the weaker will be the chain of command. Many of these
conclusions are more or less conventional wisdom inside the field of
organizational theory. The more positive precepts offered by Tullock
include the desire to limit and decentralize the role of the bureaucratic
apparatus: 'Only by frankly recognizing the limits on our ability to
control giant organizations can be obtained the benefits which can be
bestowed by a well-functioning government.'[52] Tullock's book was
published when the American bureaucracy was expanding, before the
'Great Society' experiment went sour and was almost obliterated by
the polarization of American society over Vietnam. In 1965 it seemed
inconceivable that a bureaucratic theory based on a diminishing role
for the bureaucrat in the modern state would be welcomed. A few
years later it seems more acceptable but it is still unlikely in the
foreseeable future that theory will be translated into action.

The drawbacks of Presthus and Tullock may well lie in the
relatively normative concepts that permeate their work and which
detract from what are essentially descriptions and models of the
working of a bureaucracy. What may be seen as the latest in the line
which stemmed from Simon is Anthony Downs' large-scale delineation of the bureaucracy; it certainly genuflects towards Tullock's book
but is much more comprehensive. Like Tullock, Downs has been
mainly interested in the past in democratic theory and, as is made
plain in Chapter Six, he is one of the most persuasive theorists in this
area. His method of work when trying to elaborate an 'economic
theory of democracy' is paralleled by his penetrating into the world
of the bureaucrat; his three central hypotheses are 'not directly testable' and therefore resemble the 'assumptions' in the earlier book.
Other hypotheses are generated as 'laws' and 'propositions', the whole
adding up to an impressive word-picture of the workings of the
bureau.[53] He avoids the temptation of an opening polemic and readily

admits that 'bureaus are amongst the most important institutions in every part of the world'.[54] The three central hypotheses themselves form as succinct a starting-point as we have for a general theory of bureaucracy, even though it is again suffused with a definite point of view reflective of the 'economic rationality parallel' typical of a whole group of American writers:

> Bureaucratic officials (and all other social agents) seek to attain their goals rationally. Every official is significantly motivated by his own self-interest even when acting in a purely official capacity. Every organization's social functions strongly influence its internal structure, and vice versa.[55]

Downs builds on the previous work of the 'school' that has developed the decision-making approach to bureaucratic theory. He largely follows Simon's approach to the problem of achieving rational choice in administrative decisions. Tullock's illustration of the way in which communication difficulties up and down the hierarchy allow junior decision-makers a considerable leeway in interpreting the instructions of their superiors in a sovereign position is also drawn upon. However, he extends the typology of officials into five types; two are purely self-interested, either 'climbers' who value power, income and prestige above all else, or 'conservers' who value convenience and security above these. The three mixed-motive officials will adopt wider goals and can be classed as 'zealots', loyal to narrowly based policies, 'advocates', loyal to a broader range, and 'statesmen', those who try to perceive and uphold the general welfare.[56] Although Downs tends to use these types as being dependent on individual psychology, expectations and the nature of the official's position, he does not see them as necessarily fixed for any length of time; dependent on the situation at the moment, a certain amount of movement from one type to another is eminently possible. Obviously, some individuals will always be predisposed towards one type or another, but the belief in rationality means that goal-attainments will largely condition the orientation of the official at a given point in time.

Downs presents a detailed behavioural study of the bureaucracy in action, seeking information, making decisions, balancing off tendencies to inertia and change within a given organization. There is an implicit model of the effective bureau, one that is relatively small, where the divisions between the upper and lower ranks of the hierarchy are not great, and where there is a high degree of goal concensus among bureau members. Downs breaks some new ground in his argument that bureaucracies usually need ideologies 'because they are efficient means of communicating with certain groups both inside and outside their bureaus', though to some degree it links with Simon's concept of the relationship between individual and group (see n. 45).[57] The 'ideology' of a bureau is essentially a limited one compared to that of a political party but, in presenting a cohesive *raison d'être* for the bureau and its work for society, it helps to unify the membership of the bureau and to attract support from clientele and those whose political guidance is essential if the bureau is to be allowed to continue and possibly expand its work. The final point of substance made is an imaginative defence of the present level of bureaucracy in modern democratic societies, a level made necessary by the complexity and rate of technological change in those societies and, on the whole, enlarging choice without inhibiting freedom to any marked degree. There are dangers of a change in this balance but they have yet to be seen outside a few totalitarian regimes.

A bald summary does *Inside Bureaucracy* less than justice, for it is one of the most comprehensive studies of the inner workings of the bureaucracy yet to appear. It leans heavily on much of the earlier writing but scores on the range of reference-points for the model and the large number of hypotheses which, like his list in the theoretical construct of democracy which formed the core of Downs' earlier writing, supply one with a number of possible schemes for future case-studies. Much depends on the degree to which one accepts his initial trio of assumptions cited above. A degree of rationality would seem to be acceptable in the context of bureaucratic decision-making, probably more than with the voter–politician relationship which is central to the 'economic theory of democracy'; in the case of the administrator, conscious limitation of choice takes place while he is also trained to make choices to a degree rare among the voting population at large. 'Self-interest' is a more abstract concept than it seems at first sight, for it depends on the filtering process of the individual intellect when more than the basic 'wants' are introduced to the argument. Since change in bureaucracy is often a slow process, it may be difficult for the individual official to decide whether a specific act is directly in his long-term self-interest, even if he is, say, a convinced 'climber'. As we have remarked elsewhere, perception of self-interest is an area where a great deal of basic fieldwork is needed if political science is to use the concept accurately. Case-studies have tended to confirm the validity of the third of his three assumptions (linking formal and informal structures) and there is therefore a reasonably sound basis for Downs' reasoning, though one might not always want to carry through with him to the conclusions cited. For example, the evidence relating the size of bureaux with their relative efficiency still seems too inadequate to allow his rather sweeping generalization in this area. As a look at the 'inside' of bureaucracy though, this is a good summary of our present knowledge.

Given the advances made by the 'decision-making' school, what more is there to say about the administrative structures of the modern state? Unfortunately, quite a lot. Apart from the tentative nature of much of the theory engaged in the internal analysis of bureaucracies, more needs to be known about the relationship between the bureaucracy and the remainder of the political system. Something of a start has been made in this direction by the attempts of the last decade or so to analyze whole political systems, and a certain amount has been discovered about possible relationships in this way.

Bureaucracy and systems theory

In an earlier chapter we reviewed the contribution made by certain theorists to an appreciation of how the political system works as a unit performing a variety of specific functions. As yet, the 'systems theorists' have made comparatively sporadic references to the sub-system that carries on administration in the polity, but these do give some idea of what sort of contribution this type of analysis can make to setting the bureaucracy into the political system as a whole. Systems approaches lean very heavily on the sociological analysis of the so-called 'functionalists', which is why, once again, one needs to use them as a starting-point. In fact, Parsons himself pointed out in a book published in 1960 that: 'Most of the recent literature in the field of formal organization has tended to deal with internal structure and processes: such problems as line authority, staff organization, and the process of decision-making.'[58] Of the material which he examines, in this context, it is especially that of the external relations of the organization which interests the political scientist.

In some of his writing Parsons gives the impression that he distinguishes little between elective and appointive members of the political hierarchy. In a fairly recent paper he states that 'the bureaucratic or administrative subsystem . . . is concerned primarily with the implementation of collective goals', but goes on to describe this as the set of goals that the whole polity is geared to, such as the maintenance of internal order or the setting up of specific policies in the field of welfare.[59] As one would expect, he does follow the Weberian concept of responsibility, suggesting that legitimacy can only be accorded the bureaucracy if there is some overriding control or ethos present; presumably, in a democratic system, this would be provided by the various constitutional checks from elective institutions, and in a Marxist state by the collective will expressed through the party (or party bureaucracy?).

Parsons' pupil, Robert Merton, a more pragmatic theorist as we saw in an earlier chapter, does not try to place the bureaucracy in a great scheme for he has none as such, but he does develop a minor theoretical model of the bureaucrat's relationship with the public. This arises from his observation about the bureaucratic personality and the 'displacement of goals' whereby, as Merton sees it, the means become the ends, that is, those characteristics of bureaucracy with which we are now familiar (discipline, depersonalization, hierarchical power) tend to produce a reversal of roles in that the bureaucrat, instead of serving the members of the particular society to which he belongs, becomes an arrogant surrogate for a master. For Merton, the discovery of informal group activity is proof of the existence of primary group activity inside the bureaucracy, which he regards as 'a secondary, formal group'. The norms of the bureaucracy as a whole tend to exercize a restraining effect on the influence of primary group activity in case it 'takes over' and destroys the structure itself. Personalized relationships may develop inside the organization, but rarely do so between bureaucratic and client, for this is to invite disintegration of the bureaucracy.[60] There is certainly some evidence for this point of view in the case-study material, but it is far from certain that impersonality between bureaucrat and client is as universal as Merton suggests. His example of the English employment exchange is extreme in one sense in that the unemployed man is in a position of supplication and sensitivity. Where the bureaucrat is seeking help and information from his clientele (for example, when a government department is trying to frame a new policy affecting its clientele), the relationship may be less one-sided, almost that of equals, for the atmosphere is one of mutual benefit without any master–servant overtone.

When the political scientist adopted systems approaches and the concept of 'function', it was obvious that he would be more preoccupied with the way in which parts of the political structure operated than was the sociologist with his wider preoccupations. Now that sociologists have tended to move away from functional approaches, it is less likely that we can learn a great deal from them about general problems of interrelation inside the political system. Those few political scientists who have tried their hand at macro-theory have often found it difficult to fit the bureaucracy into a notional scheme explaining interrelationships on a functional or similar basis. Both Easton and Almond refer to the place of the bureaucracy as a vital structure in the political system, although Easton's citations are comparatively rare and brief. He describes public (and some private) bureaucracies as important 'gatekeepers' in the process of want conversion, with the governmental bureaucracy being included for most purposes in that general structural and authoritative part of the political system known simply as 'the authorities'.[61] In a diagrammatic representation of the system used to illustrate the concept of feedback, an 'administrative agency' appears as one of the four output-producers on the threshold between the system itself and the point at which outputs travel outwards into the general social system.[62] In the course of a reference to the administrative subsystem, Easton seems to hint at the variety of functional positions that it can assume in the political system. This implied multifunctionality also appears in one of Almond's early sketches towards a macro-theory in which he shows how the bureaucracy can be an 'associational' interest group, can aggregate interests, and be active in the communications process as well as fulfil its chief role as applier of rules in developed societies (though sometimes appearing as a rule-maker in less-developed ones).[63] Since then, Almond has treated the bureaucracy more fully, emphasizing two points, namely multifunctionality and the powerful position held by the bureaucracy in many political systems:

> Bureaucracies dominate the output end of the political conversion process; they are indispensable in the rule-making and adjudication processes as well as influential in the political processes of interest

articulation, aggregation and communication. Other governmental structures, such as political executives, legislatures, and courts, must be viewed in relation to the functioning of the bureaucracy. They cannot be functionally effective save through bureaucracy.[64]

We have quoted Almond at length here because he expresses both a sweeping view of the potential power of the bureaucracy and gives some idea how the analysis of whole systems can illuminate its especial position. Looking at the bureaucracy in this way has the advantage of pulling together a great deal of the previous research work, both the case-studies and the more theoretical approaches. The idea of output-domination by the bureaucracy involves the monopoly of rule-enforcement by bureaucrats and most observation would tend to reinforce this. It might well be argued though that there is no fundamental reason why the output side should not include a function of rule-enforcement as well as those of making, application and adjudication. 'Separation of powers' theory, as we saw in an earlier examination of Almond's theories, is an evident influence on the output categories used in the general Almond model. That rule-enforcement is subsumed under the power of applying or executing rules or laws, with a genuflection in the direction of adjudication, is no reason for considering this tripartite division as being immutable. The importance of bureaucratic power in the modern state, barely touched upon by early 'separation of powers' theorists, tempts one to delineate outputs under four heads, rather than three, with the bureaucracy dominating the administrative or rule-enforcement function. Even if one accepts a wider range of output functions, the importance of the bureaucracy at other stages of the process in any systems analysis is still evident even if the position is as one of many in, say, the input stages of a political system. Systems theory does give some shape to the interrelationship between the bureaucracy and the rest of the political system. It also emphasizes that, among the structural components of political systems in modern society, the bureaucracy is the most pervasive and therefore one of the most powerful.

Bureaucracy and political development

As well as the general impetus given to the analysis of political systems by the internationalization of comparative government in the post-war period, the particular study of individual political phenomena has also received a fillip from this direction. Some of the most interesting and useful attempts to explain bureaucratic power and its setting in the political system stem from the consideration of the administrative structures of 'new' governments, those controlling political life in countries that have received independence from metropolitan rule in the post-1945 years. When political scientists attempted to transfer the received Western methodology of bureaucratic and organizational analysis to the administrative structures of these new nations, certain discrepancies were soon apparent. The models would not quite fit with the facts. Research has now produced enough generalizations about the position of the bureaucracy in the newer nations for us to recognize that the earlier models have to be modified to take account of what at first seemed deviant behaviour but is now recognized as being rational in terms of the situation in these nations. This has become allied to the general concept that the systems analysis approach is only really useful if it can explain the way in which political systems 'change', a term which may be less ethnocentric than 'develop', and the manner in which institutions alter, suddenly appear, or otherwise contribute to this process that we attempt to define and explain. The administrative sub-system is one of the more important ones in the modern state and therefore its isolation for special study in those political systems that are trying to become 'modern' in some way is hardly surprising.

Before examining some of the more detailed theory linking bureaucracy and what we will still term political development, it is worth noting that the discussion of the place of bureaucracy in developing countries had led to yet another round of questioning of the fundamental beliefs about bureaucracy that have been developed from the original Weberian model. Weber had seemed to make an administrative system a prerequisite of a 'modern' society as that concept was understood in the first few decades of the twentieth century. Most of the theorists who followed him into bureaucratic analysis, whatever they may have disagreed with in his formulation, agreed with this and the allied concept that bureaucracy represented rationality as far as any political system could possess this attribute. Yet a writer like S. N. Eisenstadt could examine a whole class of pre-modern societies where a form of bureaucracy came to be a highly important source of strength—the 'historical bureaucratic empire'—and show how the changes that these societies underwent usually took place because of social and economic forces unique to each and the internal contradictions that often resulted. In many of the examples taken by Eisenstadt, the bureaucracy seems to have worked against 'modernization' in the sense that we mostly use the term, either by resisting the enlargement of social mobility or (as in pre-Revolutionary France) by becoming a conserving aristocracy.[65] The late Peter Nettl went even further. Whereas Eisenstadt recognizes that even in the 'historical bureaucratic empires' the bureaucracy could carry out a certain amount of 'initial modernization', Nettl, when examining the concept of political mobilization, tends to downgrade the contribution that the bureaucracy makes to this process. Quoting from Crozier's case-study in particular, he finds the bureaucracy as generally understood to be essentially conservative and 'dysfunctional . . . in a change-oriented modern society'; that is, in fairly static societies like Eisenstadt's empires, the bureaucracy would be likely to accord with the functions of the system.[66] He is able to do this by distinguishing bureaucracy as a concept from administration in general; for him, it is the structural representation of the concensus and tends to be prominent in societies where change is not greatly desired.

Peter Nettl was one of the few English contributors to the theories of political analysis in the 1960s and much of his writing is persuasive; however, to state that the bureaucracy can never work for change is patently overstating a thin case. Although he draws heavily on Crozier, he glides over the emphasis that Crozier places on the unique cultural context in which the French administrative system is rooted and the admission that such a context may be overriding for the primary orientation of the bureaucracy. When considering the part that bureaucracy plays in certain post-colonial societies, Eisenstadt insists that the bureaucracy can play a major part in modernization because of its unique position as a reservoir of trained personnel who can seek appropriate social and economic objectives for the nation and which can also exert the necessary pressure to carry them through. He goes as far as to say: 'The emerging bureaucracies are also the major instruments of social change and political socialization in their respective countries.'[67]

It seems likely that the attitude of an administrative system to change depends on a number of variables. These will consist of the social and political context in which it finds itself, the behavioural characteristics that have developed as a result of its history and the specific attitudes of its political directors. Where a set of administrators have taken their values from a metropolitan culture, it is quite likely that a limit will be instinctively placed on the amount of change that is found to be acceptable. In Burma a Westernized administration achieved some degree of modernization, yet lost its self-confidence to some degree when faced with nationalist politicians after independence, men who wanted modernization to take new and unfamiliar forms; in such a context friction was inevitable, leading eventually to a ruling bureaucracy in the shape of army rule.[68]

What has come to be the received view of the place of bureaucracy in developing countries can be found by correlating the contributions to La Palombara's collection of papers on the subject by the better-known American theorists of the 1960s. The political systems of countries emerging from the tutelage of metropolitan states are often lacking in that diverse range of institutions that one has become accustomed to studying in most Western systems. Where a working bureaucracy has been left intact, this can enter the vacuum and carry a disproportionate amount of the responsibility for economic development especially; there are obvious limitations on its encouragement of what was then regarded as 'pluralist' institutional development on the political front. The Weberian model, assumed to fit in broad outlines the bureaucracies of the Western world, is found to be too ethnocentric for some of the administrative contours found in non-Western countries and elements considered to be dysfunctional in the West may be functional elsewhere.[69] The existence of corruption is a case in point. At some stages of development a degree of corruption may aid the integrative function of the bureaucracy, if only as a temporary expedient, a possibility which cuts right across the virtues of incorruptibility and impartiality that are claimed for the best of Western administrative systems and which forms part of the 'ideal type' of bureaucracy from which our theorizing has largely developed. As La Palombara puts it: 'The point seems to be that classical bureaucracy is not necessarily a precondition of development.'[70]

Although classical bureaucracy may not be a precondition, some form of bureaucracy obviously is and it is the exact nature of this new form that one hopes to see delineated by future research.

The only fully formulated bureaucratic theory that seems completely orientated towards political development has been that variant of functionalism associated with the name of Fred W. Riggs. This is known as the 'theory of prismatic society' for, unlike any other political theorist, Riggs has gone to the science of optics for his analogy. He compares the development of societies with the passage of light through a prism; on one side the light is white or fused, whereas on the other it is split into the rainbow colours—it is diffracted. Riggs views the range of world societies in terms of this metaphor by postulating two ideal types of society based on the concepts of fusion and diffraction of functions. At the one extreme, one basic institution carries on all the requisite functions for the society, while at the other, diffracted, extreme each function has its own structure (although Riggs sometimes uses 'structure' and 'institution' almost interchangeably, the former is the more all-inclusive term). Since these are ideal-type situations, they are rarely, if ever, found in the real world, and most societies are in an in-between situation which can be likened to the position inside the prism where light is beginning to be diffracted but before it has been completely separated out. The industrialized societies are relatively diffracted while those we consider to be traditional or still awaiting development are relatively fused.[71]

The point of all this for the administrator is that at the one extreme —the 'fused' one—there will be no independent administrative structure, and that at the other, diffracted, extreme the administrative function will be carried out by one structure as a specialism. In prismatic societies a hybrid situation occurs, and this leads to certain behavioural characteristics that are quite marked in non-Western societies where the pace of change, through the prism so to speak, has suddenly accelerated. Riggs uses a considerable number of neologisms resulting in a range of jargon that many find unattractive. For the prismatic bureaucracy, he uses the term 'sala', a Spanish word used in South America; the 'sala' has some of the connotations of fused and diffracted administrative structures. Thus some specialism is beginning to appear but impartiality is usually absent, and the client is treated in a discriminatory way depending on the influence that he can bring to bear on the sala official or on his ascribed status, the two often going hand in hand. The result is rather unsavoury:

> Corruption becomes institutionalized in the sala. Some officials enjoy positions which enable them to extort bribes and other favors from interest groups. Part of this extra intake must be passed on to superiors or influential members of the prismatic bureau who furnish protection.[72]

There is a degree of normative thinking in all of this since the presumption must be that with diffraction come those necessary checks on the bureaucracy which will cut down or even eradicate corruption; adequate salaries and an emphasis on achievement—orientation by means of examinations for entrance and promotion are two structurally simple, if politically difficult, methods to aid diffraction in the bureaucracies of 'new' nations. Elsewhere, Riggs has forecast that these bureaucracies may have to find their salvation by methods other than those used in the West, but that the polities concerned cannot 'escape the necessity for building viable political institutions—whether democratic or despotic—to control their burgeoning bureaucracies'.[73]

There is a consensus among these relatively few writers who have examined the bureaucracy in the developing nations about the need for a great deal more in the way of specific case-study material on the working of the structure under these especial conditions. Riggs' concepts are the most sophisticated yet to come to light, even if they are weighted down with jargon that has not been widely accepted as yet. Certainly, any model which attempts to describe the role of bureaucracies in the 'newer' nations will need to show the relative weight of bureaucratic power at the differing stages of development and the interrelation of the administrative structure with the other structures at each stage. It may not need to depend on the functional differentiation developed by Riggs but will need to supply clear referents for those roles that the bureaucracy is called upon to assume at each level of development. It is unlikely that any model will ignore the functional demands that call for a body like the bureaucracy which can provide the necessary degree of mobilization for the new nation; under certain conditions, for example, it is noticeable how military 'counter-bureaucracies' assume much of the mobilization initiative.

Conclusion

There is probably a wider range of empirical study and theory relating to the working of the bureaucracy than with any other set of partial theories in political analysis. There is certainly little tendency to underrate its potential power today; if anything, the danger lies in the reverse, in the temptation to see the bureaucracy as an inhibiting force in the development of responsible political institutions. Although one no longer believes that administrative structures are essentially neutral, it is equally unlikely that we need to go to the other extreme and believe that they are uncontrollable. Except in unusual or temporary phases of political development, there tends to be some counterbalance to the power of the bureaucracy, even if only in terms of a quasi-bureaucracy like the army or a monolithic political party.

We now know a great deal about the behaviour of bureaucrats under a range of conditions. What is probably needed is a convincing model which will set the bureaucracy against a number of variables in the political system and suggest the relationship between these and certain patterns of behaviour. The unit is likely to be the role of the individual and the organization behaving in a corporate fashion, although there is still likely to be some underlying functional concept until we find a better frame of reference. There will have to be room among the variables for some measurement of stages of political development, perhaps expressed in the relative salience of other institutions at a particular point in time. The degree of expectations engendered inside and outside the bureaucracy in terms of what an administrative organization in government can or should effect in the direction of political outputs will inevitably be conditioned by cultural factors, which is why a basic understanding of this latter concept is so fundamental to any scheme of systemic analysis in politics. Much of the more recent writing that we have reviewed points the way towards these general goals, and it is likely that the future study of bureaucracy will be among the more precise areas of delineation in the field of political analysis.

CHAPTER 8
CONCLUSION

If, as we suggested at the start of this book, there were some 'revolutionary' aspects about the intrusion of behavioural approaches into the study of politics, this revolutionary wave has not only passed by and been assimilated into the mainstream but has, more recently, bred its own counter-revolution. In its turn, the impetus of this latter phase seems to have been partially spent. The attack on behavioural political science had two strands at least. One came from those older political scientists who have never felt at home with the move to downgrade the philosophic element in the study of political phenomena, the other from a younger set who equated the value-free quest with the American political attitudes associated, in their view, with neo-colonialism and the Vietnam war.

The older group of critics based their standpoint on the excesses of behaviouralism as they saw them, principally the claim to create a value-free discipline out of the study of politics. As was mentioned in the introductory chapter, '*wertfrei*' is a claim which touched a nerve in many who feel that it is difficult or impossible to separate out facts and values at any time in the study of a political process. This viewpoint has been expressed eloquently by several writers, notably by Charles Taylor, barely one of the 'older' generation but a major sceptic about the 'thesis that political science is value neutral'. One would now tend to agree that the mere choice of subjects to study involves the value-judgment that each is worthy of the attention of the academic mind, that selection itself is a type of value-position and that each trained student of political activity will, despite his training, bring a set of values to both selection and study of events, beliefs and other phenomena making up the political system. As suggested in Chapter Three, it is difficult to be certain what Weber, the most important name associated with the early quest for neutrality in political science, intended as the limits of value-freedom; it may well have been an aspiration which he realized could never be completely attained. Even Taylor recognized the utility of this as a goal: 'There is nothing to stop us making the greatest attempts to avoid bias and achieve objectivity. Of course, it is hard, almost impossible, and precisely because our values are also at stake. But it helps, rather than hinders, the cause to be aware of this.'[1] Some disputants are now pushing this argument even further, maintaining that neither the normative nor the empirical theorists have correctly understood the problem which, it is argued, involves not so much the state of mind of the student of politics as the need to be sure about the subject-matter of the study. In other words, they pinpoint the difficulty inherent in producing a satisfactory definition of politics. Once such a definition is produced and generally accepted (because it will satisfy all the logical criteria) it will be self-evident, so the argument continues, whether or not description and evaluation can be separated or whether they must remain intertwined.[2] Although there are super-ficial attractions about such an approach, the evident difficulties that have been encountered in elaborating a definition that would command general acceptance almost preclude this method of settling the 'is–ought' controversy. It may be that, as Professor Mackenzie has contended, one should 'proceed ostensively, seeking the meaning of "politics" in the speech and perceptions of ordinary men', although many of us would retain the hope that quite useful definitions like David Easton's 'authoritative allocation of values' could be refined still further and sharpen our perception of the boundaries of political activity.[3] At least there are indications that the normative theorists, perhaps comforted by the disillusion that is now general about grandiose claims for grand theory, are prepared to settle for eclecticism and coexist with those who still prefer the emphasis on indicating 'how it works' rather than that on 'how it should work'.

The controversy that surfaced in the later 1960s overlapped the earlier one to an extent but contained some new elements. In our comments on democratic theory we noted the attack on pluralism as a specifically American ideology mounted by some of the members of the Caucus for a New Political Science. The Caucus, founded in 1967, had as its aim:

> . . . the reformation of American political science. It hopes to stimulate a redirection of the scholarly energies of the profession

into a sustained and critical concern for what is happening in America today. . . . It believes that, in the light of our contemporary situation, political scientists should be asking serious, even shocking questions—questions which for too long went unasked, much less answered.[4]

Although it was soon opposed by other factions inside the American Political Science Association who feared that the Caucus was attempting a take-over, Marxist style, and the acute divisions of the late 1960s now seem to have settled back into more normal patterns of scholarly dispute, the criticisms voiced have left their mark.

The chief charges laid by Caucus members against American political science and, by implication, against the behaviouralist orientation of its leading practitioners were its complacency, its conservatism, its government links and its irrelevance to current political problems, the latter being perhaps the basic and most pervading sin in the eyes of this group. Certainly, many research contracts were being funnelled through political science departments by overt and covert government agencies at this time and this must have had some effect on the choice of research subjects, thus affecting the 'value positions' of some political scientists. The total amount of this funding may have been exaggerated and will have had only a marginal effect on methodology itself. It seems odd to describe the techniques of behaviouralism as being essentially conservative since it was an attempt to curtail the influence of held values on research, but the genesis for this is the belief that many of the conclusions of behavioural research support the status quo, while the Caucus critique comes from those who feel that radical change is necessary in the American system and in political systems that resemble it. Lewis Lipsitz has tabulated what he believes to be an alternative course to behaviouralism which includes a call for broader standards for evaluating regimes, chiefly in terms of welfare measures provided for their citizens, the exposure of the bureaucratic and oligarchic tendencies in American life, the 'restructuring' of political life so as to encourage radical movements and for a 'new burst of utopian thinking' which will reorganize social life.[5] Much of this attitude seems an outcrop of the subculture of the young in the late 1960s; it is mostly highly charged, emotive and completely normative. There is of course nothing wrong with that as a social attitude but there is as much danger in this viewpoint achieving only the results implied in the premises as there is when the research worker is guided by excessively behaviouralistic methodology. Marvin Surkin stated that 'American society is in need of a radical reorganization of social priorities'.[6] Many of us would agree with this and add the majority of other political systems to the list, but to link this, as Surkin and other critics of behaviouralism do, with the rejection of the style of relatively dispassionate inquiry that American political science developed in the mid-twentieth century is surely a confusion of separate ends. It used to be said in defence of Congressional investigating committees that 'to legislate, one must investigate' (something that is likely to be more accepted in the era of the Ervin committee than it was in Joe McCarthy's heyday). Similarly, 'to prescribe, we should first describe' and there is still a need not only for information but for analytic tools with which to present facts in a meaningful manner.

As suggested early on, it may be that one is running after a straw man in taking this counter-attack on behaviouralism so seriously, just as the critics sought straw men in those who in their view took behaviouralism to extremes. That the counter-attack has had some impact is illustrated by David Easton's celebrated Presidential Address to the APSA in 1969. Professor Easton recognized that there was some validity in the cry for research to be more relevant to the problems of the real world and for political scientists to 'prescribe and to act so as to improve political life according to humane criteria'.[7] However, he recognized this as a challenge and not a threat to the technical expertise that the political scientist has built up over the years and which it is not necessary to abandon. The 'post-behavioural era', in his view, 'supports and extends behavioral methods and techniques by seeking to make their substantive implications more cogent for the problems of our times'.[8] One concrete suggestion made as a result of this gloss on post-behaviouralism is that less time should be spent, in Easton's view, on small-scale empirical inquiry and more on examining the ethical basis of political action.[9] He defends behaviouralism and the methodology flowing from it and the change from his earlier writing is one of emphasis only, a recognition that the times demand a somewhat altered strategy or allocation of time from the political scientist.

What is certain is that few now believe in the 'end of ideology' thesis and the attitude that there is little division in Western society about the ends of political activity. There are dangers, though, in a too-ready desire to be guided by value-frameworks when attempting to examine political systems and their components. The tendency for research to be conditioned by the preconceptions of the researchers is a stick which the critics of behaviouralism have used to beat its practitioners mightily during the last few years, but it cuts both ways, in that those who parade their value-systems as a paramount ingredient of their academic expertise must expect to meet with equal suspicion from those who try to keep ideology as a light injection in the mixture. Perhaps this can be achieved in the way in which William Connolly suggests: 'The responsible ideology is one in which a serious and continuing effort is made to elucidate publicly all of the factors involved in its formulation and in which a similar effort is made to test the position at strategic points by *all* available means.'[10] Only if this is done can the academic credentials of political scientists who favour an ideological guiding star be kept intact.

If the 'post-behavioural era' has now begun, it should be easier to define what 'behaviouralism' is (or was) than when Dahl, in the article cited at the beginning of this book, claimed that 'one can say with considerable confidence what it is not, but it is difficult to say what it is'.[11] It is doubtful whether even now one can be completely exact for there have been several meanings of the term, all overlapping to some extent. A possible list would include:

1. The study of political behaviour as a way of understanding the nature of politics.
2. The development of a value-free political science.
3. The elaboration of quantitative and other analytical methods to make for exactitude in the study of politics.
4. The creation of a 'science' of politics which would be as rigorous as the natural sciences.
5. The establishment of a comprehensive explanatory theory of political systems and political behaviour.

Because of the organization of the text, we have touched on some of these points much more than others and one (the quantitative method) hardly at all. Yet the value of this 'movement' or 'mood'— to use Dahl's term—is dependent on the many able minds who were able to find a challenge in the problems that its early practitioners uncovered. If, like Icarus, some of them flew a little too near the sun, they were comparatively few, and the rest, like Daedalus, have avoided disaster and have produced an enormous amount of constructive work which has enriched the discipline. One should remember the state of political science before the new 'American Revolution'. Narrow institutional and legal frameworks *have* been superseded and, subsequently, the dangers of basing all on 'inputism' have been recognized. In the future, one can envisage a more freebooting and eclectic approach to problem-solving in political science, merging strands of behaviouralism and the reactions to it that we have described. The overwhelming stamp of American political science—and therefore much of the non-American patterns which have been influenced by it —is still behavioural and will remain so for some time. In the most limited sense of the term, interest in political behaviour will survive as long as an interest in political arrangements remains and that would seem to be for a very long time indeed.

NOTES

Chapter One Introduction

1 Robert A. Dahl 'The Behavioral Approach in Political Science. Epitaph for a Monument to a Successful Protest' *American Political Science Review* vol. LV (December 1961) reprinted in Nelson W. Polsby, Robert A. Dentler, Paul A. Smith *Politics and Social Life* Boston, Houghton Mifflin (1963) p. 23
2 See below, Conclusion, pp. 179 *et seq.*
3 For an example of this which relates to all of the social sciences, see Peter Winch *The Idea of a Social Science* Routledge & Kegan Paul (1958)
4 Benjamin Disraeli *Coningsby* (1844) John Lehmann (1948) p. 238
5 Richard Hofstadter *The Age of Reform* New York, Knopf (1955); Bernard Crick *The American Science of Politics* Routledge & Kegan Paul (1959); A. J. Beitzinger *A History of American Political Thought* New York, Dodd, Mead (1972) ch. 21, etc.
6 The best-known example in print of this is Daniel Bell *The End of Ideology* New York, Free Press (1960)

Chapter Two The Search for Value-Free Political Theory

1 David Easton *The Political System* New York, Knopf (1953) p. 202
2 Graham Wallas *Human Nature in Politics* Constable (1948) p. 38. A recent biographer argues that 'Wallas himself remained poised between two worlds—having pushed the Victorian assumptions of his youth into uncharted territory, but never finding rest in these new lands of thought, and ending a critic of his successors.' Martin J. Weiner *Between Two Worlds: The Political Thought of Graham Wallas* Oxford, Clarendon Press (1971), p. 216. This argument, although interesting, seems relatively unimportant when placed alongside the remarkable fact of Wallas's foresight in perceiving a new line of development for the study of politics.
3 ibid., pp. 161–4, 150–52
4 ibid., p. 136
5 ibid., pp. 5–11
6 Graham Wallas *The Great Society* Macmillan (1914) pp. 341, 45
7 Arthur Fisher Bentley, ed. Peter H. Odegaard *The Process of Govern-*

ment Cambridge, Mass., Harvard University Press (1967) p. 208

8 A. J. Beitzinger *A History of American Political Thought* New York, Dodd, Mead (1972) p. 503

9 Charles B. Hagan 'The Group in Political Science' in Richard W. Taylor (ed.) *Life, Language, Law: Essays in Honor of Arthur F. Bentley* Kent, Antioch Press, Kent State University Press (1957) p. 121

10 Bentley, op. cit., p. 222

11 Robert MacIver *The Web of Government* Macmillan (1947) p. 220

12 ibid., p. 223

13 ibid., p. 229

14 ibid., p. 348

15 Leo Weinstein 'The Group Approach' in Herbert J. Storing *Essays in the Scientific Study of Politics* New York, Holt, Rinehart & Winston (1962), p. 220

16 Paul F. Cress *Social Sciences and the Idea of Process: The Ambiguous Legacy of Arthur F. Bentley* Urbana, University of Illinois Press (1970) p. 182

17 Arthur F. Bentley *Makers, Users and Masters* Syracuse, Syracuse University Press (1969) p. 257 *et seq.*

18 David B. Truman *The Governmental Process* New York, Knopf (1951) p. ix. (There is now a second edition, 1971, with a useful Introduction.)

19 ibid., p. 106

20 ibid., p. viii

21 ibid., pp. 210, 219–20

22 Earl Latham *The Group Basis of Politics* Ithaca, Cornell University Press (1952) p. 10

23 ibid., p. 1

24 ibid., pp. 12–13

25 Bertram M. Gross *The Legislative Struggle: A Study in Social Combat* New York, McGraw-Hill (1953), p. 10

26 Walter Lippmann *A Preface to Politics* New York, Mitchell Kennerley (1913) p. 106

27 Reinhold Niebuhr quoted in E. L. and F. H. Schapasmeier *Walter Lippmann, Philosopher-Journalist* Washington DC, Public Affairs Press (1969) p. 136

28 Lippmann, op. cit., p. 306

29 Charles E. Merriam *New Aspects of Politics* Chicago, University of Chicago Press (1925, 1931) p. xv. (A third edition was published long after Merriam's death in 1953.)

30 ibid., pp. 52–3

31 ibid., p. 125

32 ibid., pp. 3–4

33 ibid., pp. xxi

34 Stuart A. Rice *Quantitative Methods in Politics* New York, Knopf (1928) p. 17

35 ibid., p. 30

36 G. E. G. Catlin *The Science and Method of Politics* New York, Knopf (1927) p. 200

37 George Catlin *For God's Sake, Go: An Autobiography* Gerrards Cross, Colin Smythe (1972) p. 60

38 See for example Robert Dahl 'The Concept of Power' in Polsby, Dentler, Smith, op. cit., pp. 116–19

39 Charles E. Merriam *Political Power* New York, McGraw-Hill (1934) p. 10
40 Charles E. Merriam *Systematic Politics* New Haven, Yale University Press (1944) p. viii
41 Harold D. Lasswell *Psychopathology and Politics* New York, Free Press (1930) Viking Press (1960) p. 184
42 Harold D. Lasswell *Politics: Who Gets What, When, How* New York, McGraw-Hill (1936) p. 3
43 Harold D. Lasswell *The Analysis of Political Behaviour* Routledge & Kegan Paul (1948) p. 17
44 Harold D. Lasswell *Power and Personality* New York, Norton (1948) p. 11
45 Harold Lasswell and Abraham Kaplan *Power and Society: A Framework for Political Inquiry* New Haven, Yale University Press (1950) p. xi
46 ibid., p. 75
47 Heinz Eulau 'H. D. Lasswell's Development Analysis' *Western Political Quarterly,* vol. XI (June 1958) pp. 229–42 (Bobbs-Merrill Reprint PS-74 p. 241). Also see Eulau's 'The Maddening Methods of Harold D. Lasswell: Some Philosophical Underpinnings' in Arnold Rogow (ed.) *Politics, Personality and Social Science in the Twentieth Century* Chicago, University of Chicago (1969)
48 Bernard Crick *The American Science of Politics* Routledge & Kegan Paul (1959) *passim*
49 Quoted in Arnold A. Rogow *Graham Wallas* in The International Encyclopaedia of the Social Sciences, Crowell Collier and Macmillan (1968) vol. XVI, p. 440

Chapter Three Sociology and Political Thought

1 H. H. Gerth and C. Wright Mills *From Max Weber* Routledge & Kegan Paul (1948) Introduction, p. 56
2 W. G. Runciman *A Critique of Max Weber's Philosophy of Social Science* Cambridge University Press (1972) p. 75
3 Gerth and Mills, op. cit., p. 78 ('Politics as a Vocation')
4 Max Weber *The Theory of Social and Economic Organization* (Pt. I of *Wirtschaft und Gesellschaft*) transl. A. M. Henderson and Talcott Parsons, New York, Free Press (1947, 1964) p. 153
5 Max Weber *Gesammelte Politische Schriften,* transl. and quoted in L. M. Lachmann *The Legacy of Max Weber* Heinemann (1970) pp. 118–19
6 Weber *The Theory of Social and Economic Organization* p. 152
7 In Otto Stammer (ed.) *Max Weber and Sociology Today* Oxford, Blackwell (1971) p. 100
8 Weber *The Theory of Social and Economic Organization* p. 110
9 Reinhard Bendix *Max Weber: An Intellectual Portrait* Methuen (1966) p. 292
10 Gerth and Mills, op. cit., pp. 78–9
11 ibid., p. 80

12 Talcott Parsons 'Value-Freedom and Objectivity' in Stammer, op. cit., p. 42

13 For example, see S. M. Eisenstadt *The Political Systems of Empires* New York, Free Press (1963, 1969) *passim*; Gabriel Almond and G. Bingham Powell *Comparative Politics* Boston, Little, Brown (1964) pp. 17, 44 etc.; Gabriel Almond and James S. Coleman *The Politics of Developing Areas* Princeton, Princeton University Press (1960) pp. 22, 57 etc.; David Easton *A Systems Analysis of Political Life* New York, Wiley (1965) pp. 301–2; Karl Deutsch *The Nerves of Government* New York, Free Press (1963, 1966) pp. 45–7

14 H. H. Brunn *Science, Values and Politics in Max Weber's Methodology* Copenhagen, Munksgaard (1972) p. 211

15 Reinhard Bendix and Guenther Roth *Scholarship and Partisanship*: *Essays on Max Weber* Berkeley and Los Angeles, University of California Press (1961) p. 173

16 Gerth and Mills, op. cit., pp. 262–3

17 Quoted by Bendix and Roth, op. cit., p. 49

18 This appears to be the conclusion drawn by Alan Dawe in 'The Relevance of Values' in Arun Sahay *Max Weber and Modern Sociology* Routledge & Kegan Paul (1971)

19 Runciman, op. cit., vols. III–IV, *passim*

20 In Stammer, op. cit., p. 79. Ralf Dahrendorf has also emphasized the contemporary relevance of Weber's ideas to the intellectual condition of German society then and perhaps now. Quoted in Ilse Dronberger *The Political Thought of Max Weber* New York, Appleton-Century-Crofts (1971) p. 65

21 Bronislaw Malinowski *A Scientific Theory of Culture and Other Essays* Chapel Hill, University of North Carolina Press (1944) p. 36

22 A. R. Radcliffe-Brown 'The Present Position of Anthropological Studies', a Presidential Address to the British Association for the Advancement of Science, Section H, 1931, p. 13, quoted in E. E. Evans-Pritchard *Social Anthropology* Cohen & West (1951) pp. 54–5

23 Bronislaw Malinowski *Sex, Culture and Myth* Hart-Davis (1962) p. 174

24 Evans-Pritchard, op. cit., p 58

25 A. R. Radcliffe-Brown, Preface to M. Fortes and E. E. Evans-Pritchard *African Political Systems* Oxford University Press (1940) p. xxii

26 ibid., pp. xxii–xxiii

27 I. Schapera *Government and Politics in Tribal Societies* Watts (1956) p. 219

28 A. R. Radcliffe-Brown *A Natural Science of Society* New York, Free Press (1948) p. 106

29 See Anthony Giddens (ed.) *Emile Durkheim: Selected Writings* Cambridge University Press (1972) and Steven Lukes *Emile Durkheim* Allen Lane, The Penguin Press (1973). Durkheim's views on democratic theory, 'pluralism' and the 'mandate' are especially worthy of examination by political scientists.

30 Note how C. Wright Mills in *The Sociological Imagination* (Oxford University Press 1959, 1967) manages to break down a page of Parsons's dense prose into a handful of sentences which express much the same thoughts (ch. 2).

31 Talcott Parsons *The Structure of Social Action* New York, McGraw-

Hill (1937) New York, Free Press (1949) p. 44

32 Talcott Parsons *The Social System* Routledge & Kegan Paul (1951) pp. 5–6

33 Talcott Parsons and Edward Shils (eds.) *Toward a General Theory of Action* Cambridge, Mass., Harvard University Press (1951) New York, Harper & Row (1962) p. 23

34 Parsons *The Social System* p. 27 and note

35 Percy Cohen *Modern Social Theory* Heinemann (1968) pp. 58–9. Cohen also cites Robert Merton's contention that 'functionalism could equally be used to justify a policy of total revolution' since interdependence suggests that one should destroy everything or nothing.

36 Talcott Parsons *Politics and Social Structure* New York, Free Press (1969) pp. 27, 29. Much of this part of the analysis draws its initial inspiration from one of Parsons' colleagues, Robert F. Bales, and his *Interaction Process Analysis* (Addison-Wesley Press 1950). See for example Parsons, Bales and Shils *Working Papers in the Theory of Action* New York, Free Press (1963) p. 64

37 Parsons *Politics and Social Structure* p. 444

38 ibid., p. 239

39 ibid., p. 239

40 S. M. Lipset *Politics and the Social Sciences* Oxford University Press (1969) p. 146

41 Initially, it is the 'actor' who must place himself near to these alternatives; he selects whichever direction he wishes to face along the spectra. See Parsons and Shils (eds.), op. cit., pp. 76–88

42 William C. Mitchell *The American Polity* New York, Free Press (1962); William C. Mitchell *Sociological Analysis and Politics* Englewood Cliffs, Prentice-Hall (1967)

43 Mitchell *Sociological Analysis and Politics* p. 83

44 ibid., *passim* esp. pp. 101–3, 125, 145

45 ibid., p. 171 and *passim*

46 J. P. Nettl 'The Concept of System in Political Science' *Political Studies* vol. XIV, no. 3 (October 1966) pp. 305–38

47 Nettl also used the Parsonian approach as the basis of his book *Political Mobilization* (Faber & Faber 1967), political culture being here analyzed in pattern-variable terms.

48 Robert K. Merton *Social Theory and Social Structure* New York, Free Press (1949, 1957) pp. 71–2

49 ibid., p. 82

Chapter Four   General Theory and the Political System

1 See the introduction to the second edition for Professor Easton's comparison of the situation then with that applying in the early 1970s.

2 David Easton *The Political System* New York, Knopf (1953, 2nd edn. 1971) p. 5

3 ibid., p. 134

4 ibid., p. 305

5 ibid., p. 232

6 David Easton 'The Analsis of Political Systems' *World Politics* vol.

IX, no. 3, reprinted in Roy Macridis and Bernard Brown *Comparative Politics* Homewood, Dorsey Press (1961) p. 85

7   ibid., p. 88
8   ibid., p. 85
9   ibid.
10   David Easton *A Framework for Political Analysis* Englewood Cliffs, Prentice-Hall (1965) p. 56
11   ibid., p. 83
12   ibid., pp. 92–3
13   ibid., p. 109
14   ibid., p. 132
15   David Easton *A Systems Analysis of Political Life* New York, Wiley (1965) p. 479
16   ibid., p. 475
17   ibid., p. 157
18   ibid., pp. 232, 299–300
19   ibid., p. 93 *et seq.*
20   ibid., ch. 20 *passim*
21   Gabriel Almond *Political Development: Essays in Heuristic Theory* Boston, Little, Brown (1970) p. 277
22   Gabriel Almond 'Comparative Political Systems' *Journal of Politics* (1956) p. 391 (also reprinted in Almond *Political Development: Essays in Heuristic Theory*)
23   ibid., p. 193
24   S. E. Finer 'Almond's Concept of "The Political System": A Textual Critique' *Government and Opposition* vol. V, no. 1 (1969–70) pp. 3–4
25   Samuel Patterson 'The Political Cultures of American States' *Journal of Politics* vol. 30, no. 1 (February 1968)
26   Gabriel Almond and Sidney Verba *The Civic Culture* Princeton, Princeton University Press (1963) Boston, Little, Brown (1965) p. 13
27   ibid., p. 32
28   Carole Pateman 'Political Culture, Political Structure and Political Change' *British Journal of Political Science* vol. 1, pp. 291–305
29   W. J. M. Mackenzie *Politics and Social Science* Harmondsworth, Penguin Books (1967) pp. 319–20
30   ibid., p. 321
31   Gabriel Almond 'A Functional Approach to Comparative Politics' in Almond and Coleman *The Politics of the Developing Areas* Princeton, Princeton University Press (1960) p. 33 *et seq.*
32   ibid., pp. 17–18
33   Gabriel Almond and G. Bingham Powell *Comparative Politics: A Developmental Approach* Boston, Little, Brown (1966) p. 24
34   Almond *Political Development: Essays in Heuristic Theory,* p. 283 (from the Benedict Lectures given at Boston University, March 1968)
35   ibid., p. 289
36   Gabriel Almond 'Approaches to Political Causation' in Gabriel Almond, Scott C. Flanagan and Robert Mundt *Crisis, Choice and Change: Historical Studies of Political Development* Boston, Little, Brown (1973) p. 20
37   Scott C. Flanagan 'Models and Methods of Analysis' in ibid., pp. 67 *et seq.*
38   Gabriel Almond and Robert Mundt 'Crisis, Choice and Change:

Some Tentative Conclusions' in ibid., p. 237

39 Lucian W. Pye *Politics, Personality and Nation Building: Burma's Search for Identity* New Haven, Yale University Press (1962) p. 11

40 Lucian W. Pye *Aspects of Political Development* Boston, Little, Brown (1966) p. 10

41 Zbigniew Brzezinski and Samuel P. Huntington *Political Power: U.S.A./U.S.S.R.* New York, Viking Press (1965) p. 436. See also Donald R. Kelley 'The Soviet Debate on the Convergence of the American and Soviet Systems' *Polity* vol. VI, no. 2 (Winter 1973) pp. 174–96

42 Morris Janowitz *The Military in the Political Development of New Nations* Chicago, University of Chicago Press (1964) p. 1. Other writing in this area includes Samuel Huntington *The Soldier and the State* Cambridge, Mass., Harvard University Press (1956); Henry Bienen (ed.) *The Military Intervenes* New York, Russell Sage (1968); Samuel Finer *The Man on Horseback* Pall Mall Press (1957). The place of the bureaucracy is touched on in Chapter Seven, below.

43 Samuel P. Huntington *Political Order in Changing Societies* New Haven, Yale University Press (1968) p. 400

44 ibid., p. 408

45 Karl Deutsch 'Social Mobilization and Political Development' in Jason L. Finkle and Richard W. Gable (eds.) *Political Development and Social Change* New York, Wiley (1966, 1971) pp. 385–6

46 ibid., p. 397

47 Karl Deutsch *The Nerves of Government* New York, Free Press (1963, 1966) ch. 11. Karl Deutsch *Politics and Government* Boston, Houghton Mifflin (1970) p. 5

48 David Apter *The Politics of Modernization* Chicago, University of Chicago Press (1965, 1967) p. 11

49 ibid., p. 387

50 David Apter *Some Conceptual Approaches to the Study of Modernization* Englewood Cliffs, Prentice-Hall (1968) p. 338

51 ibid., pp. 349n. Also Apter *The Politics of Modernization* chs. 11 and 12, *passim*

52 Karl von Vorys 'Use and Misuse of Development Theory' in James C. Charlesworth (ed.) *Contemporary Political Analysis* New York, Free Press (1967) p. 359

53 Kenneth S. Sherrill 'The Attitudes of Modernity' *Comparative Politics* vol. I, no. 2 (January 1969) pp. 184 *et seq.*

54 Dankwart A. Rustow 'Modernisation and Comparative Politics' *Comparative Politics* vol. 1, no. 1 (October 1968) p. 47

55 Barrington Moore Jr *Social Origins of Dictatorship and Democracy* (1966) Harmondsworth, Penguin Books (1969) p. 486

Chapter Five   Partial Theory I: Voting

1 See William Albig *Modern Public Opinion* New York, McGraw-Hill (1946) p. 181. The sample was huge (over 2 million) but, being based on mailing-lists derived from telephone directories and automobile registrations, it was a poor one. The error approached 20% of the

total vote (*Literary Digest* prediction for Roosevelt was 40.9%; actual vote was 60.2%).

2 Peter H. Rossi 'Four Landmarks in Voting Research' in Eugene Burdick and Arthur J. Brodbeck *American Voting Behavior* New York, Free Press (1959) pp. 8–15. Stuart A. Rice *Quantitative Methods in Politics* New York, Knopf (1928)

3 Rice, op. cit., pp. 92–3

4 ibid., pp. 154–5, 181

5 ibid., pp. 258 *et seq.*

6 Walter Lippmann *Public Opinion* (1922) New York, Free Press (1965) p. 11

7 Gosnell's books include: C. F. Merriam and H. F. Gosnell *Non-Voting: Causes and Methods of Control* Chicago, University of Chicago (1924); H. F. Gosnell *Getting Out the Vote* Chicago, University of Chicago (1927); H. F. Gosnell *Negro Politicians* Chicago, University of Chicago (1935); H. F. Gosnell *Machine Politics: Chicago Model* Chicago, University of Chicago (1937) plus numerous articles, etc.

8 Gosnell, *Machine Politics* p. 124

9 Paul F. Lazarsfeld, Bernard Berelson and Hazel Gaudet *The People's Choice* New York, Duell, Sloan & Pearce (1944) pp. 6–7

10 ibid., p. 137

11 ibid., p. 158

12 Bernard R. Berelson, Paul F. Lazarsfeld, William N. McPhee *Voting* Chicago, University of Chicago (1954) p. ix (Introduction)

13 ibid., p. 137

14 ibid., p. 279

15 ibid., ch. 13, *passim*

16 Angus Campbell, Gerald Gurin, Warren E. Miller *The Voter Decides* Row, Peterson (1954) p. x

17 ibid., p. 215

18 ibid., p. 135

19 ibid., pp. 17–18

20 ibid., p. 183

21 Angus Campbell, Philip E. Converse, Warren E. Miller, Donald E. Stokes *The American Voter* New York, Wiley (1960) p. 5

22 ibid., p. 558

23 ibid., p. 24

24 ibid., pp. 24–41

25 ibid., ch. 3

26 ibid., p. 67; see also pp. 524–8

27 ibid., p. 64

28 C. W. Wahl 'Psychiatry and the Group Sciences' in Burdick and Brodbeck, op. cit., pp. 270–72

29 See Angus Campbell 'The Passive Citizen' in Edward C. Dreyer and Walter A. Rosenbaum (eds.) *Political Opinion and Electoral Behavior* Belmont, Wadsworth (1966) pp. 175–88 (reprinted from *Acta Sociologica* vol. VI (1962) pp. 9–12

30 Angus Campbell, Philip E. Converse, Warren E. Miller, Donald E. Stokes *Elections and the Political Order* New York, Wiley (1966) Preface, p. vii

31 V. O. Key, Jr 'A Theory of Critical Elections' *Journal of Politics*

vol. XVII (February 1955) pp. 3–18; reprinted in (for example) Nelson W. Polsby, Robert A. Dentler, Paul A. Smith *Politics and Social Life* Boston, Houghton Mifflin (1963) pp. 465–75

32   Campbell, Converse, Miller and Stokes *The American Voter* pp. 531–5. The classification refers especially to the American context with a two-party situation but it can be adapted to a multi-party alternative.

33   Campbell, Converse, Miller and Stokes *Elections and the Political Order* p. 14

34   ibid., ch. 6 ('Religion and Politics: the 1960 Election')

35   ibid., p. 124

36   Walter Berns 'Voting Studies' in Herbert J. Storing (ed.) *Essays on the Scientific Study of Politics* New York, Holt, Rinehart & Winston (1962) p. 56

37   Louis H. Bean *Ballot Behavior, a Study of Presidential Elections* Washington DC, American Council on Public Affairs (1940); *How to Predict Elections* New York, Knopf (1948); *The Mid-Term Battle* Washington DC, Cantillon Books (1950); *The Art of Forecasting* New York, Random House (1969); *How to Predict the 1972 Election* Quadrangle Books (1972)

38   Gerhard Lenski *The Religious Factor* New York, Doubleday (1961) p. 158

39   ibid., p. 141

40   Laurence Fuchs *The Political Behavior of American Jews* New York, Free Press (1965) *passim*. Fuchs has also written on other aspects of the ethnic vote; cf. his *Presidential Politics in Boston;* 'The Irish Response to Stevenson' *New England Quarterly* (December 1957); *John Kennedy and American Catholicism* New York, Meredith Press (1967); and (as editor) *American Ethnic Politics* New York, Harper Torchbooks (1968)

41   ibid., ch. 9

42   John Fenton *The Catholic Vote* New Orleans, Hauser Press (1960)

43   Raymond E. Wolfinger 'The Development and Persistence of Ethnic Voting' in Fuchs *American Ethnic Politics*. Ruth C. Silva, using a regression analysis of the 1928 presidential election, showed that the most likely motive behind ethnic voting at that time was the identification with Smith of a growing body of voters whose common denominator was that their families were relatively recent immigrants to the United States. See Ruth C. Silva *Rum, Religion and Votes: 1928 Re-examined* Philadelphia, Pennsylvania State University Press (1962)

44   Ithiel da Sola Pool, Robert P. Abelson and Samuel L. Popkin *Candidates, Issues and Strategies: A Computer Simulation of the 1960 and 1964 Presidential Elections* Cambridge, Mass., MIT Press (1964, 1965) preface and ch. 1 *passim*

45   ibid., pp. 24–39

46   See, for example, Fred Greenstein *Children and Politics* New Haven, Yale University Press (1965)

47   The literature on the 'alienated voter' includes the following: Murray B. Levin and Murray Eden 'Political Strategy for the Alienated Voter' *Public Opinion Quarterly* (Spring 1962) pp. 47–63 (reprinted in Heinz Eulau (ed.) *Political Behavior in America* New York, Random House 1966 pp. 390–409); Murray B. Levin *The Alienated Voter* New York,

Holt, Rinehart & Winston (1962); Murray B. Levin with George Blackwood *The Compleat Politician* New York, Bobbs-Merrill (1962)

48 Levin, op. cit., pp. 61–2

49 There have been several critics of Levin's approach, perhaps the most penetrating being Allen Schick 'Massachusetts Politics: Political Reform and "Alienation" ' in Robert Robbins (ed.) *State Government and Political Responsibility 1963* Medford, Massachusetts, Tufts University (1963)

50 Levin and Eden, op. cit., p. 393

51 Herbert McClosky and John A. Schaar 'Psychological Dimensions of Anomy' *American Sociological Review* vol. XXX (February 1965) pp. 14–40, reprinted in Eulau, op. cit., pp. 466–514

52 ibid., pp. 473–4

53 Donald R. Matthews and James W. Prothro *Negroes and the New Southern Politics* New York, Harcourt, Brace & World (1966) p. 312 (chapter on 'Psychological Factors on Negro Political Participation'). Also see W. R. Keech *The Impact of Negro Voting* New York, Rand-McNally (1968) *passim*

54 Dwaine Marvick 'Political Socialization of the Negro' in Fuchs *American Ethnic Politics,* p. 265

55 V. O. Key Jr *Southern Politics* New York, Knopf (1949); Duane Lockard *New England State Politics* Princeton, Princeton University Press (1959); Samuel Lubell *The Future of American Politics* 2nd edn, New York, Doubleday Anchor (1956); *The Revolt of the Moderates* New York, Harper (1956); *The Hidden Crisis in American Politics* New York, Norton (1970)

56 Lubell *The Future of American Politics* ch. 7

57 See for example Key *Southern Politics* pp. 37–41, 110–11, 251–3, etc., Lockard, op. cit., pp. 24–6

58 V. O. Key Jr *The Responsible Electorate: Rationality in Presidential Voting 1936–60* Cambridge, Mass., Belknap Press, Harvard (1966) *passim*

59 R. B. McCallum and Alison Readman *The British General Election of 1945* Oxford University Press (1947) Cass (1964) p. 269; H. G. Nicholas *The British General Election of 1950* Macmillan (1951) pp. 303, 328

60 D. E. Butler *The British General Election of 1951* Macmillan (1952) p. 11; D. E. Butler *The British General Election of 1955* Macmillan (1955) p. 4

61 D. E. Butler and Richard Rose *The British General Election of 1959* Macmillan (1960) p. 199

62 D. E. Butler and Anthony King *The British General Election of 1964* Macmillan (1965) p. 300

63 D. E. Butler and Anthony King *The British General Election of 1966* Macmillan (1966) p. 267

64 D. E. Butler and M. Pinto-Duschinsky *The British General Election of 1970* Macmillan (1971) Appendices I–III. D. E. Butler and Denis Kavenagh *The British General Election of February 1974* Macmillan (1974)

65 See especially Mark Benney and Phyllis Geiss 'Social Class and Politics in Greenwich' *British Journal of Sociology* vol. I (1950) pp. 310–27; A. H. Birch and Peter Campbell 'Voting Behaviour in a

Lancashire Constituency' in ibid., pp. 197–208; R. S. Milne and H. C. Mackenzie *Straight Fight* Hansard Society (1954) and *Marginal Seat* Hansard Society (1958); Mark Benney, A. P. Gray, R. H. Pear *How People Vote*: *A Study of Electoral Behaviour in Greenwich* Routledge & Kegan Paul, New York, Grove Press (1956)

66 Milne and Mackenzie *Straight Fight* p. 43
67 Benney, Gray and Pear, op. cit., p. 119
68 ibid., p. 170
69 Milne and Mackenzie *Marginal Seat* p. 198
70 Mark Abrams, Richard Rose, Rita Hinden *Must Labour Lose?* Harmondsworth, Penguin Books (1960) ch. 1 *passim*
71 ibid., p. 64
72 ibid., ch. 4 *passim*
73 ibid., p. 96
74 'Working-class Toryism' has been investigated by Eric A. Nordlinger *The Working Class Tories* (Macgibbon & Kee 1967) and Robert MacKenzie and Allan Silver *Angels in Marble* (Heinemann 1968). Both accounts find that working-class respondents who tend to vote for the Conservative party split into two types, 'deferential' and 'pragmatist' in Nordlinger's schema, 'deferential' and 'secular' in the MacKenzie-Silver classification. The 'pragmatist-secular' type of working-class Tory votes this way, not because he believes that the Tory party has a right to rule, but because he perceives a Conservative government providing him with more material benefits than a Labour one. 'Embourgeoisement' as an ingredient of working-class Toryism tends to be discounted; see John H. Goldthorpe, David Lockwood, Frank Bechhofer, Jennifer Platt *The Affluent Worker*: *Political Attitudes and Behaviour* Cambridge University Press (1968). When dealing with 'that small minority of the middle class which endorses left-wing political and social views', the other main 'deviant' political phenomenon in this area, Frank Parkin suggests that the 'main pay-off' for middle-class radicals is that of a psychological or emotional kind—in satisfactions derived from expressing personal values in action. In other words, personal interests as such are not involved but rather a general view of society and the ways in which it can be improved. See Frank Parkin *Middle-Class Radicalism* Manchester University Press (1968) p. 2 and *passim*
75 Mark Abrams 'What the Floating Voter Wants' *Observer* 5 April 1964
76 Hugh Berrington 'The General Election of 1964' *Journal of the Royal Statistical Society* Pt I (1965) p. 62 (discussion on Mr Berrington's paper)
77 A. H. Birch *Small-Town Politics*: *A Study of Political Life in Glossop* Oxford University Press (1959) pp. 110–11
78 ibid., pp. 111–12. Frank Bealey, Jean Blondel, W. P. McCann *Constituency Politics*: *A Study of Newcastle-under-Lyme* Faber & Faber (1965) ch. 8 *passim*
79 Richard Rose and Harve Mossawir 'Voting and Elections: A Functional Analysis' *Political Studies* vol. XV, no. 2 (June 1967) p. 188
80 ibid., pp. 192–3 and 200–201
81 Joseph Trenaman and Denis McQuail *Television and the Political Image* Methuen (1961) pp. 192–3

82   Jay G. Blumler and Denis McQuail *Television in Politics: Its Uses and Influence* Faber & Faber (1968) p. 265

83   David Butler and Donald Stokes *Political Change in Great Britain* Macmillan (1969) p. 35

84   ibid., p. 249

85   The Butler–Stokes sampling process deliberately excluded Northern Ireland from its purview.

86   ibid., pp. 337–8

87   ibid., p. 318

88   ibid., pp. 307, 369

89   ibid., pp. 347–8

90   ibid., p. 404

91   Iain MacLeod 'The Private World of Political Science' *The Times* 30 October 1969

92   Roy Pierce *French Politics and Political Institutions* New York, Harper & Row (1968) p. 140

93   André Siegfried *Table Politique de la France de l'Ouest sous la Troisième République* Paris, Librarie Armand Colin (1913, 1964) p. v

94   ibid., p. 17

95   André Siegfried *La Géographie électorale de l'Ardèche sous la IIIe République* Paris, Librarie Armand Colin (1949) p. 113

96   François Goguel 'L'élection présidentielle française de décembre 1965' *Revue Française de Science Politique* (April 1966) p. 242. Also see his *Géographie des Elections Françaises* Paris, Librairie Armand Colin (1951) and numerous articles, especially in *Revue Française*.

97   See for example Alain Lancelot and Pierre Weill 'The Political Evolution of French Electors between February and June 1969' *Revue Française de Science Politique* vol. XX (1970) pp. 249–81. This article charts the shifts of opinion in 1969 between the referendum and the presidential election, with the moderate-right Gaullist coalition eventually maintaining itself in power.

98   Cf. Mogens N. Pedersen 'Recent Electoral Research in Denmark' *Scandinavian Political Studies* vol. III (1968) pp. 253–5, with Jan Stehouwer and Ole Børre, 'Four General Elections in Denmark, 1960–1968' *Scandinavian Political Studies* vol. IV (1969) pp. 133–48

99   Angus Campbell and Henry Valen 'Party Identification in Norway and the United States' in Campbell, Converse, Miller, Stokes *Elections and the Political Order* pp. 245–68. Also see Stein Rokkan and Henry Valen 'The Election to the Norwegian Storting in September 1969' *Scandinavian Political Studies* vol. V (1970) pp. 287–300 for an updating of some of this material.

100   Klaus Liepelt 'The Infra-Structure of Party Support in Germany and Austria' in Matter Dogan and Richard Rose (eds.) *European Politics: A Reader* Macmillan (1971) pp. 183–202.

101   Heinz Eulau, Preface to Glendon Schubert (ed.) *Judicial Decision-Making* New York, Free Press (1963)

102   Glendon Schubert *The Judicial Mind* Evanston, Northwestern University Press (1965) p. 15

103   ibid., pp. 273–4

104   ibid., *passim*. See also the articles on the Court by Schubert, Eloise Snyder and Sidney Ulmer in *Introductory Readings in Political Behavior* New York, Rand-McNally (1961)

105 Kenneth N. Vines 'The Selection of Judges in Louisiana' in Vines and Jacob *Studies in Judicial Politics* New Orleans, Tulane University (1963) p. 118

106 S. S. Ulmer 'Leadership in the Michigan Supreme Court' in Schubert *Judicial Decision-Making* p. 14

107 Warren E. Miller and Donald Stokes 'Constituency Influence in Congress' *American Political Science Review* (March 1963) reprinted in R. L. Peabody and N. W. Polsby (eds.) *New Perspectives on the House of Representatives* New York, Rand-McNally 2nd edn. (1969) p. 51. More recent research seems to confirm that some correlation is possible between support for Congressmen and their relative positions on issues as perceived by their constituents. See Robert S. Erickson 'The Electoral Impact of Congressional Roll Call Voting' *American Political Science Review* (December 1971) pp. 1018–32

108 For a first-class bibliography of the general field, see the Bibliographical Note in Samuel C. Patterson (ed.) *American Legislative Behavior* New York, Van Nostrand (1968) pp. 449–51

109 David R. Mayhew *Party Loyalty Among Congressmen* Cambridge, Mass., Harvard University Press (1966) *passim*

110 Duncan MacRae *Issues and Parties in Legislative Voting* New York, Harper & Row (1970) p. 286. Both factor and cluster analyses produce 'blocs' or 'sets' of legislators linked by communal attitudes towards specific pieces of legislation.

111 John C. Wahlke, Heinz Eulau, James Buchanan, Le Roy C. Ferguson *The Legislative System* New York, Wiley (1962) p. 410. Also see articles by Ralph K. Huitt and Corinne Silverman in John C. Wahlke and Heinz Eulau *Legislative Behavior* New York, Free Press (1957)

112 Wahlke, Eulau, Buchanan, Ferguson, op. cit., p. 69

Chapter Six   Partial Theory II: Democracy

1 *The Politics of Aristotle* transl. Ernest Barker, Oxford, Clarendon Press.(1948) esp. Book IV

2 Jean-Jacques Rousseau *The Social Contract* transl. G. D. H. Cole, Everyman's Library (1913) p. 84. John Locke *Two Treatises of Civil Government* Everyman's Library (1924) p. 242. Rousseau looks forward to the problems of democratic theory—'there never has been a real democracy, and there never will be. It is against the natural order for the many to govern and the few to be governed.'

3 Alexis de Tocqueville *Democracy in America* Fontana (1968) p. 82

4 Alexander Hamilton, James Madison, John Jay *The Federalist Papers* Mentor Books (1961) p. 17

5 John Stuart Mill *On Liberty* Everyman's Library (1910) p. 143

6 ibid., p. 208, pp. 254–5

7 See especially Karl Britton *John Stuart Mill* Harmondsworth, Penguin Books (1953) p. 93. Human beings are 'self-protecting' when they are able to stand up for their rights and interests, 'self-dependent' when they can concentrate their energies on bettering themselves and their fellows. This is somewhat reminiscent of John Kennedy's 'ask not what your country . . .'

8   Richard B. Friedman 'A New Exploration of Mill's Essay "On Liberty" ' *Political Studies* vol. XIV (October 1966)

9   James H. Meisel *The Myth of the Ruling Class: Gaetano Mosca and the 'Elite'* University of Michigan Press (1958) p. 10

10   Gaetano Mosca 'Storia delle dottrine politiche' (1933), translated and included in Meisel, op. cit., p. 388

11   Vilfredo Pareto *The Mind and Society: A Treatise on General Sociology* (1963) p. 1427

12   ibid., p. 1430

13   Vilfredo Pareto *Sociological Writing* Pall Mall Press (1966) p. 120 (from *Cours d'Economie Politique* 1896)

14   Robert A. Dahl 'A Critique of the Ruling Elite Model' *American Political Science Review* vol. LII (June 1958) p. 463, reprinted in the Bobbs-Merrill (New York) Reprint Series, no. P5–52

15   Harold Lasswell *Politics: Who Gets What, When and How* New York, McGraw-Hill (1936) Peter Smith (1950) p. 3

16   John Plamenatz 'Electoral Studies and Democratic Theory: A British View' *Political Studies* vol. VI, no. 1 (1958) p. 5

17   Robert Michels *Political Parties* New York, Free Press (1962) ch. 2 and *passim*

18   C. Wright Mills *The Power Elite* New York, Oxford University Press (1959) p. 296

19   G. William Domhoff *Who Rules America?* Englewood Cliffs, Prentice-Hall (1967) p. 156

20   Dahl 'A Critique of the Ruling Elite Model' p. 469

21   Robert A. Dahl *A Preface to Democratic Theory* Chicago, University of Chicago Press (1965) p. 133

22   ibid., p. 133

23   ibid., p. 138. It is worth noting that the three methods suggested by Dahl whereby groups can gain entry to the political arena include one —'abnormal' political activity, usually violent—which he thinks irrelevant to the 1950s but which became much more relevant to the black campaigns of the 1960s.

24   Robert A. Dahl *Pluralist Democracy in the United States: Conflict and Consent* New York, Rand-McNally (1967) p. 24

25   Robert A. Dahl *Polyarchy: Participation and Opposition* New Haven, Yale University Press (1971) p. 94

26   ibid., p. 203

27   Robert A. Dahl *After the Revolution* New Haven, Yale University Press (1970) p. 78

28   See, for example, Robert S. Lynd and Helen M. Lynd *Middletown* New York, Harcourt, Brace (1929) and *Middletown in Transition* New York, Harcourt, Brace (1937)

29   Floyd Hunter *Community Power Structure: A Study of Decision Makers* Anchor Books (1963) p. 257

30   ibid., p. 102

31   Robert A. Dahl *Who Governs?* New Haven, Yale University Press (1961) p. 227

32   ibid., p. 315

33   Arthur J. Vidich and Joseph Bensman *Small Town in Mass Society* Princeton, Princeton University Press (1958) Anchor Books (1958) p. 146

34 ibid., p. 215

35 ibid., p. 288

36 Nelson W. Polsby *Community Power and Political Theory* New Haven, Yale University Press (1963) pp. 123–4

37 Robert E. Agger, Daniel Goldrich, Bert E. Swanson *The Rulers and the Ruled: Political Power and Impotence in American Communities* New York, Wiley (1964) *passim* but esp. pp. 524–6 and ch. 14

38 Robert Presthus *Men at the Top: A Study in Community Power* New York, Oxford University Press (1964) p. 50

39 ibid., p. 59

40 ibid., pp. 137–8

41 Peter Bachrach and Morton S. Baratz 'Two Faces of Power' *American Political Science Review* (1962) pp. 947–52

42 Peter Bachrach and Morton S. Baratz 'Decisions and Non-Decisions: An Analytical Framework' *American Political Science Review* (1963) pp. 632–42

43 Richard M. Merelman 'On the Neo-Elitist Critique of Community Power' *American Political Science Review* (1968) p. 454

44 See for example K. Newton 'City Politics in Britain and the United States' *Political Studies* (June 1969) pp. 208–17, and Teresa Brown, Maurice Vile, Fred Whitemore 'Community Studies and Decision-Taking in Ashford' *British Journal of Political Science* (January 1972)

45 Darryl Baskin 'American Pluralism: Theory, Practice and Ideology' *Journal of Politics* (1970) pp. 94–5. Also see articles by Michael Parenti in Marvin Surkin and Alan Wolfe (eds.) *An End to Political Science: The Caucus Papers* New York, Basic Books (1970) and by Shin yu Ono and Todd Gitlin in McCoy and Playford (eds.) *Apolitical Politics* New York, Thomas Y. Crowell (1967)

46 Surkin and Wolfe, op. cit., dustjacket

47 Duane Lockard *Power in Newark* (unpublished paper delivered in March 1973)

48 For example, the following additional selection have added much to the argument: W. Kornhauser *The Politics of Mass Society* Routledge & Kegan Paul (1959); Edward Banfield *Political Influence* New York, Free Press (1961); Henry S. Kariel *The Decline of American Pluralism* Stanford, Stanford University Press (1961); Suzanne Keller *Beyond the Ruling Class* New York, Random House (1963); Arnold M. Rose *The Power Structure* Oxford University Press (1967); Peter Bachrach *The Theory of Democratic Elitism* University of London Press (1969); Geraint Parry *Political Elites* Allen & Unwin (1969); T. Bottomore *Elites and Society* Watts (1964) Harmondsworth, Penguin Books (1966). An exhaustive listing of the literature on community power from the 1920s to 1971 will be found in Willis O. Hawley and James H. Svara *The Study of Community Power* Santa Barbara ABC–CLIO Press (1972).

49 Our reference here is to a relatively narrow view of the application of economic theory to political analysis, and not to total theories of society which include political and economic dimensions such as the Marxist thesis.

50 Joseph A. Schumpeter *Capitalism, Socialism and Democracy* Allen & Unwin (1943) p. 262

51 Robert A. Dahl and Charles E. Lindblom *Politics, Economics and*

Welfare New York, Harper Torchbooks (1963) p. 39

52 Anthony Downs *An Economic Theory of Democracy* New York, Harper & Row (1957) p. 11

53 This is made clear in Downs' reply to W. Haywood Rogers' critique (which appeared in the *American Political Science Review*, 1959, pp. 483–5) 'Dr Rogers's Methodological Difficulties—A Reply to this Critical Note' *American Political Science Review* (1959) pp. 1094–7

54 Downs *An Economic Theory of Democracy* chs. 2 and 3

55 ibid., ch. 4

56 ibid., chs. 7 and 8

57 Harold Hotelling 'Stability in Competition' *Economic Journal* (March 1929) p. 54

58 Downs *An Economic Theory of Democracy* ch. 9 *passim*

59 ibid., ch. 10 *passim*

60 ibid., chs. 11–14 *passim*

61 Brian Barry *Sociologists, Economists and Democracy* Collier-Macmillan (1970) p. 177. The Olson book which expresses that writer's views most fully is Mancur Olson *The Logic of Collective Action* Cambridge, Mass., Harvard University Press (1965). Olson believes that, *apart from special cases*, 'rational, self-interested individuals will not act to achieve their common or group interest' (p. 2). The result is to downgrade the power commonly believed to be held by *large*, well-organized groups, where the collective interests of the group do not provide directly for the perceived self-interest of the individual. Olson argues that large groups succeed by developing selective benefits for individual members. It is an intriguing, if not altogether convincing, theory.

62 ibid., ch. 6 *passim*

63 James M. Buchanan and Gordon Tullock *The Calculus of Consent* Ann Arbor, University of Michigan (1962, 1965) p. 297

64 ibid., chs. 9 and 10 *passim*

65 James Bryce *Modern Democracies* Macmillan (1921) p. viii

66 Giovanni Sartori *Democratic Theory* New York, Praeger (1965) p. 126

Chapter Seven   Partial Theory III: Bureaucracy

1 Walter Bagehot *The English Constitution* (1867) Fontana (1963) p. 195

2 A. L. Lowell *The Government of England* Macmillan (1917) pp. 193–4. See also Martin Albrow *Bureaucracy* Macmillan (1970) ch. 1 for a very useful introduction to the use of the term.

3 The two most useful translations for English readers are: Max Weber *The Theory of Social and Economic Organization* ed. Talcott Parsons New York, Free Press (1947, paperback edn. 1964); H. H. Gerth and C. Wright Mills *From Max Weber* Routledge & Kegan Paul (1948)

4 Karl Loewenstein *Max Weber's Political Ideas in the Perspective of Our Time* Amherst, University of Massachusetts Press (1966) p. 30

5 Gerth and Mills, op. cit., p. 244

6 ibid., pp. 196–204; Weber, op. cit., pp. 333–4

7 Gerth and Mills, op. cit., p. 214

8   ibid., p. 245
9   ibid., p. 232
10 Reinhard Bendix *Max Weber: An Intellectual Portrait* (1959) Methuen
    & Co. University paperback edn. (1966) p. 457
11 Loewenstein, op. cit., p. 39
12 ibid., p. 234
13 Karl Mannheim *Ideology and Utopia* Kegan Paul, Trench, Trubner
    (1936) p. 105
14 ibid., p. 143
15 ibid., pp. 105–6
16 Karl Mannheim *Man and Society* Kegan Paul, Trench, Trubner
    (1940) p. 322
17 ibid., pp. 319–27 *passim*
18 Talcott Parsons *The Structure of Social Action* New York, McGraw-
    Hill (1937) New York, Free Press (1949) p. 665
19 Carl J. Friedrich *Constitutional Government and Democracy* Ginn
    (1950); *Man and His Government* New York, McGraw-Hill (1963);
    'Some Observations on Weber's Analysis of Bureaucracy' in Robert
    Merton *et al. Reader in Bureaucracy* New York, Free Press (1952)
20 Friedrich 'Some Observations on Weber's Analysis of Bureaucracy' p.
    29
21 Friedrich *Constitutional Government and Democracy* p. 44 *et seq.;*
    Man and His Government pp. 468–9; 'Some Observations on Weber's
    Analysis of Bureaucracy' p. 29
22 Friedrich *Constitutional Government and Democracy* pp. 52–7; *Man
    and His Government* pp. 470–71. The term 'discretion' is now used
    mainly to describe the flexible application of rules by junior officials.
    See Michael J. Hill *The Sociology of Public Administration* Weiden-
    feld & Nicolson (1972) ch. 4
23 Friedrich *Constitutional Government and Democracy* pp. 397 *et seq.;*
    'Some Observations on Weber's Analysis of Bureaucracy' pp. 30–31
24 F. J. Roethlisberger and W. J. Dickson *Management and the Worker*
    Boston, Harvard University Press (1939, 1964) p. 581. The Hawthorne
    research is also described in other standard texts of the 1930s, princi-
    pally those by Elton Mayo and T. N. Whitehead.
25 ibid., esp. pp. 379–84 and 583–4
26 Chester I. Barnard *The Functions of the Executive* Cambridge, Mass.,
    Harvard University Press (1938, 1962) p. 116 (my emphasis). Barnard
    drew largely on the Hawthorne material for proof of his contentions
    in this area.
27 ibid., p. 122
28 ibid., p. 286
29 Peter M. Blau *The Dynamics of Bureaucracy* Chicago, University of
    Chicago Press (1955, 1963) pp. 260–61
30 ibid., p. 231. Robert Michels *Political Parties* (1915) New York, Free
    Press (1962, 1966) Pt II, ch. 7. Blau also cites Roethlisberger and
    Dickson in this connection.
31 Michels, op. cit., p. 365
32 Blau, op. cit., p. 243
33 Seymour Martin Lipset, Martin A. Trow, James S. Coleman *Union
    Democracy* New York, Free Press (1956) pp. 414–17. As well as those
    previously mentioned, the twenty-two include the decentralized nature

of the industry, the autonomy of the member locals, the degree to which members associate with each other off the job, the pressure of independent channels of communication and the general 'institutionalization' of opposition as being legitimate within the union structure.

34 Philip Selznick *TVA and the Grass Roots* (1949) New York, Harper Torchbook (1966) p. 259

35 Richard Fenno *The President's Cabinet* New York, Vintage Books (1959) pp. 234–47

36 Alvin W. Gouldner *Patterns of Industrial Bureaucracy* New York, Free Press (1954, 1964) pp. 79–83

37 ibid., p. 228. Gouldner argues in his follow-up study on the same organization that increasing bureaucratization at least cuts down the liklihood of *unanticipated* conflict within an organization. See Alvin Gouldner *Wildcat Strike* Routledge & Kegan Paul (1965), ch. 8. Also Charles Perrow *Complex Organizations* Glenview, Scott, Foresman (1972), pp. 1–8

38 Michel Crozier *The Bureaucratic Phenomenon* Tavistock Publications (1964) p. 208

39 ibid., pp. 225–6

40 ibid., p. 299

41 Martin Landau 'The Concept of Decision-Making' in Sydney Mailick and Edward H. van Ness (eds.) *Concepts and Issues in Administrative Behavior* Englewood Cliffs, Prentice-Hall (1962) p. 15

42 Herbert Simon *Administrative Behavior* Free Press, New York (1945, 1947, 2nd edn. 1957) p. 3

43 ibid., ch. 3. Also Introduction to 2nd edn., p. xxxiv

44 ibid., Introduction, p. xxv and pp. 80–4 2nd edn.

45 ibid., p. 243. See also Nicos P. Mouzelis *Organisation and Bureaucracy* Routledge & Kegan Paul (1967) pp. 123–7

46 ibid., p. 251

47 These include: J. G. March and H. A. Simon *Organizations* New York, Wiley (1958); R. M. Cyert and J. G. March 'A Behavioral Theory of Organizational Objectives' in M. Haire (ed.) *Modern Organizational Theory* New York, Wiley (1959); R. M. Cyert and J. G. March *Behavioral Theory of the Firm* Englewood Cliffs, Prentice-Hall (1963); Mailick and van Ness, op. cit.; Ira Sharkansky *Public Administration* Chicago, Markham (1970)

48 Charles E. Lindblom *The Policy-Making Process* Englewood Cliffs, Prentice-Hall (1968) p. 75

49 Alec T. Barbrook 'The Making of a Department' *Urban Affairs Quarterly* March 1971

50 Robert Presthus *The Organizational Society* New York, Vintage Books (1962) p. 17

51 Gordon Tullock *The Politics of Bureaucracy* Washington DC, Public Affairs Press (1965) ch. 9

52 ibid., p. 224

53 Anthony Downs *Inside Bureaucracy* Boston, Little, Brown (1967) pp. 261–81

54 ibid., p. 1

55 ibid., p. 262

56 ibid., pp. 88–9

57 ibid., p. 237

58 Talcott Parsons *Structure and Process in Modern Society* New York, Free Press (1960) p. 59

59 Talcott Parsons 'The Political Aspect of Social Structure and Process' in David Easton (ed.) *Varieties of Political Theory* Englewood Cliffs, Prentice-Hall (1966) p. 81. This essay has been reprinted in Talcott Parsons *Politics and Social Structure* New York, Free Press (1969) pp. 317–81.

60 Robert K. Merton *Social Theory and Social Structure* New York, Free Press (rev. edn. 1957) ch. 6 ('Bureaucratic Structure and Personality'). Chapter 7 ('Role of the Intellectual in Public Bureaucracy') deals largely with the clash of personality between the intellectual and the true bureaucrat working inside the same organization. Merton's arguments in the first edition of this book had a considerable influence on certain of the studies of the period, such as those by Gouldner (see the Introduction to *Wildcat Strike*).

61 David Easton *A Systems Analysis of Political Life* New York, Wiley (1965) pp. 96–7, 137

62 ibid., pp. 374–5

63 Gabriel Almond and James Coleman *The Politics of Developing Areas* Princeton, Princeton University Press (1960) pp. 33, 40, 46–7, 57–8

64 Gabriel Almond and G. Bingham Powell *Comparative Politics* Boston, Little, Brown (1964) p. 158

65 S. N. Eisenstadt *The Political Systems of Empires* New York, Free Press (1963, 1969) ch. 12

66 J. P. Nettl *Political Mobilization* Faber & Faber (1967) p. 377. Cf. S. N. Eisenstadt 'Bureaucracy and Political Development' in Joseph La Palombara (ed.) *Bureaucracy and Political Development* Princeton, Princeton University Press (1963, 1967)

67 Eisenstadt 'Bureaucracy and Political Development' p. 52

68 Lucian W. Pye *Politics, Personality and Nation Building* New Haven, Yale University Press (1962) *passim*

69 La Palombara (ed.), op. cit., especially the contributions of Eisenstadt, Riggs and La Palombara himself.

70 ibid., p. 11

71 See Fred W. Riggs *Administration in Developing Countries* Boston, Houghton Mifflin (1964) ch. 1 *passim*. Riggs' *The Ecology of Public Administration* (Asian Publishing House 1961) contains an earlier version of the scheme.

72 ibid., p. 270

73 Riggs in La Palombara (ed.), op. cit., p. 167

Chapter Eight Conclusion

1 Charles Taylor 'Neutrality in Political Science' in Peter Laslett and W. G. Runciman (eds.) *Philosophy, Politics and Society: Third Series* Oxford, Blackwell (1967) p. 57

2 See especially Fred M. Frohock 'Notes on the Concept of Politics: Weber, Easton, Strauss' *Journal of Politics* vol. XXXVI (1974) pp. 379–408

3 W. J. M. Mackenzie 'Political Science: Between Analysis and Action'

New Society (25 July 1974) p. 218

4　*PS*, the Newsletter of the American Political Science Association, vol. II, no. 3 (Summer 1969) p. 368

5　Lewis Lipsitz 'Vulture, Mantis and Seal: Proposals for Political Scientists' in George J. Graham Jr and George W. Carey (eds.) *The Post-Behavioral Era: Perspectives in Political Science* New York, David McKay (1972) pp. 171–91. Also see Charles A. McCoy and John Playford (eds.) *Apolitical Politics: A Critique of Behavioralism* New York, Thomas Y. Crowell (1967) Introduction *passim*

6　Marvin Surkin 'Sense and Non-sense in Politics' in Marvin Surkin and Alan Wolfe (eds.) *An End to Political Science: The Caucus Papers* New York, Basic Books (1970) p. 26

7　David Easton 'The New Revolution in Political Science', reprinted from *American Political Science Review* in David Easton *The Political System* New York, Knopf 2nd edn. (1971) p. 329

8　ibid., p. 348

9　David Easton 'Continuities in Political Analysis' in ibid., pp. 349–77 *passim*

10　William E. Connolly *Political Science and Ideology* New York, Atherton Press (1967) p. 152

11　Robert Dahl 'The Behavioral Approach in Political Science' in Nelson W. Polsby, Robert A. Dentler, Paul A. Smith (eds.) *Politics and Social Life* Boston, Houghton Mifflin (1963) p. 15

INDEX